Diane Amans, a leading practitioner in community dance, provides a clear and practical introduction to dance with older people. This accessible text combines discussions of key debates with useful guidance on facilitating dance activities with older adults. Accompanying exercises bring alive the contexts in which dance for 'mature movers' takes place, and the Resources section is packed with a wealth of toolkit materials.

Age and Dancing is designed as a complementary volume to *An Introduction to Community Dance Practice*, also by Diane Amans, making it the ideal resource for students, practitioners and dance artists alike. This book contains contributions by:

- Ken Bartlett
- Elizabeth Coleman
- Fergus Early
- Sara Houston
- Ruth Pethybridge
- Pegge Vissicaro

Diane Amans is the founder of Freedom in Dance and is a leading dance practitioner and training consultant. Her career has included work in education (schools, further and higher education), management of dance projects in diverse community settings and continuing professional development in the arts as well as in health and social care.

Age and Dancing

Older People and Community Dance Practice

Edited by

Diane Amans

First published 2013 by
PALGRAVE MACMILLAN

Palgrave Macmillan in the UK is an imprint of Macmillan Publishers Limited,
registered in England, company number 785998, of Houndmills, Basingstoke,
Hampshire RG21 6XS.

Palgrave Macmillan in the US is a division of St Martin's Press LLC,
175 Fifth Avenue, New York, NY 10010.

Palgrave Macmillan is the global academic imprint of the above companies
and has companies and representatives throughout the world.

Palgrave® and Macmillan® are registered trademarks in the United States,
the United Kingdom, Europe and other countries.

ISBN 978–0–230–29380–9

This book is printed on paper suitable for recycling and made from fully
managed and sustained forest sources. Logging, pulping and manufacturing
processes are expected to conform to the environmental regulations of the
country of origin.

A catalogue record for this book is available from the British Library.

A catalog record for this book is available from the Library of Congress.

10   9   8   7   6   5   4   3   2   1
22 21 20 19 18 17 16 15 14 13

Printed and bound in Great Britain by
the MPG Books Group

This book is dedicated to the memory of Jean and Bob McKay:
inspirational dancers, wonderful parents

Contents

List of Images   ix

Notes on Contributors   x

Acknowledgements   xii

Foreword   xiv

Preface   xvi

Introduction   xviii

Part One   Societies and Cultural Contexts

Chapter 1   Definitions   3
              Diane Amans

Chapter 2   Ageing and Society in the UK   13
              Sara Houston

Chapter 3   Ageing, Creativity and Dance in the United States   21
              Pegge Vissicaro

Chapter 4   Ageing and Society in Other Cultures   30
              Diane Amans

Chapter 5   What Sort of Dance and Who Is Dancing?   43
              Diane Amans

Chapter 6   Contexts, Partnerships and Funding   53
              Diane Amans

Chapter 7   The Beauty of Reality: Older Professional Dancers   64
              Fergus Early

Chapter 8   Cross-Generational Dance or Just Communities Dancing?   73
              Ruth Pethybridge

Part Two   Practical Considerations

Chapter 9   What Happens When We Age?   93
              Elizabeth Coleman

Chapter 10   Conditions That May Affect Older People   100
              Elizabeth Coleman

Chapter 11   Dance and Dementia   116
              Diane Amans
Chapter 12   Dance and Parkinson's Disease   125
              Diane Amans
Chapter 13   Duty of Care: Keeping Older Bodies Safe   132
              Diane Amans
Chapter 14   Continuing Professional Development, Training
              Opportunities, Gaining Skills and Qualifications   146
              Diane Amans
Chapter 15   Evaluation   155
              Sara Houston
Chapter 16   Choreography and Performance with Older People   163
              Diane Amans
Conclusion   178

Part Three   Resources

Index   242

Images

1.1	Diane Amans and Bisakha Sarker in Rehearsal	9
5.1	Auntie Mary Dancing	45
5.2	Growing Older (Dis)Gracefully Dance Company, Taken at the NDTA Conference at Elmhurst School for Dance, Birmingham, November 2009	48
5.3	Carl Campbell Recycled Teenagers Dance Theatre	49
5.4	Crows Feet Dance Collective: Anglepoise	50
7.1	Fergus Early with Jreena Greene in Green Candle Dance Company's Production for Older Dancers, *Falling About*	70
13.1	Freedom in Dance Class, Lincolnshire	136
14.1	Rebecca Seymour: Movement for the Mind, Wiltshire	152
16.1	Time to Dance, Stockport	170
16.2	Freedom in Dance Performers at Big Dance – Commissioned by Dance Initiative Greater Manchester 2006	174

Contributors

Ken Bartlett is currently Creative Director of the Foundation for Community Dance. He was previously Head of Arts and Cultural Services in Walsall in the West Midlands. Before that he worked in education as a teacher, school advisor and a member of the local authority schools inspectorate service. Ken has taught and lectured in Europe, North and South America, and Australia.

Elizabeth Coleman has a clinical background in physiotherapy. She has worked with psychotherapists to look at links between physical and psychological wellbeing. She is one of the founder members of the Pathway of the Biscuit training team and specialises in devising innovative, fun ways to deliver dance and movement work with older people.

Fergus Early is a dancer, choreographer and pioneer in community dance. He is Founder and Artistic Director of Green Candle Dance Company, working for and with young and older people in community and educational contexts. In 2009 he received an OBE for services to dance, and in 2011 he co-wrote and co-edited *The Wise Body: Conversations with Experienced Dancers*.

Sara Houston is Senior Lecturer in Dance Studies at the University of Roehampton. Her research is focused on community dance practice, particularly with marginalised people. Sara received the Bupa Foundation Vitality for Life Prize 2011 for her research examining dance for people with Parkinson's. She is Chair of the Foundation for Community Dance.

Ruth Pethybridge is an independent dance artist who has delivered dance in diverse settings and with all ages. Her practice emphasises creativity in choreographic processes, forming people's unique ways of moving into performance work. She continues to choreograph and perform whilst undertaking a practice-based PhD at University College Falmouth. Ruth presents her academic work at key conferences and lectures regularly. In 2008 she facilitated the first 'age inclusive' specialist training course for the Foundation for Community Dance.

Pegge Vissicaro has served on the Arizona State University School of Dance faculty for the last 30 years. She facilitates undergraduate and graduate courses focusing on movement, creative and ethnographic dance practices. She directs the Office for Global Dance Research and Creative Partnerships, which promote community-based, cultural development initiatives. Institutional collaborations include working with the Foundation for Community Dance and as a Fulbright Scholar at the Universidade Técnica de Lisboa, Faculdade Motricidade de Humana. She is also the president of the non-profit organisation Cross-Cultural Dance Resources, founded by Dr Joann Kealiinohomoku, and continues evolving her own artistic practice, terradance®.

Acknowledgements

Thanks to the dance artists and practitioners who shared their experience by responding to questionnaires and attending seminar discussions about dance work with older people.

Thanks to Marple Movers for allowing me to try out my choreographic ideas. I appreciate their sense of fun and their honest feedback. Thanks to Greenwich Dance, Company of Elders at Sadler's Wells and Time to Dance for allowing me to observe their sessions and rehearsals.

Thanks to the contributors who have written chapters, and the many organisations and individuals who have allowed me to include their material in the Resources section of this book.

Thanks to Olivia McKay, Harry Paschkowski, Scilla Dyke, Ken Bartlett and Sylvia Christie, who have helped with the research and given valuable comments and support during the writing.

Thanks to Arts Council England for funding research and development activities. Thanks to Jenni Burnell and Palgrave Macmillan for advice with publishing the book. I also wish to thank the two anonymous reviewers for their help in the drafting process.

The author and publisher wish to thank the following for permission to reproduce copyright material:

Foundation for Community Dance and Fergus Early for *Charter for the Older Dancer*

Foundation for Community Dance and Antony Smith for Animated article *Mind Your Rhetoric*

Marple Movers for 'Sample Constitution for a Community Dance Group'

Lincolnshire Dance for 'Risk Assessment Form'

Elizabeth Coleman for 'Further Information about Conditions Which May Affect Older People'

Powys for the *Lucky Me* dance performance and workshop package

English National Ballet, Roehampton University, Sara Houston and Ashley McGill for 'Executive Summary of ENB Dance for Parkinson's report'

Lincolnshire Dance and Jacky Simpson for dance leader case study

Wendy Thomas and Merseyside Dance Initiative for Redholme Memory Care Home session plan

Bethan Smith and Powys Dance for Llys Hafren case study

Rosie Perdikeas and Arts for Health Cornwall for *Let's Tango Fiesta* session plan

Sylvia Christie for *Mirroring and String of Pearls* poems by Sylvia Christie

John Killick for *On the Other Side* and *The Key* poems by John Killick

Every effort has been made to trace rights holders, but if any have been inadvertently overlooked the publishers would be pleased to make the necessary arrangements at the first opportunity.

Foreword

A couple of years back I began contemplating my looming retirement date and entered into a state of panic about my life coming to an end – no economic security, no social function or role relating to employment, and an increasing feeling that social isolation would be my lot.

Fortunately, that period has passed and I have begun to look forward to retirement from full-time employment with all the excitement that a fulfilling future will offer.

Spending time with my mother, now aged 92, as she plans her future has demonstrated that for her, and now for me, having a sense of a future is a crucial part of our humanity – one that participating in dance can engender through all our ages. The following comments illustrate this:

> 'I'm looking forward to seeing everyone in the group next week, we get on so well.'

> 'I'm looking forward to our next performance.'

> 'It's great that we are going to be working with the primary school in our next project, young and old together.'

Whilst recognising that funds for our work with older people increasingly originate from the areas of health and physical exercise, it's really important to set out that work in dance at its best is not simply a health and exercise regime. It is also, and perhaps more importantly, about creativity, expression and making meaning through the art of dance.

I may be approaching retirement but I still have tales to tell and dances to dance, and I don't necessarily want to spend all my creative time and energies reminiscing about what my life *was* like. I want to dance into my future.

This book, written by Diane Amans, together with contributions by colleagues and friends of many years' standing, pulls together many of the ideas and issues we began to contemplate at the very first UK conference on dance and older people: 'Beyond the Tea Dance', way back in 1997. The dance sector seems to look at this field of work roughly every five years or so, and it seems to me that we revisit the same issues and largely listen to the same people every time.

In putting this book together, Diane Amans has done us all a great service, first of all capturing the key issues emerging from the politics of ageing and the stereotypes of older people in dance. She has also provided us with practical guidelines together with detailed resources from artists, practitioners and projects that illuminate our thinking and offer us answers to the questions that plague our practice. When we all come together next, the political, social, artistic and health-related questions she has brought together in this volume will form a new stepping-off point for developing future debate and practice.

Ken Bartlett
Creative Director, Foundation for Community Dance

Preface

This book is a companion to *An Introduction to Community Dance Practice*, and is intended for students and dance practitioners who are interested in work with older adults. It will also be of value to activity leaders and other professionals engaged in arts and health. With the global trend in population ageing, there is an increasing number of initiatives to promote active ageing, resulting in a demand for information and resources that will equip people to work in this developing field. Whilst the book has a mainly UK focus, there is discussion of ageing and society in other countries, with examples of projects and dance initiatives outside the UK.

When I first began to be involved in community dance work in the 1970s, there was little in the way of written material and professional support. I started dancing with older people in hospitals and residential homes; initially this work was voluntary because I wanted to gain experience with an age group that was unfamiliar to me. As a young dance practitioner I was familiar with children, young people and active adults. Older people – particularly frail older people – were unknown territory. I was very nervous before that first session: would they want to dance? How do I keep them safe? Will they want to be playful or would that be seen as patronising?

Like countless other dancers – then and now – I 'winged it'. Some sessions were marvellous; others were not so good. Over the years I gained experience, skills and understanding. Now I am an 'older person' myself and, though I'm still developing my practice, I want to share what I have learned. Hopefully this book will provide some reassurance for anyone who is a little wary of starting up dance sessions with older people. It includes contextual information, guidelines and practical ideas together with exercises to promote discussion and debate. Case studies and comments from participants and choreographers serve to bring alive the contexts of this dance work.

There are a number of different 'voices' in the book, as I have included contributions from artists, practitioners and academics – each with their own unique perspective. This has resulted in a range of different writing styles, which I hope will appeal to the book's diverse readership. Some people seek in-depth analysis and critical discussion; others prefer shorter experiential accounts and practical examples of actual community projects.

Depending on the context, a reader will need different styles at different times. In the Introduction I have suggested ways in which the reader might engage with this text.

> ... older people are not a category apart. We will all grow old one day – if we have that privilege, that is. Let us therefore look at older people not as people separate from ourselves but as our future selves. And let us recognize that older people are all individuals with individual strengths and needs, not a group that are all the same because of their age.[1]

In the above extract from the United Nations World Assembly on Aging, Kofi Annan says, 'older people are not a category apart.' He is right; however, in the field of community dance there are particular issues to consider in relation to working with older people. If you are young, and have yet to appreciate what some of the dancers in this book have experienced, you may unwittingly lead sessions that are unsafe or inappropriate. These chapters offer suggestions, invite challenges and propose ways forward.

These are exciting times for participatory artists. Despite financial uncertainties that are likely to remain for some time, there are some indisputable facts: numbers of older people will continue to increase, together with government-backed imperatives supporting active healthy ageing. The so-called silver tsunami brings opportunities for community dance artists to contribute to an expanding range of programmes. Whether you choose to do a specialised training course in leading dance activities with older people, or put together your own professional development programme, I hope you will find something of interest here.

Diane Amans

Note

1. Kofi Annan (2002) UN World Assembly on Aging, Madrid
http://www.globalaging.org/agingwatch/index.htm.

Introduction

As you begin to look at this book, you will probably not want to read every chapter in turn – from the beginning of the book to the end. For example, if you are a dance practitioner who is fairly new to this work, you may want to begin with Chapter 5, which will give you an idea of the range of places in which older people are dancing. You could then look at some of the practical examples in the Resources section. Other readers may prefer to start with factual information about changing demographics and then move on to the chapters dealing with issues and debate. The book is divided into three sections, which are described briefly below.

In Part One you will find contextual information and an introduction to some of the key issues relating to a study of older people dancing. Chapter 1 deals with definitions – looking at the language and labels that are used to describe older people. The chapters 2 to 4 compare ageing and society in Britain with a global picture of ageing.

Chapter 5 gives an overview of the wide range of dance activities that mature movers take part in. These include mainstream classes for people of any age, and performance projects and dance sessions specially aimed at older people. Chapter 6 offers an outline of contexts and agendas; it looks at who is funding and delivering the work and how projects are set up.

In Chapter 7, Fergus Early presents an interesting perspective on older professional dancers – he describes the advantages and challenges of life as an older dancer and choreographer in the UK. In Chapter 8, Ruth Pethybridge discusses the history, terminology and values of cross-generational dance practice.

Part Two deals with practical considerations in facilitating dance with older people. First, there are two chapters describing what happens to us as we age, and outlining some of the conditions that may affect older people. As dance practitioners it is essential for us to understand the effects of ageing – if you are not yet an older dancer you will find it useful to learn about some of the ways in which growing older might impact on dance participants.

There are separate chapters on 'Dance for People Living with Dementia' and 'People Living with Parkinson's'. Chapter 13 covers duty of care and includes guidelines for ways in which dance artists can keep people safe.

You may have already taken part in training or other activities that have given you the knowledge and skills to lead effective and appropriate dance sessions with older participants. If you are interested in continuing professional development in this field, Chapter 14 offers information and discussion about informal and formal ways of gaining skills and experience.

One essential element in a practitioner's professional practice is the ability to document and evaluate the effects of dance work. In Chapter 15, Sara Houston discusses the challenges of finding effective ways to evaluate our practice, and Chapter 16 looks at the tension lines that exist in choreography and performance. What do dancers say about their choreographers? How does the media present dance by older performers? What do we want the audience to see?

The Resources section contains a range of 'toolkit' materials. Practitioners have generously shared their experience and bright ideas. There are:

- suggestions for dance activities in different settings
- starting points for choreography
- a sample constitution and health form for community groups
- duty of care guidelines
- case studies
- contact details and useful publications

This section also contains supplementary material relating to individual chapters. I hope these practical guidelines are helpful and that the book offers some interesting food for thought.

Part One
Societies and Cultural Contexts

1   Definitions

Diane Amans

. . . .

This chapter offers an introduction to terminology and is one of a number that discuss the language and labels used to describe older people. The term 'older dancers' includes mature people who work as dancers and also those who are participants in dance sessions. The focus in this chapter is mainly on community dance projects. In Chapter 7, Fergus Early discusses issues relating to older professional dancers.

Service provision is often linked to specific ages – for example, people need to be over a certain age to qualify for a pension, health care and subsidised transport. Some charities, such as Age UK, and companies like Saga target specific age groups. Who should community dance practitioners be aiming at and which labels will be most effective in marketing dance sessions?

The chapter includes older people's views on ageist language and the stigma attached to certain labels. These themes are discussed further in Chapter 2, where Sara Houston examines ageing and society in the UK, and in Chapter 4, which includes an overview of how older people are perceived in some other countries. In Chapter 8, Ruth Pethybridge also considers language in the context of cross-generational dance practice.

. . . .

Older people – who are we talking about?

The terms 'older people' and 'older adults' are often used in community dance work with mature movers, but who are we referring to? How old are 'older people'?

Literally speaking, the term might refer to anyone older than the person who is speaking or writing. Does it make sense for dance practitioners to treat dance with older people as a sort of specialism within community dance? Why not just offer general adult classes that are open to all comers? What is so different about older participants?

The term 'older people' can include independent, active mature adults, people with limited mobility, frail care home residents and people with dementia. The differences between these groups have less to do with chronological age and more to do with physical and mental function.

However, in some contexts, service provision is linked to specific ages – we need to consider whether we want to mention age limits when we are planning dance projects or marketing dance classes.

Service provision linked to specific ages

The Office for National Statistics refers to older people as those 'aged 50 [or] over'.[1] In the UK, state pensions are age related – someone who was 30 years old in 2011 will receive a state pension at the age of 68. As people are living longer, this age limit is rising – the parents of today's 30-year-olds will have become eligible for their pensions at 60 years (women) and 65 years (men).

People over 60 receive free prescriptions, winter fuel allowance and a free bus pass for local travel. People over 75 receive a free television licence. Within this range of statistics and statutory provision, the government links older people to a variety of different ages.

Other companies and agencies mention a range of different age limits in their services for older people:

- Saga offers insurance and holidays to people over 50.
- Elders Councils are forums to make sure the voice of the over 50s is taken into account in policy making.
- Various housing associations advertise retirement properties for the over 55s.
- Some car hire companies require a doctor's letter if applicants are over 70. Others have an upper limit of 75.
- Some companies specialise in travel insurance for the over 80s.
- The Ministry of Justice is considering plans to raise or abolish the upper age limit for becoming a juror (70 years in 2011).

Within this range of statutory and other provisions there is a considerable spread of age limits. Older people are variously considered to be over 50, 55, 60, 65, 68, 70, 75 or 80 years.

Specialists in ageing are dividing older people into an increasing range of different categories. They refer to 'young old', 'old', 'older old' and 'oldest old', the latter term relating to the Fourth Age, which is generally associated with more dependent, infirm older people. These different categories do not usually specify a particular age group. The University of the Third Age,[2] for example, does not have a lower age for membership but caters for those who are described as 'young old' – still in fairly good health and socially active.

Third Age and Fourth Age

The terms 'Third Age' and 'Fourth Age' came into use in the 1960s by sociologists and researchers in fields associated with demography and gerontology. They recognised the need for a means of differentiating between people in older age groups.

The Baring Foundation report, *Ageing Artfully*, uses the concept of a Third Age and a Fourth Age:

> (…) Third Age is used to denote an older person who remains physically and mentally fit and in full possession of all their capacities. Fourth Age suggests someone who has begun to experience significant limitations to these capacities. Beyond the fact that both terms are applied to older people they cease to be chronological. So, for instance, someone aged 90 in excellent health would be in their Third Age while another person could be 60, suffering dementia and mobility problems and be in their Fourth Age. Physical and mental health are not, however the only determinants to a full life. So someone in their Third Age could feel that the arts are not open to them due to their class or ethnic background. These categories are not static though, someone can move back and forth between Third and Fourth Age due to changes in health.[3]

Language and labels

Service providers such as the National Health Service and individuals working in the care services still refer to 'the elderly', usually when they are describing more frail older people. By contrast, the charity Age UK has rewritten policies and information sheets, replacing 'the elderly' with 'older people'. The media often refer to 'pensioners' and 'senior citizens', and some specialist groups use terms such as 'silver surfers' and 'recycled teenagers'.

In a recent survey (Amans 2010),[4] dance agencies and artists were asked about the language they use to describe their target participants. Most commonly used labels are 'older people' and 'older adults'; the terms 'over 50s' and 'over 60s' are also widely used. 'Elders' is popular with some groups – the Sadler's Wells based 'Company of Elders' is an long-established UK performance group.

Some dance artists have asked their group members how they like to be described, and labels that are disliked include 'old people', 'pensioners' and 'the elderly'. In one such discussion there was general consensus about the term 'pensioners':

Mary I hate being called a pensioner

John Yes – it makes you feel so old

Mary Mind you – I don't mind being called a pensioner if it means I get in free . . . (chorus of agreement)

Unsurprisingly, researchers find that many people reject age-related labels when they are applied to themselves (Setterston and Trauten 2009).[5] In the 1990s a consumer study in the United States found that people would forgo a discount rather than be associated with the 'perceived stigma of "senior citizen" or "pensioner" ' (Tepper 1994).[6] It would be interesting to examine whether or not this is still the case in the more austere financial climate some 20 years later.

Whilst I have not carried out research into discounts and stigma, I have interviewed people aged over 50 about the kind of language that would attract them to or discourage them from taking part in activities aimed at older people. Kath, aged 66, dislikes references to 'young at heart' and adds:

. . . I don't like anything that implies everyone wants/needs the same thing or that I should conform to their perception of older people – lumping us all under one label.

I'd be more likely to attend an activity that mentioned individuality, fun, laughter, personal journey and social interaction. A chance to explore what you *can* do, not highlight what you can't do.

So what language should we use in community dance?

If a project or class is aimed at older people, how should we describe it in our marketing material? First, we need to be clear whom the class is for and why we want to specify that it is a class for older people. Are we working with partners? If so, what labels do they use? Would the target participants be happy to use these labels to describe themselves?

If a project is funded by partners who have a remit for promoting healthy ageing, they may have a target group in mind – for example, active over 50s. This helps us with the wording of publicity – though by including a lower age limit it may exclude other people who would benefit from such a class. It may be better to invite people who would describe themselves as 'mature movers' and then add a clarifying sentence describing the kinds of activities that will be offered.

When a dance artist is working with a group in community settings such as day centres, care homes and hospitals, these organisations will have their own language to describe the participants; they may be service users, residents or patients. Whilst it is important to be aware of the terminology of any host organisation, community dance practitioners are free to develop their own language. Sometimes I use the host organisation's labels when I am writing reports and project updates, but I more frequently use the generic term 'participants' or 'dancers' when referring to the people who join my sessions.

I think it is important to try to avoid language that reinforces stereotypes, such as those outlined in the next section.

Challenging negative stereotyping

For some years, dance artists and other activists have been challenging the use of language in relation to older people. In his presentation at the *Beyond the Tea Dance* conference, Antony Smith raised the issue of what he called 'limited lexicons'.

How much do we limit our vision of the role of older people in dance by the language we use to describe them, however well-intentioned our choice of words might be? To mind our language is not just to tackle the negative lexical stereotyping of old age, but also to take on the vague and altogether limited terminology we use when attempting to talk positively. In the context of older people and dance we are almost all guilty of using the same small reference book of platitudes at least once when we are asked for our comments. The words go something like: 'Older people bring a sense of calm/of dignity/of serenity to dance; they bring a lifetime's rich experience'.

There is nothing intrinsically wrong with the words; they are perfectly agreeable. But they are just not enough, and we do an injustice to older dancers by continuing to be limited by them (. . .). The problem of this limited lexicon is compounded by the fact that it is so difficult to come up with any realistic alternatives...

Smith goes on to point out that

there is no continuity. The visible dancer becomes invisible at thirty-something [...]. If she or he reappears at all it is as something of a novelty several decades later. We can celebrate the fact that colleagues in dance are still challenging this state of affairs, but we are still left with a major generational divide – lissom young bodies alongside considerably older ones

(...) Inevitably those of us promoting the role of the older dancer fall back at some point on the word 'experience', but how do we honestly translate this word into dance terms? 'Dignity', 'serenity' and 'calm' are at least tangible concepts in movement terminology – even though all we may mean when we use them is 'tries hard but moves rather slowly'. In theatre, music, the visual arts good artists are perceived to grow in stature as they grow in experience. Not so in dance. We may respect dancers' past work. We may marvel that they're still dancing at 40, let alone 60, 70 or 80. But we tend to get embarrassed when we actually see them on stage, because the contrast with what we're used to is so immense. Again we have lissom young bodies on one side and almost nothing on the other until we reach the dancer-as-novelty stage.[7]

In Chapter 7, Fergus Early offers a more recent perspective: he refers to older, professional dancers as 'formidable artists in their own right' and describes mature dancers who are challenging ageism within the dance world.

Multiple identities, roles and boundary management

Implicit in many definitions and labels is the notion of identity. Identity theorists maintain that our identity is our answer to the question 'Who am I?' and that the responses will be linked to our roles.[8] Most of us will have several answers and may focus on different ones depending on the situation. Dance artist, mother, gardener, friend, consultant, mentor and granny are just some of my identities and many of them are linked to roles – work, family and social roles.

Figure 1.1   Diane Amans and Bisakha Sarker in Rehearsal
Source: Simon Richardson

The identities listed above are all ones I accept; they are roles that I occupy. However, sometimes other people confer a role or identity onto us. When I am working in a care home I see myself as a dance practitioner involved in participatory arts. The care staff may see me as a fitness instructor and the residents may see me as a health professional.

Actually I do not accept either of these role identities; I am not a fitness instructor or a health professional and, if that is how others see me, I need to be careful about managing boundaries and expectations. When Errol asks my opinion about the pain in his shoulder, I suggest he has a word with his doctor about it. Even if I happen to know the answers to medical or health questions, I refer them to the appropriate source. I am there to invite people to join me in dancing, not to advise them about their aches and pains or to 'instruct' them.

It is worth considering your role in the context of dance in community settings. Who are you? How do people see you? What are you qualified to do?

Role identities and participants in community dance classes

The residents mentioned above also have a number of role identities. In their lives before they entered a care home they had a range of roles – both work related (cook, head teacher, lorry driver, research assistant, factory worker) and in their family and social lives (sister, husband, neighbour, churchgoer, babysitter, football supporter). Some of these identities remain, but those that are connected to roles that they no longer occupy may seem like distant memories.

Whether our dance work is with independent, active, older people or frail residents in care homes, we are dancing with individuals who have occupied many different roles during their lives. We need to recognise and respect these important aspects of their unique individuality. In our sessions they are dancers (I remember one woman coming to me after a session to tell me she was thrilled to hear herself referred to as a 'dancer' – that was a new identity for her).

Respectful language – managing tricky situations

We have considered the language we, as dance practitioners, use to describe participants in our sessions. What about situations where an older person's language and behaviour are not respectful of others?

Discussion points

You are just preparing to begin leading your dance session when Emily starts to talk very loudly to the woman next to her. She is referring to one of the new support workers and is using racist language to describe them.

- How would you feel?
- What would you do?

The above example occurred in a residential home in the north of England. The dance artist felt very uncomfortable and found this difficult to deal with. Emily was in her own home, talking to her friend; the support worker in question was out of earshot and the dance session had not yet started. However, the dance artist found the racist language offensive and did not want to ignore it. What should she do? The dance artist chose to have a quiet word with Emily after the session. She used the Describe Express Specify Consequences (DESC) script,[9] which is useful for giving feedback to someone whose behaviour causes a problem for us.

Conclusion

This chapter has considered labels and definitions and the part these play in contributing to our sense of self. The language we use as dance practitioners has the potential to challenge negative stereotypes of older people – or, unwittingly, reinforce them.

Discussion points

- What do you understand by the term 'older people'?
- How do other people see you? Which roles or labels could be applied to you?
- What do you understand by ageism in relation to older people?
- If you were designing marketing material to attract older people to a dance project, what language would you use?

Notes

1. 'Focus on Older People', UK Office for National Statistics, http://www.statistics.gov.uk/hub/population/ageing/older-people (accessed 6 August 2012).
2. Universities of the Third Age (U3A) are learning co-operatives for older people who are not in full-time employment. They are run by volunteers and offer educational, creative and leisure opportunities, http://www.u3a.org.uk (accessed 3 May 2012).
3. Cutler, D. (2009) *Ageing Artfully: Older People and Professional Participatory Arts in the UK*. Baring Foundation: London.
4. Amans, D. (2010) Original interviews during research carried out for this book.
5. Setterston, R.A. Jr. and Trauten, M.E. (2009) The New Terrain of Old Age: Hallmarks, Freedoms, and Risks. In *Handbook of Theories of Aging* (Vern L. Bengtson, Merril Silverstein, Norella M. Putney, Daphna Gans, eds). Springer Publishing Company: New York, pp. 455–470, available at http://www.amazon.co.uk/Handbook-Theories-Aging-Vern-Bengtson/dp/0826162517/ref=sr_1_fkmr1_1?ie=UTF8&qid=1344268890&sr=8-1-fkmr1.
6. Tepper, K. (1994) The role of labelling processes in elderly consumers' responses to age segmentation cues. *Journal of Consumer Research*, 20, 503–518.
7. Smith, A. (1997) Mind your rhetoric. *Animated*, Winter 1997. This article is reproduced in full in Part Three.
8. Stryker, S. and Burke, P.J. (2000) The past, present and future of identity theory. *Social Psychology Quarterly*, 63, 284–297.
9. Bower, S. and Bower, G. (2004) *Asserting Yourself – Updated Edition: A Practical Guide for Positive Change*. Da Capo Press: Boston, MA. The Describe Express Specify Consequences (DESC) script is a tool for assertive communication. In giving feedback to someone using the DESC script we would describe the behaviour, explain how

it makes us feel, say what we'd like to happen and outline any consequences (both positive and negative). For further explanation see the Caring with Confidence website www.caringwithconfidenceonline.co.uk (accessed 6 August 2012).

Further Reading

Simmons, M. *Getting a Life: Older People Talking*. Peter Owen Publishers: London.

2   Ageing and Society in the UK

Sara Houston

....

This chapter includes further debate about who we actually mean when we are referring to older people, together with information on changing demographics and the role of older people in society.

Sara Houston also discusses:

- how legislation and service provision contribute to perceptions of senior citizens in the UK
- popular culture and representations of older people in the media
- negative stereotypes and the ways these impact on society

....

The UK, like many places around the world, has an ageing society. In 2009, 16% of the population were over 65. By 2034, the Office for National Statistics predicts that 25% of the population will be aged 65 and over. Only 18% will be under 16.[1] Despite a more aged population with, one might assume, an increasing influence, there are still issues concerning older people that remain endemic in society. These issues centre on health, social care, finance and a general lack of awareness about older people.

The Health Service Ombudsman's 2011 report is an example of how lack of awareness has infiltrated into health care for frail older people. In February 2011, the Health Service Ombudsman, Ann Abraham, produced a report[2] that detailed accounts of lack of care, compassion, due process and procedure for older people in hospital at the end of their lives. The report was written because Abraham noticed that she was receiving more than twice as many complaints about undignified care of older people than for any other population group.[3] Abraham argues that time and human and financial resources need to be allocated by the National Health Service to cope with an ageing population. She points out, however, that many older people requiring care often have 'multiple and complex needs',[4] which will only be adequately addressed by changing attitudes regarding the social and emotional needs of older people.

The lack of awareness and compassion towards vulnerable older people shown in Abraham's report could arguably be seen as ageist. Ageism has been an issue for some people as they have grown older. In legal terms, there was a change in UK law on age discrimination in employment, training and education in 2006 and again as part of the Equality Act in 2010. The issue of ageism in the UK had become pressing in the 1990s and 2000s as people in their forties and even thirties were refused jobs because they were considered too old.[5] Or rather, the issue had become pressing because the problem had started to encroach on the lives of those who would not consider themselves to be typically thought of as 'old'. For those older than the official retirement age of 65, the problem of ageism was, and still is, amplified.[6] The systematic discrimination against, and stereotyping of, people because they are perceived to be 'old' pervades many aspects of life; the area of the ability to work is just one.

Stereotyping of a grouping of people works, in cultural theorist Stuart Hall's words, 'to reduce, essentialise, naturalise and fix difference'.[7] By making absolute the various general characteristics of a type of person,[8] a boundary is created between that marginalised grouping and those who do not align themselves with it. Whilst through empirical data it is difficult to distinguish any visible demarcation that essentially separates one social category from another, Richard Dyer comments: 'the role of stereotypes is [...] to make fast, firm and separate what is in reality fluid and much closer to the norm than the dominant value system cares to admit'.[9] In her workbook *The Arts and Older People*, Fi Frances lists some negative stereotypes of older people.

Older people are often seen as:

- unattractive (wrinkled, sagging, bent)
- peculiar movers (slow, swaying, rickety)
- cranky or temperamental
- incompetent, inefficient or inactive
- ignorant or 'senile'
- useless (have no role in life or no contribution to make)[10]

The stereotypes force together a large swathe of the population who are very diverse in culture, experiences, preferences, education, family situation, class, financial status, health and well-being, where and how they live, work status, age, aspirations. In addition, they may not identify with any of the characteristics listed above. The diverse nature of British society can be seen in people whether they are considered mature or young.

In terms of the older person, the demarcation line between old and young is extremely hard to define. When does a person become 'old'? What is 'older'? Older than me? Older than you? Is it someone who has grey hair and wrinkles? Someone who is drawing a pension? Someone of 65, or someone a generation older of 95? Is it solely about how one feels, or acts? If a list were drawn up of possible answers, there would nearly always be a contrary claim to disprove each of them.

Many of the possible answers would of necessity centre around defining oldness as being different from other 'stages' of life. It would be possible to find many of the definitions taking on a negative quality in relation to what they were measured against. Frances argues in simple terms that it is precisely negative images of difference that allow the 'non-aged' to look on old age as a problem: '...older people are often seen as *different* from the rest of us, and different in ways that for some reason can make some of us feel superior'.[11] Sociologist Dick Hebdige's notion of subcultures can be seen in the situation Frances lays out. Although writing about those who *choose* to rebel against mainstream lifestyles, Hebdige notes that to deal with the other, the dominant culture labels and redefines the subculture to make it manageable.[12] In a culture of youth, older adults are first metaphorically ghettoised and then labelled because they apparently do not conform to the position that the dominant culture idealises.

In a body-conscious society, the computer games industry and the Hollywood and Bollywood film industries survive on a diet of young, impossibly flawless flesh. Take Lara Croft for example, the virtual tomb raider, the action heroine of computer games since 1996. She is a symbol of the young, fertile female with a phenomenal capacity to keep running, jumping and karate kicking monsters that stand in her path to the treasures of past civilisations. Croft is a fantasy figure, but her attributes stand in opposition to the stereotypes associated with older people in much of the UK.

Popular culture in the UK is fed by a tabloid media and advertising industry that aggressively champions a young, flawless aesthetic. Many popular lifestyle magazines tartly scorn well-known women for putting on weight, for revealing frown lines or cellulite and avidly collect gossip on which celebrity may have had cosmetic enhancements to prolong a youthful appearance. In line with gossip, the number of cosmetic surgery procedures in the UK has risen from approximately 26,400 in 2006 to 36,400 in 2010.[13] Non-surgical procedures, such as Botox, have been even more popular. Targeted at those below 50, those more mature, on the whole, are ignored: 'Defining markets has been a rigorously unforgiving process for years; if you're a mature female, you're somewhere between 25 and 44 or you're nowhere. The fact that you might be a glamorous, active, consumer-hungry 50 still puts you in marketing no man's land.'[14]

Anthropologist Haim Hazan points out that old age as a problem relies on the assumption that old people are separate from society: 'There is an unbridgeable gap between the "aged" and "society". We tend to speak of the "adaptation of the aged person to society", "what society can do for the aged"'.[15] He continues: "Paradoxically, whereas the aged are seen as having long, rich, personal and social histories, we relate to them as discrete beings detached from their previous lives and from the social frameworks of the non-aged."[16]

Different from the young models gracing colourful lifestyle magazines, due to inevitable grey hair and softening of facial features (provided there is no hair dye or facelift), the older person is perceived to have hardly any outer recourse to expressing his or her personality. If he or she does through unusual dress, hair colour or behaviour, he or she becomes branded as 'dotty' or 'eccentric'.[17] The subversion of the norm, of the expectations perpetuated by an ingrained representation, causes those 'rebels' to be ostracised further.

Mainstream theatrical dance in the UK is a specific example where replication of negative representations of older people has occurred, or where mature dancers have been ignored as artists. Apart from some distinct counter-examples, dance is often associated with young people. Most professional dancers in the UK are young and retire around the age of 35. On the whole, dance repertory does not cater for the dancer past their athletic prime. Some principle dancers, especially in ballet companies, are kept on as character dancers, but this invariably means either becoming token kings and queens or becoming the ugly sisters, the wicked witch or fairy, or the rather stupid and ugly comic loner. The association of the older person with unattractiveness, with crankiness and above all with witches is played out in dance. These myths and representations of the older person are still endemic in Western culture and are still active in dance.

The example of dance traditions illustrates how stereotypes of older people pervade the social structures that make up society. One repercussion of this is the adoption of these attitudes by older people themselves, thereby relinquishing activities they might have done and even self-identities they might have had before retirement, or, for example, before entering a residential home. In this way, stereotypes become enacted for real, even though possibilities still remain open to enjoy activities, such as dance, in all its facets. Anthropologist A.P. Royce notes in *Ethnic Identity*[18] that minority groupings often recognise that they have to acknowledge the rules and roles laid out by the dominant group in order to 'fit in' so as not to be totally disadvantaged. Since, she argues, the dominant order has no need to know the complexity of minority living as it enjoys the luxury of power and norms, stereotypes suffice. The minority grouping therefore appropriates stereotypes of themselves laid out by the dominant group.[19] Hazan puts it slightly differently:

> We see ourselves as we imagine others see us and therefore the behaviour of older people and their attitudes towards themselves are shaped and reinforced by society's prevailing images of them. By adopting these images, the elderly in turn confirm and strengthen them.[20]

Whereas Royce argues that the individual belonging to a minority group, in this case the elderly person, manipulates the dominant system, Hazan maintains that it is a far less cunning appropriation of dominant representations. Either way, the outcome is similar.

Whilst there are growing numbers of glamorous older actors and broadcasters who champion the ability of an older person to be active, youthful and clever, the problem of being different is highlighted after a person stops working, whether as an actor, banker or supermarket assistant. Despite the recent lifting of the default retirement age in the UK Equality Act, being left to claim either a comfortable pension or low value benefits once an individual has excluded themselves, or has been excluded from, the workforce sometimes can lead to a sense of devaluation for such a person. This is especially the case when the government puts so much emphasis on the ethics of work. In their welfare policies, recent UK governments have laid stress on getting people back to work so as to be responsible citizens.[21] Participating in the growth of the economy then is important for being seen to be socially useful and responsible. This idea can be detrimental to the person who is seen only as a receiver of state welfare, as in the case of many pensioners, or if they themselves feel that they are not producing work and being successful at it any more.

As 25% of the population head towards old age, there are fears for an ageing society. One well publicised fear is that many more older people will be forced into poverty following retirement or ill health because public and private financial provision will not be able to cope with the demand.[22] Yet it is clear from UK studies on quality of life issues for older people that financial stability is only one concern amongst many indications of quality of life. Following several large scale studies, sociologists John Bond and Lynne Corner[23] have suggested that the four major elements that older people say give their lives quality are family, social contacts, health, mobility and ability. After these factors comes material circumstance and participation in activities. Relationships between people and keeping healthy are therefore key to maintaining or developing the quality of life for an ageing population.

Organised arts activity, including dancing, is one way that people have developed their social networks. In contrast to the representations of older people in dance mentioned above, much community dance has welcomed mature participants, and outlets for creativity through dance are growing for this section of the population. In conducting interviews with a group of older people with Parkinson's who attended a dance class in London, I asked them why they came to the class.[24] Their answers were broadly similar, spanning reasons to do with health, confidence, sociability and because they liked dancing, or felt they could give it a go. Many decided to dance because they found it difficult to keep up exercises on their own. Dancing, many of them confided, was also much more interesting than straightforward exercise. The social impact of dancing was immense. All of the group had stopped working and the dance sessions were a way of feeling productive, active and sociable. These responses mirror other findings.[25] Comedia's report *Use or Ornament? The Social Impact of Participation in the Arts*[26] testifies to positive outcomes of participation in arts activity internationally, in particular regarding social cohesion, community empowerment and self-determination, health and well-being. In 2003 Everitt and Hamilton's UK-wide study into the connection between the arts and health likewise concluded that participating in the arts for both younger and older people enhanced, amongst other things: '[...] positive mental health, emotional literacy ... healthy communities'.[27]

As these examples testify, arts activities can be illustrations of positive acts that give meaning and purpose to people's lives whatever their age. As British society engages with the challenges of an ageing population, it is also useful to document the channels of expression and fulfilment in which older people may participate.

Notes

1. Office for National Statistics. http://www.statistics.gov.uk (accessed 14 January 2011).
2. Abraham, Ann (2011) *Care and Compassion? Report of the Health Service Ombudsman on Ten Investigations into NHS Care of Older People*, London: The Stationery Office.
3. Ibid, p. 8.
4. Ibid, p. 9.

5. The 1999 GMB union equality briefing on age discrimination cited findings in conjunction with the 1993 Labour Force Survey and the 1989 report of the Select Committee in the Employment Patterns of the Over 50s, disclosing that the over 40s were being bypassed for promotion, the over 50s were finding it hard to obtain a job interview and the over 55s were more likely to be in long-term unemployment. GMB (1999) *Equality Briefing: Age Discrimination*. http://www.gmb.org.uk (accessed 5 April 1999).

6. See the numerous publications by Age UK, also findings by sociologists, such as Christina Victor, Haim Hazan and Bill Bytheway: Bytheway, Bill (1995) *Ageism*, Buckingham: Open University Press; Hazan, Haim (1994) *Old Age: Constructions and Deconstructions*, Cambridge: Cambridge University Press; Victor, Christina (1994) *Old Age in Modern Society*, London: Chapman & Hall (first published 1987).

7. Hall, Stuart (1997) *Representation: Cultural Representations and Signifying Practices*, London: Sage, p. 258.

8. Roger Brown argues that a 'type' of person, where they are classified by their 'role' in society, differs from that of a stereotype of a person. Although generalised, types do not reduce the individual to simple essentialisms that tie that individual to certain social representations. Brown, Roger (1965) *Social Psychology*, New York: Macmillan, pp. 152–154.

9. Dyer, Richard (1993) *The Matter of Images: Essays on Representations*, London: Routledge, p. 16.

10. Frances, Fi (1999) *The Arts and Older People: A Practical Introduction*, London: Age Concern, p. 27.

11. Frances, *The Arts and Older People*, p. 27.

12. Hebdige, Dick (1979) *Subculture: The Meaning of Style*, London: Routledge, p. 94.

13. Statistics obtained from the British Association of Aesthetic Plastic Surgeons, February 2010, http://www.baaps.org.uk (accessed 4 April 2011).

14. O'Sullivan, Sally (2004) 'A Stiff Shot of Botox for the Over 40s Market', *The Observer*, http://www.guardian.co.uk/media/2004/jul/11/condenast.pressandpublishing, 11 July 2004 (accessed 4 April 2011).

15. Hazan, *Old Age*, p. 18.

16. Ibid.

17. It is interesting to note that 'dotty' is usually used in the UK to denote females who are financially poor and 'eccentric' to describe wealthy old people of both sexes, 'dotty' being the more pejorative term.

18. Royce, Anya Peterson (1982) *Ethnic Identity: Strategies of Diversity*, Bloomington: Indiana University Press.

19. Royce, *Ethnic Identity*, p. 191.

20. Hazan, *Old Age*, p. 33.

21. See publications such as Department of Health and Social Security (1998) *A New Contract for Welfare: Principles into Practice*, London: Stationery Office and the *Welfare Reform Bill 2011*. http://www.publications.parliament.uk/pa/cm201011/cmbills/154/11154.i-v.html (accessed 20 February 2011).

22. This fear is noted in public and private organisation initiatives to alter pension contributions.

23. Bond, John and Lynne Corner (2004), *Quality of Life and Older People*, Buckingham: Open University Press, p. 5.

24. Interviews conducted from October 2010 to February 2011 as part of research for English National Ballet: Dance for Parkinson's pilot project. Houston, Sara and Ashley McGill (2011) *English National Ballet, Dance for Parkinson's: An Investigative Study*, London: Roehampton University.

25. Brinson et al. (1992) *Arts and Communities. The Report of the National Enquiry into the Arts and the Community*, London: Community Development Foundation; Matarasso, François (1997) *Use or Ornament? The Social Impact of Participation in the Arts*, Leicester: Comedia; Shaw, Phyllida (1995) *Changing Places: The Arts in Scotland's Urban Areas*, Edinburgh: Scottish Office and Scottish Arts Council; Cooper, Lesley and Helen Thomas (2002) "Growing Old Gracefully: Social Dance in the Third Age", *Ageing and Society*, Vol. 22, pp. 689–708; Everitt, Angela and Ruth Hamilton (2003) *Arts, Health and Community: A Study of Five Arts in Community Health Projects*, Durham: University of Durham.

26. Matarasso, *Use or Ornament?*

27. Everitt and Hamilton, *Arts, Health and Community*, p. 77.

3   Ageing, Creativity and Dance in the United States

Pegge Vissicaro

In the previous chapter Sara Houston gave an overview of ageing and society in Britain. Here Pegge Vissicaro gives an insight into ageing in the United States, together with an example of community dance practice with older people.

   Her chapter includes:

- an overview of changing demographics in the United States
- a section on 'creatively ageing through dance'
- a description of the Moving Communities Model, which is a community collaboration with residents in a low-cost housing facility for seniors and disabled adults

   Pegge's observations on current changes in ageing populations offer a US perspective on the points made elsewhere in this book, particularly chapters 2, 4 and 7.

The United States and ageing

The United States is ageing at the fastest rate ever in history. Research presented on the website transgenerational.org (Transgenerational Design Matters, 2009) indicates that a person turns 50 every eight seconds as the average age continues to rise. In 2010, the population census revealed that one out of eight people is 65 or older. Although it is not a unique occurrence worldwide, Americans acknowledge that the shifting demographic landscape has significant socio-cultural, economic and political ramifications. This fact has become even more obvious during the current presidential campaign cycle since the elder votes, representing over 40 million people, will likely determine the election outcome and the future of our country.

Many conditions are responsible for creating this watershed moment, which shapes and is shaped by the ageing population. Some factors include technological advancements in medicine that lengthen lifespans. Another major effect is information access and delivery to promote health awareness and prevention. However, the greatest impact on this extraordinary time is the rapidly growing number of older people due to the baby boom following the Second World War. During the 19 years from 1946 to 1964, over 76.4 million children were born in the United States. In 2011 'boomers' represented 26% of all Americans (Federal Interagency Forum on Aging-Related Statistics, 2010). In the same year 13% of these individuals reached the traditional retirement age of 65, although that age has increased to 67 for people born after 1959. In 2030 one in five US citizens, or approximately 18% of the population, will be 65 or over.

The state of Arizona plays a pivotal role in defining and transforming the US social tapestry. Recognised as a destination for retirees and 'snowbirds' seeking a dry, warm climate, ageing adults flock to this part of the country. Today there are approximately 865,000 seniors over the age of 65 living in the state. In 2010 the city of Scottsdale, which shares a boundary with Phoenix, had the highest percentage of people aged 65 and older amongst places with 100,000 or more people (20%), compared with the national average of 13% (Brandon, 2012). According to the US Department of Health and Human Services Administration on Aging, Arizona is ranked first as having the largest increase of people 85 and older since 2000; the change is 50.9%. It is also estimated that between the years 2000 and 2020, the number of Arizonans over the age of 85 will surge by 102%. This profile of seniors and trends in lifestyle requires immediate and thoughtful preparation. The most critical concerns pertain to retirement planning and the health care system's ability to meet demands.

Creatively ageing through dance

First line baby boomers, or those who turned 65 in 2011, are revolutionising the ageing process. The number of years a person lives is no longer an exclusive focus. Instead, emphasis is on quality of life, which may positively impact one's health by minimising reliance on medical care. So what does quality look like and why is creativity, specifically involving dance, a strategy for meeting the needs of a 'graying' society today? As a dance artist ready to embrace the youthful age of 57, I embody the epicentre of this baby boomer generation. What has become increasingly important for me to realise is that I am also in a position to facilitate transitions for people in later stages of life using their own creative resources. Additionally my surroundings, living as I do in the heart of Arizona's largest metropolis, offer a distinctive framework to interact with and study seniors.

The greatest change in my thinking as I age is the discovery that purposeful or intentional movement has the power to provide holistic balance and serve as a stabilising mechanism for the elderly. Although numerous studies demonstrate the benefits of physical activity on slowing body–mind deterioration (Adler & Roberts, 2006; Greider, 2011; Kramer et al., 2006; Scarmeas et al., 2009; Singh, 2004), this notion of promoting the whole person is relatively unexplored. A holistic approach considers the interrelationship between physicality, emotionality, intellectuality and spirituality. Anxiety generated by fear of the unknown can easily disrupt emotional or psychological equilibrium; therefore, reducing apprehension and other stressors is vital. This happens through the acquisition of techniques for adapting to change that expressive and creative movement may facilitate. Intellectual balance involves assisting people to acquire skills or providing resources to help them become more knowledgeable about a particular phenomenon. For example, learning to dance Latin salsa, which lowers blood pressure due to increased physical activity, improves self-esteem, empowers individuals and promotes general well-being. Finally, the ability to envision oneself as an integral part of the larger world may be spiritually uplifting. The unified idea that everyone and everything is connected heightens consciousness, strongly motivating individuals to become more accountable for their actions. The whole person exemplifies these aspects as a networked system in which interdependency produces homeostasis.

Incorporation of a holistic philosophy in my own creative practice has evolved over time. These ideas were deeply influenced by personal experiences with the pioneer artist, Anna Halprin, whom I met in 2010. At 92 years young she has continued to have a profound impact on the field of dance for more than half a century. What Halprin brings to the world is an understanding that each person encounters a given context with his or her unique 'body' of history or repository of information. The inherent capacity humans have to tap into their embodied knowledge informs how, why, where, when and with what or whom we move. From that awareness emerged the Life/Art Process®, an integrative, expressive arts tool for holistic self-exploration. At the Tamalpa Institute, founded by Halprin and her daughter Daria in 1978, the Life/Art Process® was conceived based on the premise that creativity is intrinsic to all life (Restar, 2011). People's life experiences are the source for artistic expression.

The arts and creativity may be entering a new age, their golden years, just like the baby boomers who are leading innovative enterprises to change society. Fuelling the fire is an unprecedented level of co-operation between government agencies recognising the power of arts to transform the way people age. In March 2011, the National Endowment for the Arts and the

US Department of Health & Human Services hosted a first-of-its-kind event to showcase and discuss recent research on the arts and human development. Common themes amongst related studies demonstrated relationships between the arts and positive health outcomes especially amongst older adult populations. Perhaps the most compelling information to surface from this forum was the finding that 'arts engagement appears to encourage health-promoting behaviors (physical and mental stimulation, social engagement, self-mastery, and stress reduction) that can help prevent cognitive decline and address frailty and palliative care through strengths-based arts interventions' (The Arts and Human Development, 2010). The meeting also resulted in recommendations towards establishing a long-term federal partnership to promote and share research nationwide. What we see happening is a paradigm shift that will launch more collaborative and sustainable efforts to improve quality of life for senior Americans.

The Moving Communities model

My dance practice is framed by research on arts and ageing along with recent government-led health programmes such as Let's Move and Choose My Plate (daily food plan), and investigation of the Life/Art Process®. These contextual elements converge in the work I have been developing within a community collaboration at Westward Ho in downtown Phoenix, a facility for elderly and disabled adults. Established as a premier luxury hotel that opened in 1928, it once hosted celebrities like Marilyn Monroe, Elizabeth Taylor and the King of Nepal. The hotel closed in 1979 and then reopened two years later with US Housing and Urban Development subsidies as a home for nearly 300 low-income residents.

In August 2010 Westward Ho became the locus for the formation of a creative wellness programme designed to meet the needs of residents as well as staff. These needs were identified through one-on-one surveys facilitated by Judy Butzine, co-founder of the Cultural Arts Coalition, several months prior to conceiving the programme. Her work provided the foundation upon which to build a community partnership based on mutually shared missions and visions by all participants. With Judy's leadership, Arizona State University (ASU) College of Nursing and Health Innovation and Herberger School of Dance professors Kay Jarrell and I joined forces to co-design an interdisciplinary, holistic model with the intent to improve, enhance, strengthen and sustain the highest quality of life for all people, particularly those ageing citizens of Maricopa County. Together we proposed a collaborative approach to promote mind–body fitness that empowered and engaged older adults through self-awareness and group interaction. The programme, Moving Communities through Creative Wellness and Social Integration, explored how arts and wellness strategies positively impact the growth of self-sustaining, healthy communities (Butzine, 2010).

An existing community/public health course facilitated by Professor Jarrell provided a conduit for initially connecting the partnership to ASU. Her curriculum involved engaging fourth-year nursing students with Westward Ho residents and other groups of people in downtown Phoenix. Situated in a small room on the facility's second floor, these students took blood pressures, tested glucose levels and shared dietary advice, amongst other information. Some incentives for residents to actually visit the 'clinic' were socialising with Kay and her students, receiving free hygiene supplies and winning prizes for contests like 'The Biggest Loser', designed to encourage weight reduction.

The concept of Moving Communities slowly began to crystallise and generate energy. Implementation meant that from the onset our response to the insiders' interests was critical, which the Westward Ho residents had difficulty articulating. They desired physical exercise but did not explicitly mention dancing. A larger challenge we faced was that this population seldom communicated with each other, suggested feelings of distrust and fear, and a variety of other problems. The residents moved quietly through the public spaces and preferred staying in their apartments except to leave for doctors' appointments or to buy food. The strategy used to address this issue was to provide opportunities for interaction by co-ordinating events in Westward Ho public spaces that once radiated the energy of international celebrities. On September 21, 2010, the Cultural Arts Coalition (CAC) hosted the International Day of Peace in which musicians and dancers from outside Westward Ho intermingled with approximately 100 people. Together they shared a performative experience based on ideas of unity, reciprocity and balance.

Building on momentum from that event, multiple interrelated activities have been occurring in Westward Ho public spaces. The first is a series of free bimonthly art-making workshops designed to encourage creativity and social integration. The CAC buys all the materials and often pays professional artists to assist residents. Over the past several years participants have made calendars, masks, 'dreamcatchers', flower arrangements, clay pots, beaded bracelets and other items. During the creative process, they easily converse with each other and when it ends, there is a noticeably stronger bond within the group as well as an individual sense of joy and self-confidence from making art. The residents also stated they have achieved an expanded sense of well-being that demonstrates the belief that everyone can utilise the arts as a means to reflect, express and discover (Butzine & Ohm, 2008).

Another activity is a series of movement classes offered to the residents. These take place once or twice a week over an academic semester to correspond with the time Kay's nursing students are present. Her students participate by moving with us and recording each resident's vital signs before and after the 60-minute session. We explore breathing, imagery, relaxation techniques, strengthening and stretching parts of the body whilst seated in chairs, locomotor (travelling in space) and rhythmic patterns, individual expression and group collaboration. In addition to movement, we sing, tell stories, play musical instruments (mostly shakers) and draw. Healthy snacks and water also are provided along with reading material that elaborates on information presented in class, resourced by the CAC and the ASU School of Nursing and Health Innovation. In the first year of its operation, the CAC staff co-ordinated these classes and provided insurance coverage. In the second year I facilitated the movement sessions through ASU's School of Dance, requiring participants, generally averaging eight per session, to sign university liability forms.

A third layer of the CAC/ASU alliance is involvement by third-year dance majors. In their creative practices course, I introduce them to community dance, discuss methods for building community and explain the history and purpose of the Westward Ho initiative. Currently the schedules for Westward Ho movement classes and the ASU course do not coincide. However, my students make several site visits to meet residents and staff, participate in public events, including art workshops, and assist in co-producing a culminating activity for Westward Ho movement sessions to celebrate accomplishments.

This celebration best illustrates how residents draw upon the rich source material of their life knowledge to make dance. The partnership's intent is to place participants at the centre of their own experience, thereby revealing and honouring personal stories, which inform the creative process (Ohm & Butzine, 2010). The translation of experience into generating work also stimulates critical thinking, problem solving and self-discovery that lead to greater self-reliance for daily living. These are outcomes of ideal community dance programming when adhering to the guiding practices and core values that a partnership shares (Butzine, 2010). Though still far from achieving that ideal, my students use information acquired during site visits to design open scores, allowing multiple interpretations to realise common goals. For example at Harvest Fest 2011 students scored a dance that accommodated the residents' varied knowledges and abilities, and also connected them through a co-operative task. I noticed initially that the college students seemed reluctant to engage with elderly people, perhaps due to the vast age difference. However, with increased contact, relationships formed as they became aware of the residents' extraordinarily rich and interesting life experiences. One instructional objective is to help them discover novel strategies for broadening perspectives about creative ageing so that more student artists may consider pursuing this area of community dance practice.

Ageing, creativity and community

The Moving Communities model continues to solidify over time through practice, documentation, analysis and public dissemination of research. As a result of our association, Westward Ho recently received a national award given by the US Department of Housing and Urban Development (HUD) to acknowledge HUD facilities that strive to improve quality of life. Reflection on this work reveals the strong union between the arts, creativity and wellness. Yet something that warrants further mention is the investment of time to incorporate arts strategies and form communities. It is community, a fundamental way in which people organise themselves, that I believe is the missing link to developing the whole person and promoting well-being.

Anna Halprin, through the Life/Art Process®, reminds us that in the human world, diversity naturally exists because of the unique life resources each individual brings to a given setting. Every group, no matter the configuration, is as diverse as any other group. Like all species, we depend on variation to sustain healthy ecosystems; scientific research demonstrates that biodiversity adds richness to a particular environment (Midgley, 2012; Millennium Ecosystem Assessment, 2005). From a socio-cultural perspective, the rapid rate that Americans are coming of 'age' also has profound implications. The ease with which technology facilitates baby boomers to move and interact allows us to have more diverse experiences and access to knowledge. Since knowledge is power, boomers may be the most potent generation on the planet in terms of sheer numbers. This combined energy makes our presence known as we drive innovation to fulfil individual needs, significantly impacting all people.

The 21st century technological revolution, shaped by boomers such as the late Steve Jobs of Apple Corporation and other entrepreneurs, also fuels the growth of information-sharing tools. These tools foster the emergence of communities formed by people with common interests and goals.

Communities are important social spaces where collaboration yields new knowledge construction. Collaboration is a core characteristic of community, 'revealing the collective consciousness of belonging together and affirming the condition of mutual dependence' (Tönnies, 1957). Communities, similar to all social organisations, are inherently diverse. The varied knowledge each person contributes produces a natural tension, which triggers interaction as one relates information to share meaning. Since communities function to promote reciprocity, there is a greater possibility that members will be open to learning about different ideas to benefit the group. Additionally, 'negotiating difference' happens more easily in communities where interaction builds trust (Vissicaro, 2010). Trust supports members to take risks and explore more opportunities for synthesising ideas. This creative capital, which sustains communities, exemplifies the spirit of collaboration and is a powerful resource for communities in schools and online, and for initiatives such as the one at Westward Ho.

Conclusion

Like a fine wine maturing, boomers are now poised at an exciting moment in history to 'move' communities as a strategy for ageing creatively. The layered and interdisciplinary Westward Ho community model in Phoenix, Arizona emphasises purposeful interaction using dance and other forms of expression to develop collaborative skills. This exchange encourages social engagement, promotes holistic wellness and improves quality of life for seniors. Increased well-being has a phenomenal affect on society in the United States by reducing medical care costs that include fewer hospitalisations and less depressive states. At a moment of rapid growth amongst elderly Americans, the time has come for an ageing creativity explosion that thrives on diverse knowledge resources to build participatory communities through the arts. In such a dynamic and supportive network, members are able to imagine and invent life's possibilities; growing old is truly a creative process.

References

Adler, Patricia A. & Roberts, Beverly L. March/April 2006. The use of Tai Chi to improve health in older adults. *Orthopaedic Nursing, 25*(2): 122–126.

The Arts and Human Development: Framing a National Research Agenda for the Arts, Lifelong Learning, and Individual Well-Being. 2010. Retrieved April 27, 2012 from http://www.arts.gov/research/TaskForce/Arts-and-Human-Development.html.

Brandon, Emily. January 9, 2012. 65-and-Older Population Soars. US News and World Report. Retrieved April 25, 2012 from http://money.usnews.com/money/retirement/articles/2012/01/09/65-and-older-population-soars.

Butzine, Judy. 2010. Cultural Arts Coalition Current Programming at the Westward Ho. Retrieved June 1, 2012 from http://artscare.org/cac.event.83.shtml.

Butzine, Judy & Ohm, Melanie. 2008. Cultural Arts Coalition Introduction. Retrieved June 5, 2012 from http://artsCARE.org/cac.intro.shtml.

Federal Interagency Forum on Aging-Related Statistics. 2010. Retrieved April 30, 2012 from http://www.agingstats.gov/Agingstatsdotnet/Main_Site/default.aspx.

Greider, Katharine. 2011. American Association of Retired Persons. Retrieved May 2, 2012 from http://www.aarp.org/health/fitness/info-01-2011/the_real_fountain_of_youth.html.

Kramer, Arthur F. Erickson, Kirk I., & Socombe, Stanley J. October 2006. Exercise, cognition, and the aging brain. *Journal of Applied Physiology, 101*(4): 1237–1242.

Midgley, Guy F. January 2012. Biodiversity and ecosystem function. *Science 335*(6065): 174–175.

Millennium Ecosystem Assessment. 2005. Retrieved on May 5, 2012 from http://www.millenniumassessment.org/proxy/Document.356.aspx.

Ohm, Melanie & Butzine, Judy. Autumn 2010. Capturing Community. Animated, Foundation for Community Dance.

Restar, Taira. 2011. Tamalpa Life/Art Process®. Retrieved April 24, 2012 from http://www.tairarestar.com/life_art.html.

Scarmeas, Nikoaos, Luchsinger, Jose A., Schupf, Nicole, Brickman, Adam M., Cosentino, Stephanie, Tang, Ming S., & Stern, Yaakov. 2009. Physical activity, diet, and risk of Alzheimer's disease. *Journal of the American Medical Association, 302*(6): 627–637.

Singh, Maria A. F. May 2004. Exercise and aging. *Clinics in Geriatric Medicine, 20*(2): 201–221.

Transgenerational Design Matters. 2009. Retrieved on May 8, 2012 from http://www.transgenerational.org.

Tönnies, Ferdinand. 1957. *Community and Society: Gemeinschaft und Gesselschaft* (C.P. Loomis, Trans.). Lansing, MI: The Michigan State University Press (Original work published 1887).

Vissicaro, Pegge. 2010. The politics of extraordinary possibilities. *Animated*, Foundation for Community Dance, *Autumn 2010* (27–28).

4   Ageing and Society in Other Cultures

Diane Amans

....

This chapter contains a selection of data on older people in different world regions together with examples of ageing in different socio-cultural contexts. Inevitably these brief comparisons make some generalised points and these are not intended to reinforce the view that older people can be seen as a homogenous group.

In addition to presenting demographic statistics the chapter further examines age-related language, which was discussed in the previous two chapters. It also covers:

* Global ageing – issues and challenges
* Examples of positive ageing
* How older people are perceived in different countries
* Negative stereotypes
* Different responses to the International Day of Older Persons

....

Introduction

Throughout the world there are rising numbers of older people whilst, with few exceptions, there is a steady decline in birth rates. The term 'ageing population' refers to the percentage of the population aged 65 or over. In some countries the young–old balance is changing at a considerable rate and this has significant implications for all aspects of society.

Whilst population ageing is a global trend the countries with a recent ageing population are in the process of making rapid adjustments as they address some of the issues that the UK and other industrialised countries have been concerned about for years. These include concerns about pensions and the financial implications of funding long-term health care for older people.

Demographics

By 2050 more than one in five people will be aged 60+. In some world regions – namely Asia, Latin America and the Caribbean – the percentage of the population who will be over 65 in 2030 is expected to be double that in the year 2000. The oldest old are the fastest growing section of the community in many countries.

The world's population aged 80 and over is projected to increase 233% between 2008 and 2040, compared with 160% for the population aged 65 and over and 33% for the total population of all ages.[1]

In 2004, with the exception of Japan, the world's 20 'oldest' countries were in Europe and, for at least the first half of the 21st century, Europe is expected to continue to have the world's oldest population. Outside of Europe many countries have rising numbers of older people but their ageing *population* is growing more slowly as they still have higher birth rates than most European countries.

Global ageing: Issues and challenges

There have been two UN World Assemblies on Ageing – to discuss issues and challenges arising from global ageing. At the 2002 Madrid Assembly, Kofi Annan, who was Secretary General of the United Nations at the time, said:

> The world is undergoing unprecedented demographic transformation [...] Perhaps most important, the increase in the number of older persons will be greatest in developing countries [...]. Over the next 50 years, the older population of the developing world is expected to multiply by four.
>
> This is an extraordinary development that bears implications for every community, institution and individual – young and old.
>
> [...] Such a revolution will present enormous challenges in a world already transformed by globalization, migration and economic change.

He outlined some of the challenges presented by the world's changing demography:

> As more and more people move to cities older persons are losing traditional family support and social networks and are increasingly at risk of marginalisation.

The HIV/AIDS crisis is forcing many people in developing countries to care for children orphaned by the disease

In many developed countries the concept of cradle-to-grave security is fast disappearing. The shrinking size of the working population means that older people are even more at risk of inadequate pensions and medical attention[2]

In 2002, following the second international assembly on ageing, the Madrid International Plan of Action on Ageing was signed by 159 countries and adopted by the United Nations General Assembly. The plan contains three main 'priority directions':

- Older persons and development
- Advancing health and well-being into old age
- Ensuring enabling and supporting environments[3]

Global Alliance for the Rights of Older People

In 2011 the Global Alliance for the Rights of Older People was set up with the aim of strengthening 'the rights and voice of older people globally'. Nine organisations are represented on its steering group and these include Age UK, Global Action on Ageing and HelpAge International.

There is a proposal to create a 'Convention on the Rights of Older People' – calling on UN member states to make sure that older people's needs are represented at a national and international level. Opinion is divided on the need for a convention. Some take the view that existing structures are sufficient; many others point out the gap between legislation and implementation. Ageism and age discrimination continue to exist in most countries.

Speakers at the August 2011 open meeting of the Global Alliance gave an insight into the lives of older people in the different countries that were represented.[4] Here are some extracts from their discussions.

On the subject of social exclusion, which is exacerbated by poverty and little or no income support, Ellen Bortei from the University of Ghana pointed out that in Ghana only a small proportion of older people receive social pension and only 2% of people aged over 60 are registered for the National Health Insurance scheme. She highlighted the numbers of older people relying on informal support, which is diminishing as their children move away.

The representative from the Czech Republic, Oldrich Stanek, made recommendations that included the right to a minimum pension and 'adequate resources to live in dignity specifically for the most vulnerable: women, unemployed, forced early retired, older migrants'.

Himanshu Rath from Agewell International, India, argued for action to address ageism and age discrimination. 'Circumstances force old people to remain invisible. United efforts are needed.'

Insights on ageing: A report by HelpAge International

Today's '2050 generation' (those who will enter old age at mid-century) will be the policy-makers and professionals driving change in all fields of development. Demography is not destiny, and the choices they make will decide how successfully the world ages.

In 2011 HelpAge International carried out a global survey to find out what older people (60+ years) think about ageing and what action they would like their governments to take. The survey asked the views of older people in countries not featured in other worldwide surveys, such as Kyrgyzstan, Bangladesh, Mozambique and Jamaica. The project involved 1265 people from 32 countries across Africa, Asia, Eastern Europe, Western Europe and the Caribbean.

Main findings

Perceptions of ageing

- 48% of respondents over 60 think the world is becoming a better place for older people.
- 29% think that the world is getting worse for older people whilst 15% think it is staying the same.
- 72% of older people in rural areas feel valued, compared with only 56% in urban areas.

Health

- 88% of older people would like to see their governments do something to make living in older age better.
- 63% of older people find it hard to access health care when they need it.

- 65% of older people in rural areas find it hard to get health care when they need it, compared with 60% in urban areas.

Income and work

- 72% of older people say their income does not pay for basic services such as water, electricity, food and decent housing.
- 76% of older people in rural areas say their income cannot pay for basic services such as water, electricity, health care, enough food and decent housing. This compares with 67% in urban areas.[5]

Examples of positive action on ageing

The HelpAge International report also included examples of positive changes:

Kenya: In 2009, the Kenyan government introduced a social pension of 1500 Kenyan shillings (US$18) for all people over 65 years old.

Philippines: In February 2010, the government of the Philippines passed the Expanded Senior Citizen Act, which will introduce a pension for the poorest people over 60.

Nepal: The pension allowance has been increased and, since 2008, the age of eligibility reduced to 70.

Ghana: Following a meeting between older people and the Vice President in 2009, and a follow-up meeting in 2010, a National Ageing Policy and a four-year plan for implementing this were approved by the cabinet.

Bolivia: In 2007, a law was passed that awarded an annual grant of 2400 Boliviano (US$300) to people over 60 years of age throughout the country.

Tanzania: Included provisions related to social protection for vulnerable and needy groups, including older people, in its National Strategy for the Growth and Reduction of Poverty 2005–2010 (the MKUKUTA) and the National Social Security Policy, 2003. More recently, the MKUKUTA-II (2010–2015) includes people's empowerment as one of its three key pillars. It aims to improve the quality of life and social well-being of Tanzanians and to reduce inequalities across geographic areas, and as a result of income, gender and age. Targets include increasing the proportion of older people receiving the minimum social pension.

Mozambique: Older people are now included in Mozambique's national strategic plan for HIV prevention, care and treatment. Improvements like these dramatically improve the lives of older people and are likely to be the reason why 48% think the world is getting better for them.

In addition, the following positive changes were reported on the Global Action on Aging website[6]:

Mexico: In the Mexican City of Guadalajara a debit card was introduced in 2011 to help older people who have no social income. People benefitting from the programme receive 500 peso per month.

Spain: The mayor of Coruña has pledged money to cover the costs of social programmes and welfare policies as there is predicted to be a 41.6% increase by 2025 in the number of citizens aged 80+.

Russia: The local government in the Omsk region plans to spend 4.5 million roubles on a network of internet clubs for older people to learn how to use computers. They will learn how to use search engines, email and basic skills in Word and PowerPoint.

Canada: In 2011 the Nova Scotia Department of Seniors offered Age-Friendly Communities funding 'to assist communities to promote healthy, active aging by creating or adapting structures and services to be accessible for people of all ages'. They also introduced Positive Aging funding 'for non-profit community organizations to create projects that focus on health, wellbeing and community participation'. The department insists that older people are involved in the planning and delivery of projects.[7]

United States: In March 2011 a Positive Aging Act was introduced with the aim of increasing older people's access to screening for mental illness and treatment in community settings.

How are older people perceived elsewhere around the world?

First Nations elders

At the end of the 20th century the Aboriginal Liaison Office at the University of Victoria published a paper as part of a 'First Nations Sensitivity

Curriculum Review'. The paper summarised First Nations traditional values:

Emphasise connections with the past – continuity of life

- Tradition is important – even in the here and now.
- The value of respecting elders for their wisdom, age and experience particularly with regard to their knowledge of family songs, prayers, genealogy, etc. This respect represents a key element of a traditional community.
- Traditionally trained elders are often called upon during community functions to verify ancestral rights, songs, names and heredity rights. Part of their role is to ensure proper application of the process identifying ownership.
- Traditionally trained elders also provide the strongest ancestral connections to concepts of healing: a return to states of balance and strength in the modern age.

…young people may be consistently told the importance of helping others, saying hello to older people and being respectful to elders.[8]

There are similarities between the above and the preface to the Japanese Elder law (see below) which also emphasises respect for older people.

Case study: Japan and the United States

Both Japan and the United States have legislation relating to their older people. Compare the wording of the following extracts:

National Law for the Welfare of the Elders: Japan 1963

The elders shall be loved and respected as those who have for many years contributed toward the development of society, and a wholesome and peaceful life shall be guaranteed to them. In accordance with their desire and ability, the elders shall be given opportunities to engage in suitable work or to participate in social activities.

Older Americans Act of 1965: Declaration of objectives for older Americans

The Congress hereby finds and declares that, in keeping with the traditional American concepts of the inherent dignity of the individual in our democratic society, the older people of our Nation are entitled to...equal opportunity to the full and free enjoyment of the following objectives:

An adequate income...the best possible physical and mental health...suitable housing...opportunity for employment...efficient community services...participating in and contributing to meaningful activity....[9]

Allowing for the fact that the Japanese extract has been translated there are still interesting differences in language here. It would be wrong to infer that people in the United States do not love and respect their elders or indeed wish them a 'wholesome and peaceful life'; they just do not include these aspects in their legislation. However, there are undoubtedly significant cultural differences and, increasingly, some similarities between the two countries.

Japan, like the rest of the world, faces economic and social changes – which inevitably impact on people's attitudes. Despite Japan's long tradition of older people living at home with their children and contributing to family life, sociological studies are suggesting that intergenerational relationships are changing[10] and increasing numbers are moving into care homes.

Japan Respect the Aged Day

The Japanese have long been acknowledged as a society that values and respects their elders. They introduced the 'Respect the Aged' Day in 1963 – nearly 30 years before the International Day of Older Persons was launched by the General Assembly of the United Nations in 1991. Japan's national 'Respect the Aged' Day was established as a public holiday in 1966. On this day in September, Japanese people pray for older people's health and longevity, and the government sponsors cultural programmes and athletic events focusing on the elderly.

In Japan there are also well publicised festivities and traditions to celebrate people reaching significant birthdays. However, increased life expectancy and economic cuts have resulted in some changes. The Keirokai celebrations, described below, used to be held for people aged 60 and over, but because people are living longer the qualifying age has been increased to 65 or 70. As there are now so many more people reaching the age of 100 the government has reduced the size of the silver celebration sake cup, which is traditionally presented to centenarians on Respect the Aged Day. The cup, which used to be 10.5 cm in diameter, is now only 9 cm.

Keirokai

Local communities host Keirokai ceremonies where children perform songs and dances and volunteers deliver boxed lunches to older people. Keirokai is also celebrated in parts of the United States and Canada. The Japanese Canadian Community holds an annual Keirokai festival to celebrate seniors. The report of the 2010 Keirokai highlights the importance attached to this event; there is entertainment by community groups of all ages and messages from the Japanese Consulate.

If the younger generations [...] are the future of the Nikkei community, the seniors are the foundation upon which the community is built. The Greater Vancouver Japanese Canadian Citizens' Association's annual Keirokai, held at the beginning of each year, is one way of paying tribute to our seniors. On Saturday January 9, almost 200 seniors over the age of 70, along with a large contingent of volunteers, gathered at the Special Events Hall at the Nikkei Centre for a deluxe bento lunch and a variety of entertainment. Entertainers included the Tonari Gumi Minyo Dance Group, Alson Nishihara and Janine Oye, the Gladstone Japanese Language School, the Tonari Gumi Uzushio Kayo Club and Moko & Himali Kuwubara. JCCA Board member Gary Matson served as Master of Ceremonies and JCCA President Ron Nishimura gave the opening and closing remarks. Greetings from the Japanese Consulate and kampai were provided by Consul General Ito.

One component of the Keirokai that always proves popular is the post meal exercise led by long time volunteer Kay Fujishima. The exercises, which can all be done whilst seated, are a great way to get everyone involved and bring a smile to everyone's faces.

To close out the festivities, door prizes were handed out, along with gifts for selected guests as listed below:

Oldest men: Hajime Inouye 100, Jiro Kamiya 99

Oldest women: Kiyoko Ishiguro 101, Yae Kariya 101, Tsuya Imoo 100.[11]

Language and ageing

In the context of discussions about ageing populations, one of the significant differences between Japan and the United States reflects a different attitude to actually becoming older. In Japan it is customary to ask a person how old they are and to offer congratulations on their old age. In the United States it would probably be considered impolite to ask someone their age – and some marketing studies suggest that age-related labels should be avoided.

In 2010 the Omaha World Herald featured an article about older people rejecting the 'senior' label. 'You can call them Boomers, or you can call them the Me Generation. Just don't call them seniors.' Apparently a health care organisation changed the name of its retirement services to 'Immanuel Communities' rather than 'Immanuel Senior Living'.[12]

Media coverage of older people frequently uses the language of burden. In Europe's newspapers there are daily references to economic concerns and these inevitably mention the 'problem' of paying for an increasingly ageing population. Fewer younger workers and many more pensioners have resulted in references to a 'demographic time bomb' and 'silver tsunami'.

In Germany a new word emerged in the early years of the 21st century: 'Langlebigkeitsrisiko'. Literally translated as 'longevity risk' it refers to insurance liability resulting from a life expectancy which is longer than that allowed for when calculating premiums. There are negative meanings implicit in this term – living longer is causing an increase in the cost of insurance. It is actually seen as a problem! If this view is combined with other assumptions about ageing populations – for example, that they make little contribution to society – it reinforces one of many negative stereotypes of older people.

Negative stereotypes

We are regularly exposed to stereotypes of ageing, many of them seemingly harmless – such as birthday cards joking about wrinkles and memory loss. Often older people themselves contribute to the negative stereotypes leading to them becoming self-fulfilling prophecies. In Europe and other industrialised countries, we celebrate young perfect bodies and use images of youth to promote sales of anything from cars to vitamin pills. Indeed a fear of ageing prompts people to spend huge amounts of money to buy products that will keep them feeling and looking young.

In societies where becoming old is not regarded with many positive associations, young people are likely to see themselves as superior to older people. There is little to balance the negative stereotypes and myths – which shape attitudes to ageing. This is one of the reasons why intergenerational activities are being promoted as key elements in community cohesion initiatives.

In areas of the world where there is genuine respect for older people, and 'the elderly' are honoured and revered, it could be argued that there is less likelihood of stereotyping leading to negative attitudes.

Honouring older people: International Day of Older Persons

In 1991 the General Assembly of the United Nations designated October 1st as the International Day of Older Persons. Throughout the world there are special events in recognition of older people and the contribution they make to society.

HelpAge India (Orissa office) celebrated the 2010 International Day of Older Persons by presenting an Economic and Health Survey report on the care needs of India's oldest old. Another 2010 event in India was an Intergenerational Walkathon, which took place in Brahman Jharilo. This was followed by the delivery of a petition for better health care, insurance, pensions and social security and the distribution of umbrellas, bed sheets and food packets to all the older people who attended the event.[13]

In Australia there is an Every Generation Festival with a Positive Ageing Awards presentation dinner to celebrate the contributions older people have made to society. As part of the International Day of Older Persons celebrations in New Zealand, Age Concern gives awards for the best media portrayals of ageing and older people. The judge in 2010 said:

> Our Patron's Award encourages media depictions of older people that challenge negative attitudes. Lack of respect for older people in our society shows through in negative media images which, in turn, reinforce them...Judge Ken Mason issued a challenge to the media 'to get the truth about ageing out there: that older people are vital and diverse, they make a contribution, they have rights and they deserve respect.'[14]

Conclusion

Judge Mason's challenge to the media reflects the spirit of many of the positive ageing practices mentioned in this chapter. Some cultures value the role of older people in maintaining traditional connections with the past. They are seen as a source of important knowledge and wisdom. Others emphasise the growing financial burden associated with caring for their country's oldest citizens.

Discussion points

- How do the demographic predictions in the UK compare with the rest of Europe and the global picture?
- Are intergenerational connections changing?
- Do you think older people in other countries experience ageism, or age discrimination?
- How are older people perceived in other places around the world? As a burden or as a valuable source of knowledge and experience?
- What do you know about older people dancing in other cultures?

Notes

1. Kinsella, K. and Wan He (2009) *An Aging World: 2008. International Population Reports*, http://www.census.gov/prod/2009pubs/p95-09-1.pdf, accessed 14 August 2012.
2. Kofi Annan Report on the Global Action on Aging website, http://www.globalaging.org/waa2/articles/kofispeech.htm, accessed 14 September 2011. Note: In line with United Nations terminology, references to 'more developed, developed or industrialised' include all European and North American countries together with Australia, New Zealand and Japan. The terms 'less developed, developing or non-industrialised' refer to all other countries. These categories are used for comparisons, and may not indicate developmental differences between countries.
3. http://www.fam.org/docLib/20080625_Madrid_Ageing_Conference.pdf, accessed 14 September 2011.
4. http://www.globalaging.org/agingwatch/convention/un/OEWG%20August%20Day%203.html, accessed 14 August 2012.
5. Williams, J. (2011) *Insights on Ageing: A Survey Report.* London: HelpAge International.
6. http://www.globalaging.org/whatsnew/2011/September/Newsletter%2009%2012%202011.html, accessed 14 August 2012.
7. http://www.cakens.com/tag/ns-govt/, accessed 14 August 2012.

8. Pepper, F.C. and White, W.A. (1996) *First Nations Traditional Values*. Victoria, British Columbia: Aboriginal Liaison Office University of Victoria.

9. A Comparison of Japan and the United States on Issues of Aging Lesson Plans on Aging Issues: Creative Ways to meet Social Studies Standards. Adapted from *Schools in an Aging Society: Social Studies Classroom Activities for Secondary Schools*, State of Connecticut, Department of Education and Department on Aging 1992 http://www.ithaca.edu/gerontology/schools/pdf/Comparison%20Japan%20&%20U.S..pdf, accessed 12 September 2011.

10. Yamato, R. (2006) Changing Attitudes towards Elderly Dependence in Postwar *Japan. Current Sociology* March 2006, vol 54, No 2, 273–291.

11. Greenaway, J.E. *The Bulletin Journal of Japanese Canadian Community, History and Culture,* February 2010 http://jccabulletin-geppo.ca/2010-2-february/keirokai-2010/, accessed 14 August 2012.

12. Waters, P. in Omaha World-Herald 20 April 2010, http://www.omaha.com/article/20100420/NEWS01/704209899, accessed 14 August 2012.

13. http://www.orissadiary.com/ShowEvents.asp?id= 21615, accessed 14 August 2012.

14. http://www.ageconcern.org.nz, accessed 14 August 2012.

5   What Sort of Dance and Who Is Dancing?

Diane Amans

Older people are taking part in a wide range of dance activities – some of which are open to all comers and do not target a particular age group. Others are dance classes, projects and performance groups designed for older participants. This chapter introduces the reader to 14 older people for whom dance is an important part of their life. Their diverse dance experiences include a lively jive class, an intergenerational performance project, a tea dance and a gentle duet on a dementia care ward.

Older people dancing: What pictures does that term conjure up?

- Two ladies with grey permed hair partnering each other at a tea dance?
- Pamela Stephenson on the UK TV show *Strictly Come Dancing*?
- Granddad on the dance floor at a family wedding disco?
- A quiet duet in the corner of a hospice bedroom?

Here are a few more examples to illustrate the extensive range of contexts in which older people are dancing.

Geraldine and Bill: Modern jive

Geraldine is a 63-year-old college lecturer who goes to her local town hall for the weekly jive sessions.

> I enjoy getting dressed up – you don't have to but I like wearing skirts and high heels for a change. It's really good exercise too – I've lost weight and I feel much healthier since I started jiving. You don't need a partner – you can just turn up. You always get asked to dance.

Bill is 81 and goes to at least three jive sessions each week.

> I love it – gets me out there meeting people. It's given me a new lease of life since my wife died.

There are usually over 200 dancers of all ages with a beginners' class at 7:30 followed by a freestyle session.

Susan and Kath: Creative improvisation

Susan and Kath attend a weekly dance session at Marple Movers, which is based in Greater Manchester. The regular dance class is a fusion of creative dance and structured improvisation. They invite guest choreographers to help them make dance pieces that challenge stereotypes of older people. These dance works are performed at community showcase events and national conferences. Here are some extracts from their comments book.

- This is my stress buster.
- I have gained so much in confidence. I never dreamt I would be able to take part in a public performance.
- I was 54 when I was first called 'a dancer'.
- I grew about 6 inches.
- The feeling I wanted to express was being acknowledged.
- The regular sessions have helped me maintain my flexibility and stamina. On a recent holiday I noticed that I could walk further and for longer without getting tired.

Auntie Mary dancing

The above examples are of people dancing in groups; here is an example of someone dancing in the privacy of her own home. Dance artist, Amanda Fogg, recently found out that her 90-year-old auntie enjoys dancing by herself:

> [...] Frequently, when I phone her, I hear music in the background. The first time I remarked on this, she replied, 'Oh yes – it's something I put on to get myself going a bit'. Another time she said, 'I was just

Figure 5.1   Auntie Mary Dancing
Source: Amanda Fogg

flinging myself around'. Now I know that Auntie Mary dances every day. She performs a set sequence that she has put together herself and works through, to various pieces of music, 'Like "Anchors Away" – you know – lively tunes that make you feel like dancing'.

I love the image I carry in my head, of my wonderful Auntie Mary dancing in her kitchen diner, where the music player is, probably between breakfast, checking whether the birds need feeding, and then getting on with her day. It really inspires me.[1]

Patrick

A very different example of someone dancing in his own home is Patrick, dancing with Lucinda Jarrett from Rosetta Life.[2] As he was nearing the end of his life, Patrick, who had met Lucinda in the hospice, danced so that he could keep connected with people who were important to him. He valued the opportunity to be outside the medical narrative which dominated the rest of his life, and enjoyed playful movement experiences with Lucinda. He was keen to maintain his relationship with his grandson and he was able to do this though dance and movement play.

George and Edith: Dementia Care Hospital

George's wife Edith has Alzheimer's and is a resident at the hospital where he works as a maintenance man. Sometimes the activity co-ordinator organises an afternoon tea dance. On one of these occasions George decided to see if Edith wanted to dance. He carefully helped her up and she stood on his feet whilst he led her in a waltz. Afterwards, with a happy smile and a tear in his eye, he said 'I never thought we'd dance together again like that – I hope they organise another one of these'.

Margaret and Stanley: Tea dance

This is another example from a tea dance – the 2010 JABADAO[3] tea dance tour. One of the dance artists wrote:

> Margaret, the 96 year old who asks for a Cumberland waltz and dances it immaculately in a lone couple on the carpet-cum-dance floor . . .

> . . . Stanley can't stand but we dance a lot together through eyes, through hands, using scarves, feathers. We hold hands during *My Funny Valentine* and he asks if I'll marry him.[4]

Andrea: Zumba (dance fitness)

Andrea attends at least two Zumba classes each week. She goes with a group of friends who are all in their 60s. They enjoy the party atmosphere in this large class of more than 70 people:

> It's the feeling of being alive.

Andrea and her friends choose to go to the regular Zumba class, which is for all ages, rather than the Zumba Gold class which is aimed at active older people and people who are fairly new to exercise.

George and Molly

George and Molly attend weekly dance sessions at the local working men's club. George, aged 78, has just had both knees replaced and is delighted that he can dance again with his wife. His friends nickname him 'Fred Astaire'.

Judy: Member of GODS – Growing Older (Dis)Gracefully

We are a group of 25 women, aged 50 to 80+, who love dancing regularly; even better we love showing off the dances we have created together with many different choreographers: contemporary modern and Asian, musical theatre, storylines or abstract. The bigger the challenge the better. Dancing brought us together but friendship keeps us together. We perform wherever we are invited – outside a neighbourhood pub, in the city centre, local parks and museums as well as theatres. The exercise does us good but the buzz from performing keeps us vital, alert and self-confident.

Dance for Parkinson's

There is a rich variety of dance activities for participants who have Parkinson's disease. These dancers are usually active, independent people who enjoy the chance to take part in a social activity.

> I tend to shun special Parkinson's events because I do not want to be defined by my illness. Parkinson's is an unfortunate and involuntary part of my identity which I try to deny and reject. I am not a 'person with Parkinson's', I am C_ who would like to forget she has Parkinson's. Special Parkinson's events can be extremely depressing, serving only to remind me of my illness, and to suggest how much worse it will become. Getting together to dance, however, can be helpful, because it involves imaginative expression, and so enables me to transcend/forget my Parkinson's.[5]

To dance – or not to dance; whose decision?

In contrast to the above independent dancers there are people who 'have dance visited upon them'[6] in their residential homes and day centres. They are not always offered a choice about whether or not they take part – possibly because some venues only have one main activity room, or perhaps the carers assume they will enjoy it and do not offer to help them move to another room. Most people *do* enjoy the sessions but it is important to make sure that people have the freedom to choose not to dance. In some settings residents enjoy observing from a distance and may decide to join in at a later stage.

The dance styles offered in residential homes and day care settings will vary depending on the experience and interests of the dance artists who

Figure 5.2 Growing Older (Dis)Gracefully Dance Company, Taken at the NDTA Conference at Elmhurst School for Dance, Birmingham, November 2009
Source: Simon Richardson

have been employed to deliver the work. Participants may have been consulted about what kind of dance they would like to do but this is often not the case. Sometimes there is creative chair-based dance exercise and, following the success of the television show *Strictly Come Dancing*, many health and social care settings offer dance activities based on ballroom dancing.

There are also imaginative 'one-off' events, such as a Spanish party with flamenco dancing, Indian dance and storytelling and intergenerational projects linking care home residents with schoolchildren. These are often the result of a collaborative venture between dance companies and arts and health organisations – sometimes initiated by a member of staff or a local dance artist who wants to try something new. Chapter 6 looks at working in partnerships and ways of funding projects.

Performance opportunities

Many of the dancers featured at the beginning of this chapter enjoy taking part in performance projects. In the UK and other countries there are dance companies for older performers – sometimes with their own choreographer and often working with guest choreographers to help them devise and perform dance pieces.

Figure 5.3   Carl Campbell Recycled Teenagers Dance Theatre
Source: Kathy O'Brien

Company of Elders is based at Sadler's Wells Theatre in London and is a performance group for people aged 60 and over. They have performed in a diverse range of venues including the UK Houses of Parliament and the Venice Biennale Dance Festival. A number of national and international guest choreographers have created dance pieces with them.

Since they appeared on BBC2's *Imagine* series the company has had a lengthy waiting list of people keen to take part in their performance projects. Rehearsal director Simona Scotto has initiated outreach projects that have been supported by the Sadler's Wells Connect department.

Die Spätbewegten is a dance programme that takes place in the dance studios of Hannover Opera House in Germany. There are regular weekly groups together with performance opportunities and, like the Sadler's Wells Connect department, the Opera House supports the rehearsal director, Mathias Bruelmann, to develop outreach work. The label 'Spätbewegten' translates as 'late movers' – it could also be interpreted as 'people who were moved late'.

Recycled Teenagers is a programme run by Carl Campbell Dance Company 7 for people over the age of 50. There are weekly sessions in Peckham, London – using 'the dynamic rhythms of Caribbean dance to "lively up" its members'[7]

Crows Feet is an 'all women, all-comers' dance company based in Wellington, New Zealand. They create a new programme of contemporary dance every year and membership is open to any woman, provided she is over 35 years of age. Most of the choreography is by director Jan Bolwell, who founded the group in 1999.

Striking Attitudes is a professional company creating opportunities for community participants to perform alongside professionals. The company runs creative dance and movement classes in Cardiff, South Wales. The classes are mainly focused on making work for performance:

> ...and are designed to appeal to the more mature dancer (in the dance world that means anyone over the age of forty); the purpose is to enjoy. Class members have a broad range of abilities, from those working professionally in the field of community dance, to those who have never danced before.[8]

Figure 5.4   Crows Feet Dance Collective: Anglepoise
Source: Penny Towns

GODS – Growing Older (Dis)Gracefully, mentioned by Judy in the above section, is a dance company based in the Dance Department of Liverpool John Moores University. The age range is from 50 to over 80 and company members include dancers, teachers of dance and older adults who have had little previous dance experience.

> They are an important feature for the Department because they provide opportunities for dance students to meet with, talk to, be taught by, co-perform with older dancers – all of whom demonstrate that dance is not a short term career choice.[9]

Conclusion

This chapter has shown a small sample of the dance activities on offer to older people. It is an enormously diverse area of work, which attracts considerable interest both from people wishing to take part in dance programmes and from choreographers who are interested in working with a different and more varied group of bodies. Many of the above examples illustrate opportunities for possible employment for dance artists and valuable work experience or shadowing opportunities for community dance students.

Discussion points

– Why do you think people go to classes that are especially for older dancers?
– Crows Feet Dance Collective is for women aged over 35 – would you say this is a dance group for older people?
– Reread the section 'To dance or not to dance'. Do you think it is acceptable to run a dance session in a setting where people have had no chance to opt out? How would you handle such a situation?

Notes

1. Amanda Fogg interview.
2. Rosetta Life is an artist led charity developing new practice in End of Life Care and offering cultural activities to people living with long term illness. www.rosettalife.org.
3. JABADAO is a dance company organising movement play projects from very young to oldest old www.jabadao.org.
4. JABADAO Blog Rash Dash, www.rashdash.co.uk (accessed 20 June 2011).

5. Houston, S. and McGill, A. (2011) English National Ballet *Dance for Parkinson's: An Investigative Study*. London: Roehampton University.
6. Ken Bartlett interview.
7. www.ccdc7.co.uk/recycled-index.htm (accessed 14 August 2012).
8. http://www.strikingattitudes.com/Dance-and-Movement-Classes.html (accessed 14 September 2012).
9. http://www.ljmu-dance.com/thegods.htm (accessed 31 August 2011).

6   Contexts, Partnerships and Funding

Diane Amans

....

Who is funding and supporting dance with older people? What are the agendas? Who is delivering dance? Who are the target participants? Who would be likely partners in collaborative working?

This chapter will help the reader to plan projects, prepare funding applications and write marketing material. Using examples from the UK and the United States it provides the background information needed to illustrate how dance projects can connect to a variety of different agendas (health, arts, social care, leisure).

Case studies demonstrate a number of different ways of setting up dance projects with older people and challenge the reader to clarify the aims and objectives of proposed projects.

....

Who is delivering dance?

The activities described in the previous chapter include some that individuals have created for themselves and others that are provided by dance organisations and other agencies that offer regular classes and projects. Often these have been set up as part of local arts and health initiatives or in conjunction with charities such as Age UK.

Many local, regional and national dance organisations run regular weekly classes for older people. Here is a selection that was on offer in Spring 2011:

- Edinburgh Dance Base: Mature Latin Movers, Tap for Mature Movers
- Dance East: Time to Dance (over 50s)
- Cheshire Dance: Mature Movers 50+
- Glasgow Dance House: Still Dancing (for senior citizens)
- New Dance Llangollen: Strictly Fun Dancing (ideal for over 50s but open to all)
- DanceHouse Dublin: The Macushla Dance Club for over 50s

In addition to weekly sessions some organisations offer performance opportunities, either at showcase events for community groups of all ages, or as separate events. There are older people's dance companies associated with dance agencies – for example the Leap of Faith company at East London Dance and Dancing to the Music of Time based at Greenwich Dance. Chapter 5 includes further information on dance companies for older people.

Who is funding dance with older people?

There are fewer funding opportunities specifically aimed at dance with older people compared with funding streams targeting younger dancers. Nonetheless funding has been found from various sources including:

- UK Arts Councils
- Local authorities
- Voluntary agencies
- The National Lottery
- Trusts and foundations

Often dance projects in the UK have been funded by grants that have a different main focus such as healthy ageing, community cohesion and well-being.

Example 1

City Arts

City Arts is a Nottingham-based charity offering participatory arts to local communities. In 2009 they delivered an Elders Dance Project on behalf of Art in Mind.[1] Dance artist Jenny Edwards led sessions with two groups in care homes, and South Asian dance artist Vina Ladwa worked with Hindu and Punjabi/Gujarat groups at the New India Community Centre in Nottingham. This project was funded by the One Nottingham neighbourhood renewal small grants scheme, and was supported by City Arts, whose work is supported by Nottingham City Council and Arts Council England together with a number of trusts, foundations and other organisations. Their 2010 annual report listed the following funders:

Arts Council England
Arts Partnership Nottinghamshire (Nottinghamshire County Council)

Boots Charitable Trust
Esme Fairbairn Foundation
Lloyds TSB
Modernisation Fund (Capacity Builders)
Hardship Fund (Community Development Foundation)
Gedling Borough Council
NHS Nottingham City
Nottingham City Council (Arts and Event Service and Play Service)
Positive Actions for Young People (PAYP – Connexions)
Targeted Mental Health in Schools Programme
The Baring Foundation
The Co-operative Foundation
The Foundation for Sports and the Arts

The above list illustrates the wide range of possible funders for arts activity –
many of which do not have the arts as a primary focus.

Benefits, values and engaging with other people's agendas

Community dance practitioners are usually well aware of the value of taking part in dance activities; it is useful to be able to articulate these benefits in ways that connect to other people's agendas.

> [...] It doesn't dilute the art form. It doesn't mean that dance is in some way less important – but it could be that some of the partners/stakeholders/other agencies don't realise how important it is. We need to understand their priorities and help them understand how dance could become part of their action plan.[2]

In chapters 9 and 10 of this book, Elizabeth Coleman describes how dance activity contributes to physical, social and emotional health. In my own practice, participants and health professionals have reported improvements in balance, muscle strength, joint mobility, posture and co-ordination. There are also individuals who attribute a lift in mood and better sleeping patterns to their participation in dance activities.

There are numerous project reports and evidence-based research studies that describe the health impacts of taking part in physical activity in later life.[3] It is worth considering what dance can offer in addition to the physical benefits. It is an art form and has the potential to engage the whole person; dance offers an aesthetic experience and opportunities for self-expression.

...dance can have a positive impact on both the physiological and psychological status of older people.[4]

There has been some interesting research into the *Five Ways to Wellbeing*, developed by the new economics foundation (nef). The Five Ways reflect many of the characteristics of community dance projects.

Five Ways to Wellbeing

Connect . . .

With the people around you. With family, friends, colleagues and neighbours. At home, work, school or in your local community. Think of these as the cornerstones of your life and invest time in developing them. Building these connections will support and enrich you every day.

Be Active

Go for a walk or run. Step outside. Cycle. Play a game. Garden. Dance. Exercising makes you feel good. Most importantly, discover a physical activity you enjoy and that suits your level of mobility and fitness.

Take Notice

Be curious. Catch sight of the beautiful. Remark on the unusual. Notice the changing seasons. Savour the moment, whether you are walking to work, eating lunch or talking to friends. Be aware of the world around you and what you are feeling. Reflecting on your experiences will help you appreciate what matters to you.

Keep Learning

Try something new. Rediscover an old interest. Sign up for that course. Take on a different responsibility at work. Fix a bike. Learn to play an instrument or how to cook your favourite food. Set a challenge you will enjoy achieving. Learning new things will make you more confident as well as being fun.

Give

Do something nice for a friend, or a stranger. Thank someone. Smile. Volunteer your time. Join a community group. Look out, as well as in. Seeing yourself, and your happiness, linked to the wider community can be incredibly rewarding, and creates connections with the people around you.[5]

The Five Ways to Wellbeing are often linked to service provision by local and national agencies, including dance organisations. In 2010 Merseyside Dance Initiative – working in partnership with Liverpool Primary Care Trust as part of Liverpool's Year of Health and Wellbeing – incorporated the Five Ways into their evaluation of this year-long programme. They will also be using the Five Ways to Wellbeing as a framework for evaluating the impact of their recently launched dance and health strategy and programme of activity 2012–2015.

Partnership projects

A dance company or agency seeking to deliver dance work with older people will often form partnerships to support the work, both with funding and support in kind. Potential partners include organisations that have a remit for delivering services for older people, such as housing associations, residential and day care settings, leisure services, the NHS and charities like Age UK.

Sometimes collaborations have been initiated by a dance company or individual dance artist, who contacts various possible partners and outlines an idea for a project. Even if they cannot offer funding, stakeholders may be prepared to contribute other support, such as a venue/marketing/refreshments/putting artists in touch with participants.

The following example shows that it is possible for an individual to find funding, create partnerships and set up their own dance group for older people.

Example 2

Creative Dance 60+

Creative Dance 60+ is a dance group for active older people. It is small not-for-profit community organisation founded by project manager Jackie Richards, a local Tottenham resident. The group is managed by trustees and has its own constitution and bank account. The dance sessions take place in The Bernie Grant Arts Centre and are led by dance artist Simona Scotto, who is rehearsal director with the Sadler's Wells 'Company of Elders'.

Their initial six-month project, which ended in March 2011, was funded by a Haringey Council neighbourhood 'Making a Difference' grant (£4300). As well as offering creative dance opportunities for active older people the project aimed to 'encourage social cohesion... healthy living... and neighbourliness'.[6] They

---

have received further funding from the estate of an educationalist and plan to extend the work to include other communities.

Having evaluated this first project the group has decided to extend membership to people aged 50 and over, as they have received expressions of interest from this age group.

As a contrast to the above small-scale project, the next example, Life Circles, is a two-year programme with a budget in excess of £73,000 and a considerable number of partners.

Example 3

Life Circles

This is a two-year community dance programme involving eight residential settings in Somerset, Dorset and Devon. The project, jointly led by Somerset charity Take Art and a new organisation Core Dance, comprises:

- weekly sessions in each venue
- apprenticeship placements for dance practitioners
- continuing professional development for community dance artists
- creation of a Somerset Company of Elders
- development of a film and teaching resource
- mentoring for Core Dance

The partners involved in Life Circles are

- Age UK Somerset
- NHS Active Ageing
- Somerset County Council
- Activate in Dorset
- Dance in Devon
- Trinity Laban
- Foundation for Community Dance
- Arts and Health South West
- Dance South West
- Art Matrix

The project has been funded by grants from the Baring Foundation, Guildford Academic Trust and Arts Council England, with support in kind from Dance in Devon and Activate.

All three examples show evidence of organisations finding appropriate partners and working together. Funding applications are more likely to be successful when there is evidence that an idea has been carefully thought through and there is genuine collaboration between a number of organisations.

The Baring Foundation, which funded two of these examples, emphasises in their grants guidelines that they are looking for projects that 'display evidence of effective partnerships with residential care settings and in some cases other partners as well'.[7]

An example from outside the UK – partnership working in the United States

An effective partnership between the National Center for Creative Aging, New Jersey Performing Arts Center and the National Guild of Community Schools of the Arts has produced an *Arts and Aging Toolkit*. Although it has a US focus the toolkit includes some excellent advice about setting up partnerships. There are ideas for finding partners – in addition to the suggestions I have already made they suggest lifelong learning institutes, schools, houses of worship, colleges and universities.

The toolkit suggests what to say in that initial telephone call and how to prepare for the first planning meeting. In addition there are guidelines on grant applications, information on how participatory arts work can benefit older adults and suggestions for designing, implementing and evaluating programmes. It is a very comprehensive resource and, whilst some of the detail will not be relevant outside the United States, it has much valuable guidance to offer.[8]

How can partners build a sustainable future?

Successful older people's dancing projects address the issue of sustainability from the start.[9] Often there is training built in to the project, with staff in care homes and day centres working alongside dance artists and attending training sessions to enable them to support the dance practitioners and practise some of the dance activities on a one-to-one basis or in small groups. The Powys dance project, described in Resources, developed learning partnerships between dance artists and activity leaders in care settings.[10]

Where managers have seen the positive impacts of taking part in dance activities they have sometimes been motivated to put together a new grant application in order to resource continued sessions. Individual artists and dance companies could have a role to play in supporting agencies as they seek to move forward after a successful project.

What is the role of dance agencies and individual artists in supporting sustainability?

There are a number of ways to help organisations develop their dance activities with older people. It need not be a time-consuming exercise for dance practitioners to share their knowledge and contacts, and to suggest how the work may be continued beyond the initial projects. Ideally this would be considered well before the last session – but there is often a gap as evaluation is completed, more sessions are requested and funding is secured.

Here are some practical suggestions based on my experience of managing older people's dance projects.

- **Suggest sources of funding and help with the application**. For example, it is surprising how few organisations have thought of applying to the Arts Council for funding. Also, commercial businesses often have a community fund (see Boots and Lloyds TSB above).
- **Build on existing relationships and find new partners**. Celebration events can be effective opportunities for advocacy; they are an excuse to invite people to see the work. I usually distribute a questionnaire where visitors can indicate how they might become involved in future projects.[11]
- **Support groups in becoming self-sufficient**. Sometimes I suggest that groups constitute themselves as a not-for-profit organisation, like Creative 60+ and Marple Movers.[12] This works particularly well if you have several keen core members who are prepared to give time to setting up and managing the group. It is not complicated – they just need a bank account, a constitution and trustees or a small management group.
- **Negotiate support in kind from other agencies**. It can usually be mutually beneficial for organisations to offer support in kind or donate goods. It helps them meet targets. So when a theatre offers studio space it boosts their 'audience' numbers and people may decide to return and see a show. If a large supermarket donates bottles of water it demonstrates that it is giving something to the local community. It is always worth

asking; make sure you acknowledge the support from other agencies by displaying their logos.

- **Introduce or increase a charge to participants**. A small charge is unlikely to discourage people from attending the dance sessions and some practitioners have found there is more commitment when people have paid.
- **Join with practitioners in other art forms** and pool resources for a mixed media project.
- **Offer a shadowing opportunity** to emerging community dance practitioners (useful if you need additional support in a group and invaluable professional development for the practitioner).

These are a few ideas for making effective use of scare resources and increasing the likelihood of agencies further developing their dance activities with older people.

Being realistic – sustainability is not always possible

On the other hand we need to accept that it may not be realistic to expect a project to continue indefinitely. As well as sustainability we should pay attention to managing endings; finding a way to celebrate and value what has been achieved and accepting that it has passed.

If a project is planned to last for a specified number of weeks/months/ years, dance agencies and practitioners have a responsibility to manage the expectations of participants and other stakeholders such as support workers. In some cases there is a good chance that further funding will be found and sessions will continue; other projects run their course and come to an end.

Conclusion

As older populations increase and there is growing acknowledgement of the contribution that dance can make to an active old age, it follows that there are increasing employment opportunities for dance practitioners. This chapter has given some examples of the contexts in which the work takes place. If you are a practitioner who is interested in becoming involved in dance work with older people the following exercises will help you find some starting points in your local area. There is no need to wait for an existing dance programme to advertise job vacancies; sometimes the most innovative projects develop when an enthusiastic individual offers a few taster sessions and invites potential partners to observe the impact.

Exercise 1

- Collect information about services for older people in your area.
- Summarise the main activities of three providers or agencies that work with older people.
- How do you think these services support the quality of life for older people?
- Find information about any interagency partnerships. How effective are they? What is their impact on the lives of older people?

Exercise 2

Group exercise

Discuss services for older people and identify some key priorities for the following organisations:

- NHS
- Age UK
- Leisure centres
- Housing associations

Exercise 3

Make notes on possible ideas for a project with

1. Active older people
2. Frail residents in a care home
3. An intergenerational group

Choose one of your ideas and identify potential partners. Who do you think would be interested in your proposal? How could you persuade them to support you? What do you want from them? How will the older people be involved in setting up and managing the project? Identify possible sources of funding in your area.

Notes

1. Hui, A. and Stickley, T. *Elders Dance Project: Executive Summary*. The report can be downloaded from http://www.city-arts.org.uk/downloadFile.asp?fileName= userfiles/1140/pdf/Elders%20Executive%20PF.pdf (accessed 14 August 2012).
2. Amans, D. (2008) *An Introduction to Community Dance Practice*. Basingstoke: Palgrave Macmillan.
3. Connolly, M.K. and Redding, E. (2011) *Dancing Towards Wellbeing in the Third Age*. A literature review produced by the dance science department of the Trinity Laban Conservatoire of Music and Dance. It looked at project reports and evidence-based research studies that describe the health impacts of taking part in physical activity in later life.
4. Ibid.
5. *The Five Ways to Wellbeing* (2008) taken from the Foresight Mental Capital and Wellbeing project, which commissioned the Centre for Well-being at **nef** (the new economics foundation) to develop 'five ways to wellbeing'. Published as a set of postcards, they are a set of evidence-based actions to improve personal well-being. www.neweconomics.org/publications/five-ways-well-being-evidence **nef** is an 'independent think-and-do tank'. More information about their work is available at http://www.neweconomics.org.
6. Richards, J. (2011) Creative Dance 60+ Final Report (unpublished).
7. Baring Foundation (2012) *Guidelines for Applicants to the Arts and Older People Project Programme 2012*.
8. Boyer, J.M. (2008) *Creativity Matters: Arts and Aging Toolkit* published by NCCA, the National Guild and NJPAC.
9. Denholm, A. *Investigation of Sustainable Models of Dance Development Work with Older Adults in Nottinghamshire*. City Arts Dance Work with Elders: Final Report can be downloaded from http://www.city-arts.org.uk/.
10. For further information on the Powys Dance Leading Dance with Older Adults partnership see the Case Study in the Resources section.
11. See Partnership questionnaire in Resources.
12. Marple Movers is a Stockport-based community group that meets for a weekly dance session and an occasional performance project. Their constitution is included in Resources.

Further Reading

Bytheway, B. et al. (2002) *Understanding Care, Welfare and Community*. Abingdon: Routledge.

Burns, S. (2009) *Fundraising Toolkit*. Leicester: Foundation for Community Dance.

7   The Beauty of Reality: Older Professional Dancers

Fergus Early

· ·

The first six chapters have looked at definitions of ageing, and contexts and examples of community dance projects. Here there is a different focus; in this chapter Fergus Early reflects on the opportunities and challenges of being an older professional dancer. He shares some fascinating memories of watching mature performers in the second half of the 20th century. These include Leonide Massine, Martha Graham, Merce Cunningham and Jane Dudley.

Fergus also raises issues about expectations of older dancers and asks who is taking responsibility for nurturing their careers as mature artists. He outlines ways in which dancers confront stereotyped attitudes to ageing and presents a convincing case for valuing and celebrating the contribution of older performers.

· ·

When I was a young ballet dancer, there was a mysterious moment in Act II of our aged and traditional production of Swan Lake: at the end of a long and beautiful *pas de deux*, Prince Siegfried allowed the Swan Queen, with whom he is passionately in love, to fall, on the last beat of the music, into the arms of his best friend, Benno. Benno was otherwise unconnected to the scene, having just walked on stage expressly, it seemed, to snatch this culminating moment from his friend and master, the Prince. It turns out that this was not evidence of some hidden subtext of rivalry between the two men, but had a mundane and faintly comical derivation: when Swan Lake was revived in St Petersburg in 1895, the part of Prince Siegfried was allotted by right to Pavel Gerdt, a slightly portly 50-year-old, who was nevertheless the Premier Danseur Noble of the Maryinsky Ballet. Gerdt could manage the bulk of the *pas de deux*, which contained no lifts, but the final, swooning fall of the Swan Queen, to be caught only inches from the floor, was a catch too far – he refused to do it. Ivanov, the choreographer, was determined to end the duet with the fall. The result, a compromise: Benno would come on and do the catching, leaving generations of ballet goers mildly puzzled.

As an illustration of the role of the older professional dancer, this example does not cover the concept in glory – rather it reinforces some prevalent stereotypes, particularly the one of the dancer who has 'gone on too long'. For in general we have very particular expectations of professional dancers. We feel that they should be athletic, beautiful, physically powerful and possessed of real virtuosity.

What is this about? It could partly be to do with the sexualisation of dance in western society. In the early years of ballet, for example, dancers were seen as the playthings of the upper classes: in the 19th century, the Paris Opera of the Third Empire was in effect a sophisticated brothel where the aristocracy could take their pick of the young women and men as they fancied. This projection of sexual fantasy onto dance required youth above all – older people and sex was (and largely still is) a taboo concept.

Whether one considers the male roles danced *en travesti* by women dancers of the Paris Opera of the 1870s – in order to be able to show titillating glimpses of leg – or the sleek, cat-suited contemporary dancers of the last 40 years, youthful sexuality is a major engine in dance. Its resonance is immeasurably reinforced by the barrage of advertising promulgating images of young, thin, androgynous people, often, as it happens, dancing. In this virtual fantasy world, the immense beauty to be found in the reality of the human condition is disparaged and ignored.

For the reality is that humans are of all shapes, ages, sizes, colours, and that each of us moves and expresses our self with a unique character and a unique beauty. In dance, we too often limit ourselves to a ludicrously small segment of the range of humanity. Imagine a novelist limiting her or himself to writing only about young people between the ages of 18 and 35, each character weighing not more than 60 kilos (women) or 80 kilos (men), all nearly identical in musculature and physique and all corresponding to a perfume advertisement's criteria of beauty. Not a great literary prospect, I believe, and nor, in truth, is it so enticing on the dance stage.

But if we ask more of our dancers than physical perfection and a cloned beauty there are other qualities we might value: qualities associated more with experience, wisdom, an older age. What could we expect from older dancers? Perhaps economy, precision, emotional accuracy, relaxed humour, developed stagecraft, a vision of a healthful older age. I have had many vivid experiences of watching mature dancers over the years. Here are a few:

1966, Stratford upon Avon

Leonide Massine, in his seventies, a redundant hairnet ensnaring his thinning black hair, hobbled painfully down the stairs. First he would do his barrework, his muscles and joints following the ingrained patterns of 45 years, since Maestro

Cecchetti first laid out for him Monday's adage, Tuesday's rond de jambe. What he did might look a parody of the technique of the young dancers of the day, but his body and his mind needed these shapes, these repeated forms, their energy and their pulse. Later, in rehearsal, he would sit thinking darkly beneath his low eyebrows until with a cry of sheer frustration he would leap out of his seat into a ferocious rendering of the Can Can dancer from La Boutique Fantasque, his hands flapping at the wrist, his head thrown back and precisely inclined, his feet, which had seemed so arthritic, prancing like a young dressage pony. Then the moment passed. He subsided, spent and age sank over him. Painfully he regained his chair. We'd seen it though, that handsome Russian youth, filled with an almost diabolic energy, visiting us from the past, 40 years earlier, of the famous, fashionable, audacious Ballets Russes. It was no illusion; Diaghilev's young actor–dance lover had been there with us.

*   *   *

1979, The Royal Opera House, Covent Garden

At first it seemed like blasphemy. Martha Graham, the queen of anti-ballet, to appear at the Royal Opera House! But as the red curtains swept up and aside and Copeland's airy prairie music for Appalachian Spring sung out over the vast expanses of the old stage and as the chorus of young girls with their formal sweetness and the preacher with his terrifying stiff-legged sexuality started to make their choreographed magic, it was soon clear that here was a fine match – a truly classical choreographer taking a truly classical stage. On the same bill, Graham herself in Acrobats of God. There she was – long slit skirt of her figure-hugging dress, black hair flattened back with its bun pierced by crossed skewers, ludicrous up-sweeping Cleopatra-like make up – all just as it should be. Forward she came, down below the proscenium to a place where, like a true comedian, she could 'work' her public. Behind her slaved the dancers, now halted by a single gesture, now waved into ever more absurd efforts by her, Martha, God-choreographer in charge of her menagerie of acrobats. An eyebrow raised was all she needed to make us complicit in her callously mischievous schemes. We giggled, we roared. She had us, too, in the palm of her hand. Effortlessly she commanded her dancers. Effortlessly she commanded her audience.

*   *   *

1992, Queen Elizabeth Hall

The young dancers in their body tights spread, group, run off, run on, do important things in obscure corners and trivial things centre stage. Their technique is almost balletic, with just that slight skewing, that awkward angularity that is the hallmark of the old wizard of Modern Dance, Merce Cunningham. The choreographic form is satisfyingly unsatisfying. Never predictable, never derived from elsewhere. The dancers are immensely skilful, with an ability to change direction, to divert energy flow with a suddenness that is astonishing. Still something lacks; some spark that I remembered from earlier times. Then, unexpectedly (of course), a tall old man in a purple all-in-one leotard hobbles onto the stage. Someone has left a clothes horse on stage. The old man, feet recoiling gingerly from the floor as if the stage were covered in shards of glass, reaches the clothes horse. Ah, no! It's a portable barre. He clutches the barre, executing some steps, nimbly, in almost sprightly fashion. He lets go the barre and his hands do something that looks like a madly accelerated martial arts exercise. The curly hair is grey, the face more knobbly than ever, the feet tortured with arthritis, but a ripple runs through us in the audience. This man is performing. The other dancers, none even half his age, are dancing, dancing wonderfully, but he, Merce, is performing.

*   *   *

1996, A London rehearsal room

A woman in her eighties, spine, ribs, hips out of alignment, her hair white, her face alert and strong, pushes herself from her feet to standing, using the arms of her chair. She gives one hand, then the other to each of the two men standing beside her. She takes three steps diagonally forward, then three on the other diagonal. The steps are not evenly spaced on the pulse of the Schubert impromptu, but deliberately asymmetrical. She uses the support of the men without acknowledging them. Her body twists and the arms, unexpectedly long, extend wide, hands still held by the men, while her head turns in opposition. It is an effort too much and her body subsides over the back of one of the men, one arm hanging loosely down in front. On another beat of the music her shoulder seems to dislocate and the arm drops a further nine inches. It is a supreme gesture of fatigue that only this *body, in* this *position could achieve. Later, the woman walks to the front of the stage, still supported by the two men, and lets go their hands; as the piano climaxes, she lifts her hands up in a conscious re-creation of Isadora Duncan's gesture during her rendering of the Marseillaise. The moment is balanced on a knife edge of tension – can she stand alone? Will she fall? The meaning of this moment is focused through the precise physicality of its performer. No younger dancer could achieve the moment, for it could never contain this doubt and therefore this triumph. Jane Dudley, dancing after a recent hip replacement and a knee operation is showing us the power and danger of pure gesture and consummate performance.*

So what is it like to be an older dancer in the UK today? In one sense it is a privileged position. For a person such as me, who has been present as the entire panoply of late 20th and early 21st century dance has evolved in this country, it has been a wonderful journey. To have taken part as a young ballet dancer in some of the very first Graham classes taught in London (by Mary Hinkson, of the Graham Company in, I think, 1963); to have watched Cunningham, Cage and Rauschenberg in the 1964 world tour that finally established the Cunningham Company as pre-eminent in the dance world; to have first witnessed the eerie and comic abstractions of Alwin Nikolais, the soul dance of Alvin Ailey, the classical clarity of Paul Taylor as they toured in succession to London; to have been part of the creative maelstrom that was The Place in the early 1970s and then to have been instrumental in the birth of British New Dance with its seminal influence; to have watched the naissance of British Black and Asian dance; to have seen the establishment of the first dance degrees and then the burgeoning of scores of graduate and postgraduate dance qualifications in our universities; to have witnessed (and made a feeble attempt to participate in) the beginnings of hip hop and break dance; to have been closely involved in the astonishing rise of what is often called 'community dance' and integrated practice – as an older dancer and artist, I benefit immeasurably from my first-hand involvement in this long and rich history.

At another level, though, age is anything but an advantage. For all but a handful of artists (mainly those who have formed or become part of a larger institution), life as an older dancer or choreographer is tough. This is not to say that young or 'emerging' dancers or choreographers are entering an easy world: competition is fierce and many more young people graduate with BA degrees in dance than can ever find work as dancers, but there is an atmosphere of encouragement – much funding is directed towards 'youth' and new work, youth dance has a high profile and popular programmes on television foreground young dancers of various styles. All in all, this is very positive – certainly dance enjoys an entirely higher approval rating, particularly for boys and young men, than it ever did in my own youth. No one, though, seems to feel any responsibility for nurturing the careers of our artists to maturity. Certainly not the bulk of promoters, who are happy in the main to put on seasons of 'new' and 'exciting' choreographers who are not too demanding of payment and respect, and tie down a few 'serious' slots with distinguished foreign companies and the very few British companies that have been given consistent support over the years. Not the major funding bodies of the UK, either, which, apart from funding those few on a regular basis, often seem to lack a coherent sense of a developing profession in need of nurture and continuity. Wonderful artists, at the height of their powers, have often been passed over for funding, or cut off in mid-career. This is unfortunate, because the generation of dancers who are now in their fifties and sixties, as well as being formidable artists in their own right, are the very people who can best offer real support for the younger generations of dancers and choreographers, as models of longer term development, as employers and as mentors.

Dance, like many things, is very subject to fashion. Young people in particular are the targets and prey of consumerist fashion fads – and dance styles are no exception. Older dancers and choreographers, by contrast, have lived through too many fashions to take such things seriously and are usually focused on their own paths of development, taking the work beyond the diktats of fashion. In our recent book, *The Wise Body: Conversations with Experienced Dancers*, my co-author, Jacky Lansley, and I conclude that the older independent dancers we interview, from several different countries and dance cultures, share the practice of dancing for life: 'If you intend to remain a dancer until late in life, possibly until the day you die, then your physical discipline must have a meaning beyond serving the ambitions of a career' [*The Wise Body*: Lansley/Early, Bristol: Intellect Books, 2011]. These dancer–choreographers are intensely self-motivated and, whatever their age, are engaged on journeys of exploration that are ongoing and forward looking.

Within the UK, a number of choreographers have, over the years, developed a considerable body of work with casts of dancers of different ages, exploring and celebrating difference and the aesthetic benefits that such diversity can bring: Matthew Hawkins, for example, has worked with mature dancer Diana Payne-Myers, as well as continuing to perform in his own work. Jacky Lansley has included in her interdisciplinary work such mature performers as Timothy Taylor, Sandra Conley (retired principal dancer of the Royal Ballet), Tania Tempest-Hay and me, and Rosemary Lee has worked with large casts of professional and non-professional dancers of all ages.

There have also been a number of initiatives that have brought together groups composed entirely of older dancers to form companies. Probably the first was the Netherlands Dance Theatre (NDT), whose Artistic Director, Jiri Kylián, formed Netherlands Dance Theatre III, in 1991, especially for dancers of 40 years and older. This group developed a great reputation in the dance world, but was disbanded in 2006, due to lack of subsidy. In its time, though, NDT III provided a model for a company of older dancers (even if most of them were a company of very fit forty-somethings, performing work that dated from the earlier repertoire of the main NDT company).

Figure 7.1 Fergus Early with Jreena Greene in Green Candle Dance Company's Production for Older Dancers, *Falling About*
Source: Hugo Glendinning

In this country, the first venture of this kind was by my own Green Candle Dance Company. In 1996, I mounted *Tales from the Citadel*, with a cast of older dancers ranging in age from their mid-forties to mid-eighties. The piece had music by Erik Satie and Sally Davies, design by Craig Givens and choreography by the cast (which included Jane Dudley, Jacky Lansley, Tim Rubidge, Brian Bertscher and me – all very experienced creators, as well as dancers). I directed the production, which toured England and ended with performances at the Dance Umbrella Festival in London.

In 2000, former Rambert dancer Ann Dickie formed the dance company From Here to Maturity to provide opportunities for mature dancers as well as aiming to encourage creativity and the participation of older people in society through education and outreach activities. Dancers have included Lucy Burge, Joy Constantinides, Jane Dore, Irene Hardy, Jennifer Jackson, Max Reed, Tom Yang and Artistic Director Ann Dickie.

In 2006 Soma/Numa & UK Foundation for Dance presented *Body of Experience*, a dance performance celebrating the mature performer in different world dance styles, which toured nationally. *Body of Experience* brought together six leading artists, performing in their own unique styles: Chitra Sundaram (Bharatanatyam, Indian classical dance), Debbie Lee-Anthony (contemporary), Jackie Guy (Caribbean contemporary), Jacqui

Chan (physical theatre with text), Nancy King (Raqs Sharqi classical Egyptian dance) and Raymond Chai (neo-classical ballet).

Whilst these companies are totally disparate in style, they all share a desire to challenge the ageism of society and in particular the dance world. *Body of Experience* published this statement about its approach:

> We are living longer and dancing longer. The older person is often marginalised, with the younger, athletic and muscular body blazoned everywhere, and we are told dance is only for the young. But the mature dancer brings something unique: a seasoned and experienced body memory, a different aesthetic and energy, perhaps a deeper understanding of performance artistry.

From Here to Maturity said, 'It [the company] aims to encourage creativity and the participation of older people in society through education and outreach activities, and by making original and imaginative dance pieces which entertain, stimulate and touch the emotions.' And Green Candle Dance Company has this to say about 'Tales from the Citadel':

> One of the curious features of our society is the way it undervalues and discards experience. Dance, with its wanton squandering of talent almost before it becomes artistry, is a major culprit. So much is lost so soon. The experience our cast brings to the production, on the other hand, not only gives insight into dance – the value of a gesture, the dynamic of a phrase – but also other skills the performers have acquired, acting and singing, for example, to the pool of physical skills which might be expected.

It is noticeable that all of these ventures have in different ways confronted our society's prevalent ageism head on. You cannot be an older dancer without being acutely aware of the prejudice and oppressive attitudes that confront all older people, not just dancers. As dancers, though, we represent a particularly vivid challenge to people's preconceptions about what is normal and suitable for older people. To still be dancing (and what is more shocking, to be earning money from it) in one's 60s, 70, 80s or even 90s – the Japanese Butoh dancer, Kazuo Ohno, danced on stage into his hundredth year – is viewed by many as an embarrassing aberration. In one way, the situation may even have worsened in recent times: ballet companies, particularly large state-run or state-funded companies such as the Royal Ballet, Bolshoi Ballet or the Royal Danish Ballet, with their traditions of character dancers who were as much actors as dancers, used to keep quite a large number of their older dancers under contract as teachers, *répétiteurs* and performers, dancing older character roles in classical ballets. When I first saw the Bolshoi Ballet in the early 1960s, they brought to London a complete chorus of older men and women to dance the 'cushion dance' in Romeo and Juliet, to magnificent effect – but such grandeur would be regarded as an unaffordable luxury nowadays.

So, to conclude: there are probably more opportunities for the mature dancer now than there used to be; choreographers and audiences are a little more aware of the value of 'difference' on stage than once they were – the emergence of integrated companies such as Candoco, Green Candle, StopGAP and Magpie Dance, which are inclusive of performers with physical and learning disabilities, has had a significant effect on changing sensibilities, allowing people to discern expression and ability where previously they saw only disability. On a wider scale, as our age demographic tilts the balance of the population towards older age, society is slowly waking up to the fact that older people, in all spheres, have not only needs and rights, but also vast and important gifts to bestow. The 'baby boom' generation, born in the ten years that followed World War II, and now in their fifties and sixties, are far from content to retire into oblivion for some considerable time yet, and we can expect dancers, like everybody else, to claim a much increased career span. This offers the prospect of dance emerging from what can be seen as an infantilised youth into a rich and varied maturity where it can fulfil its potential across the full spectrum of human experience.

The dance of youth has often meant the dance of virtuosity, and audiences will always hunger for virtuosity – it is exciting to see someone balance longer, turn more times, jump higher, flip faster, extend a leg more impossibly high – but it is an excitement of diminishing returns: how many circuses do we want to see? Of course I do not believe for one moment that young people cannot create and perform wonderfully expressive and satisfying art, but an art form which denies the participation of its most experienced exponents is subjecting itself to a kind of lobotomy: the artist whose practice has grown and developed over many years has a voice that needs to be heard and a dance that needs to be danced.

Note

*Sections of this chapter appeared previously in the journal Cairon: Revista de Ciencias de Danza.

8   Cross-Generational Dance or Just Communities Dancing?

Ruth Pethybridge

. . . .

Ruth Pethybridge is a dance artist with extensive experience of working in community settings as a teacher, choreographer and project manager.

In this chapter she explores the emergence of cross-generational dance – examining the terminology and the politics of difference in relation to dance projects across generations. In addition to offering a theoretical context for the work, Ruth illustrates the chapter with examples drawn from her own practice and that of other experienced dance artists.

Ruth offers her own perspective on some of the themes covered in other parts of this book. She offers further discussion on terminology, a subject that was explored in the first two chapters. Also, her inclusive approaches to choreography and her argument for flexibility in the dance artist's role reinforce the community dance values that are discussed in Chapter 16.

. . . .

Introduction

The development of *cross-generational* dance as a category is a linguistic development that reflects a change in contemporary communities and dance practice. At what point an area of practice receives such a label, and it sticks, is a significant one – both within the field of dance and in the wider culture within which it sits. This chapter will examine some of the history, terminology and values of cross-generational dance and touch on some of the theoretical perspectives relevant to it.

*   *   *

I remember describing my area of research to a colleague who asked incredulously – 'cross-generational – it used to just be called community dance!' He was referring to the fact that in previous eras it was not uncommon to find different generations dancing together. In addition to artist-led projects in dance studios there was social dancing that involved people of all ages and was cross-generational without explicitly naming itself to be.

One of the earliest records of dance involving different ages dates back to the 1700s:

To commemorate the laying of the foundation stone of Blenheim Palace, Woodstock, in 1705, three teams of morris dancers performed on this occasion: 'one of young fellowes, one of maidens, and one of old beldames.'

(Green in Chandler 1951, 26)[1]

In this example, social dancing (morris in this case), does not need to be labelled as cross-generational, but rather evolves out of the relationships and practices of village life at that time. Arguably, the term 'cross-generational' has evolved out of necessity, as contemporary culture has become more fractured and communities more disparate.[2] Chris Beckett points out that:

Segregation between adults and children is really only common in industrialised societies, where children go to school while adults go to work [...] in pre-industrialised societies (and still in many developing countries around the world), both adults and children are involved in the same daily activities and routines [...] the change in role between childhood and adulthood is very much less pronounced.

(Beckett 2002, 112)[3]

The 'daily activities' or 'routines' that Beckett refers to here would have included the practice of certain forms of communal dance. The sharing of such activities by different generations is increasingly rare, as Beckett identifies, due to the fact that there has been a demographic shift in the way families operate in most developed western cultures.

As the change between children and adults becomes more pronounced, so too does the idea of generational difference – and the idea that this difference can cause a perceived gulf or 'gap' in understanding.

Generational difference has particular poignancy in Britain today, where there is an ageing population. In 2010 there was a spate of books published about this very issue: *What Did the Baby Boomers Ever Do for Us?* (Beckett, 2010), *The Pinch* (Willetts, 2011) and *Jilted Generation* (Howker and Malik, 2010) were three of the more high profile ones. Set against a climate of an ageing population, these books refer to 'baby boomers'[4] stealing future economic resources and 'intergenerational warfare' as a possible result. Whilst some of these claims may be overblown, the publication of these books does highlight the necessity of developing positive relations across generations in today's climate.

The emergence of cross-generational dance as a newly defined field, then, is timely. Dance artists such as Cecilia Macfarlane, Rosemary Lee and Luca Silvestrini are all working at the forefront of this field, each with their own artistic and political motivations. Lee, for example, states that it is simply a way for her to make work about the human condition and open up dance to wider audiences. For Macfarlane her practice evolved as she herself looked for satisfying ways to continue her career as an older dancer and to make choreographic work in an inclusive way. Silvestrini meanwhile has a mainstream professional company that runs cross-generational education projects alongside its own choreographic work. Other independent dance artists continue to work on a project basis, bringing together dancers of all ages in workshops and the creation of performance work.

Whilst the field itself is a recent development, some of the methods and values of cross-generational dance can be traced back further – to 'post-modern' or 'new dance' in the 1960s and 1970s. Macfarlane, who founded the Crossover Intergenerational Dance Company in 2003,[5] had 'strong links' (Jordan, 1992, 62)[6] with the New Dance movement in Britain, namely the London-based X6 collective. What X6 and Macfarlane's company at the time – Cycles – had in common, was an emphasis on the collective; a concern with the co-operative nature of how their group or space functioned. The emphasis on creative collaboration was a very clear departure from companies set up on the basis of a choreographer's rarefied talent or personal movement style. These egalitarian values were in keeping with a political movement in the wider arts scene that sought to overthrow the notion of the artist as an individual with special abilities. Owen Kelly refers to this as the end of a romantic idea whereby 'the artist was *different* from ordinary people, visited by a genius which stood outside geography and outside history' (Kelly, 1984, 59).[7] In the UK this movement was known as 'Community Arts'. The democratisation of art, associated with this movement, paved the way for community dance and cross-generational dance as we know it today – making dance accessible to people of all ages.

Terminology

Using the term *cross*-generational rather than *inter*-generational in this chapter is purposeful. The latter, although more commonly used, often refers to interactions between two distinct peer groups: 'the old' and 'the young'. These two terms are problematic when one begins asking at what point someone is considered to be either 'old' or 'young'. These notions are culturally specific and often more to do with policy, or perception, than how old someone is chronologically, or indeed how old they feel. What is more, using 'inter-generational' misses out a vast array of people who may fall in the middle of these categories, old and young. Instead, using 'cross-generational' implies a more fluid working definition. This is not to suggest abandoning the term intergenerational entirely, but merely highlighting how terminology and language might influence practice.

The terms cross-generational and intergenerational, however, share a philosophical problem. Both rely on an understanding of what is meant by generation. Seeing generation as a group of people born at a moment in time, who share traits or cultural preferences is problematic, as it homogenises vast groups of people. This is at odds with developments in cultural and critical theory that seek to particularise experience and provide specificity rather than generalisations. Again, it is not possible – or desirable – to do away entirely with the term generation as it reflects people's lived experience. Generational experience is often a result of how people are treated by the state as part of an age group. In order to examine some of the myths of ageing, it can be useful to think of how the body is not only a natural phenomenon but is also in fact formed through society. Structures of power such as institutions, governing bodies or indeed cultural attitudes have great influence and implications for bodies of all ages.

How state-run education functions, or when retirement age is enforced, directly affects the daily lives and experiences of those living under such laws. What is more, these laws also affect their relationship to their bodies and the practices they are willing, or not, to take part in. Feeling 'too old' to dance, for example, is often due to the cultural values of dance itself rather than its being an objective fact about physical limitations. The notion of the body as constructed by society, rather than being purely a biological phenomenon, has been addressed by numerous scholars.[8] This view can be useful to dance artists who may be trying to negate some of the negative perceptions of ageing, in that it questions the inevitable 'narrative of decline' associated with the Third Age. Social constructionism instead suggests that the body is a result of societal and institutional attitudes towards it. Through an inclusive approach that allows people to take things at their own pace dance artists too can also question what is 'natural', or the accepted wisdom about a particular person or dance form – challenging perceptions of what defines the 'older dancer'.[9]

The term generation is also referred to through the familial line. In this instance, when parents become grandparents their roles shift and they are considered to be of the third generation, regardless of their particular age.

Frith states that 'what is significant here is less the specific age of family members than the age difference between them and how this relates to domestic power and status' (Frith, 2005, 144).[10] Again, there is much more at play than simply a chronological account of how long someone has been alive. Rather, it is through relationships that generational experience becomes significant. Defining someone as 'older', for example, is always in relation to someone else, or a cultural norm. When working across generations in dance these relations come to the fore as participants do not have the usual peer group markers to rely on. Workshop participants may become aware of their ages in a different way – both in a negative and positive sense. Sarah, a 56-year-old participant of a recent cross-generational project, said that:

> Moving with young children was pure fun, a whole quality of play revived in me. Twice we played follow my leader with a child in the lead and this was particularly stretching and fun. They moved so quickly and it was absorbing to follow and made me breathless, I realised I don't dash about like that at all these days but I still can and the discovery made me feel younger and more in touch with my childhood self.
>
> (Bridge 2010)[11]

Whilst this is an extremely encouraging example, other older dancers have commented on their reticence and fear at working with younger people and not being able to keep up, or being considered slow.

There is significant difference in working with a healthy person in their 50s and someone who is entering what has been referred to by Anne Davis-Basting (1998) as '*deep* old age'; these people may be frailer or have more difficulty accepting new ideas around what is possible for them. Similarly, a younger person may feel intimidated by their lack of experience, and may also need empowering to be able to contribute positively. Planning projects appropriate to the needs of particular participants is key for dance artists working across generations.

The politics of difference

Age is one of the ways in which people experience themselves as being different from one another and this will affect how they feel and move in the dance studio. However, being 'different' can have the negative connotation of deviating from a norm. The older dancer is often subject to these connotations given the emphasis within dance practice on being young, fit and athletic. In this case the 'old*er*' may be in relation to what is considered the 'normal' age for a dancer – in their late teens to early thirties. As the previous section identified, these ideas may be deeply embedded in the people you are working with and it is the dance artist's role in cross-generational dance to gently challenge these assumptions. Being 'different' can be an asset to a choreographer interested in dance as a form of human expression.

Difference is a loaded term. It can be embodied in numerous ways and has been addressed distinctly as a political category by many writers in various disciplines. Indeed, as Ien Ang points out, 'claiming one's difference and turning it into symbolic capital has become a powerful and attractive strategy amongst those who have been marginalized or excluded' (Ang, 2003, 141).[12] 'Being different' can become a central part of how people perceive themselves. Many subcultural groups take pleasure in identifying themselves as being 'different' from the norm. In the case of older people, though, difference is often construed negatively as being 'other' in a consumer culture obsessed by youth. This attitude compounds generational difference being seen as a problem.

Davis-Basting, in her book *The Stages of Age: Performing Age in Contemporary American Society* (1998), addresses the notion of generational difference through interviews with members of two American performance groups. She establishes the similarity and bonding between people of different ages. Take, for example, the following quotation from one of the participants of the Roots and Branches Theatre:

> They come to us with maybe a little preconceived idea of older people, and they are a little wary of us – they are ready to treat us like older people. We of course look at them as young people. What's beautiful is the way it melds. All of a sudden we're all one age group. We become family. Ida – in her eighties.
>
> (Davis-Basting, 1998, 99)[13]

Whilst it is important to have such favourable examples, it can mean that some of the more complex issues get overlooked. Davis-Basting's tone is unerringly positive. She does not refer to the fact that these companies are potentially treading a fine line between reinforcing the stereotypes of different ages, or dismissing them in a project of denial, meaning that older dancers may be subscribing to the mainstream values of dance and performance rather than actually demonstrating an alternative aesthetic or value system.

In line with the desires of many political agendas for dance, what Davis-Basting does is use the intergenerational companies in this chapter as clear evidence for her assertion that 'a supportive, respectful atmosphere can absorb differences of age, personality and opinion without breeding division' (Davis-Basting, 1998, 110).[14]

This notion of 'absorbing differences' or coming together 'in spite of our differences' is common in politically left-leaning community arts projects that seek to create stronger links between people who may not normally interact. In fact, this interaction has been actively encouraged in the political climate that seeks art forms to prove their worth on the basis of merits such as 'social inclusion' and the like.

Whilst it may indeed be the case that working across generations generates cohesiveness, the notion of coming together *in spite* of our differences perhaps oversimplifies the embodied experiences of self at play in contemporary society. It glosses over differences in an attempt to homogenise for the sake of equality. Rather than seeing everyone as equal and therefore 'the same', cross-generational dance sets out explicitly to seek different ages. Therefore it can be useful to acknowledge, perhaps even encourage, this difference. Achieving this in practice is a matter of using approaches to creating choreography that encourage people to move singularly, rather than simplistically trying to 'bring people together' in order for them to 'meld'. As theologist Miroslav Volf puts it: ' "differentiation" [...] consists in "separating *and* binding" ' (Volf, 1996, 65).[15]

This is an idea that was shared by a 32-year-old participant in a mother and daughter dance workshop. She commented that:

> At one point during the process I noticed that my mum was having difficulty getting up off the floor and she tells me she's been having trouble with her hips recently, that it is in our genes to have this kind of trouble, arthritis too. I relate to a pain that I have [...] and feel the fear of wondering if that means it is inevitable for me too. The connection between us is painful at times in that as much as I love her, I also resist becoming too like her, yet the likenesses in our physicality make this very hard to ignore. I feel it is important to notice how different we are too, as well as what we share. By the end of the project mum says her hip feels much better, that moving so much more than she usually does, in a more fluid way, has done it good somehow.
>
> (Parry, 2010)[16]

In the instance of dancing with a relative, similarities and differences can come loaded with emotions. However, this differentiation often occurs in workshops with people who are unrelated too. It can be useful to think in a more pluralistic way than the binaries of either/or, and same/different.

Instead of categorising by way of 'different from [...]' or 'other than [...]', referring to people as unique is a way to indicate an alternative value system.

Cecilia Macfarlane often uses the term 'unique' in her practice, seeking ways to encourage distinct responses from everyone in a group rather than encouraging them to be the same as each other or conform to an archetype of what a dancer should be. She may provide everyone with a prop – a pebble, for example – and proceed from this by asking each member of a group to create a solo in response to it. These will vary dramatically although they begin from a common starting point. Similarly, life is lived and experienced uniquely, although it may have some of the same points of reference or commonalities. In contemporary society we define ourselves through multiple relationships and membership of diverse communities. For Macfarlane, it is important to include a wide range of ages in Crossover, in order that no one becomes a 'token' older or younger dancer. Rather than the two age groups of 'old' and 'young', Crossover purposefully includes a plurality of ages. Macfarlane has described this as being like a tapestry of different threads crossing over.

Both philosophically and in the dance studio, uniqueness is experienced in relation to others. This quotation from one of the members of Crossover also demonstrates how uniqueness is manifested in practice.

The big difference between being in an intergenerational dance company is like I think you become very aware that when you're watching somebody move, you're not thinking 'oh they did that turn very well' [...] I'll look at, say Akasha doing a turn and I won't think 'oh that's a perfect pirouette from Akasha', I'll think 'that's how Akasha turns' [...] and then I'll look at Cecilia and I'll think that's how Cecilia turns, and then I'll look at Jeremy and think that's how Jeremy turns, and then I'll do my own turn and think 'and this is how I turn', so instead of thinking of 'a turn' and seeing how everybody does that turn and deciding who's good at that turn and who is bad at that turn, you just are aware that everybody turns differently and then you celebrate that [...] we show that everybody does move differently and to try and get everybody to move the same, in a lot of ways is a little bit ridiculous and the best thing to do is to try and do your own turn in the most unique and individual way that you possibly can. And I think the more that I dance with Crossover, the more I become aware of my own identity as someone who moves and dances.

(Carline, 2009)[17]

Roly Carline's comment illustrates how, rather than striving towards an ideal in their movements or their physicality, the dancers in the company are recognised for who they are. However, this is not to suggest that they do not work hard or try to aim for the best that they can achieve, simply that each person is valued in their uniqueness. In this instance unique does not mean special or particular but simply that they are distinct from everyone else – *plural* – and that this is capitalised upon in the creation of choreography. A dance artist's uniqueness is a fantastic creative resource; it is the different body sizes, shapes and energies in cross-generational dance that can make it so compelling.

In an inclusive approach to dance, allowing each person to explore and experiment uniquely within a set task, difference can be – in Macfarlane's words – 'celebrated'.

Family dance?

Families can be a useful way in to working across generations – with parent and children groups or 'invite a grandparent' sessions, for example. However, there is a danger for the 'family' metaphor to underpin all cross-generational work, which is not always helpful. Jeremy Spafford, another dancer with Crossover states that:

> Given the gender and age breakdown of the group it is tempting to see it as a kind of family. Images created by the dancers have parental, sisterly, fraternal and grandparental resonance; indeed Cecilia used family references in the early days to set choreographic tasks. These soon came to feel distracting and unhelpful [...] it was the fact that the dancers were not related that made the experience extraordinary. As the project progressed, it became more and more obvious that intimacy across generations outside of the family is rare and, to some extent, taboo [...] and yet, within the safety of the group, there can be physical and emotional closeness. This is not a family: it is a group of friends of different ages, respectful of (and often amused by) that difference.
>
> (Spafford, 2006)[18]

Here, Jeremy points out how the explicit difference between the dancers informs their work and their relationships. 'Equality' does not necessarily mean being the same as one another. The dancers acknowledge their differences openly as part of the creative process, and the fact that they are not related makes this all the more significant.

Crossover is a unique company. It was formed by personal invitation from Macfarlane to people who have been involved in her community dance practice in Oxford, which she has been building up for over 25 years. Thus they were already committed to dance in some shape or form. The performers are a mixture of those with training and those without, but all had taken part in Macfarlane's community dance projects. Although Macfarlane is the artistic director, members of the company take responsibility for both its running and its artistic decisions – carrying on the democratic ethos that began in the 1970s.

For dance artists new to cross-generational practice, though, bringing people of different ages together can be a process fraught with obstacles. However arbitrary the divisions, lives in 21st century Britain are still very much affected by systems based on age that separate and divide outside of the family context. In practical terms this can make it problematic to bring *un*related people of significantly different ages together: how do you make a project appeal to a teenager and someone in later life at the same time? It can be easier, as in the case of Crossover, or families, when relationships are already established.

Given these difficulties, how the practice of cross-generational dance is presented to the general public, and to potential participants and their relatives, is crucial – particularly when not relying on established family ties. In my own explicitly cross-generational dance work I have tried different strategies. When starting out I led a day of introductory workshops for distinct age groups, prior to selecting people to take part in the development of choreographic work. Four workshops were offered, divided up as follows: 'Parents and children', '10–16-year-olds', '16 years+' and 'Seniors'. The process of deciding on these divisions revealed the arbitrariness of such categories. People who are 16 or just over do not necessarily consider themselves as adults, and people who are in their fifties or sixties are not always comfortable with such labels as 'seniors'. Participants struggled to place themselves within these groups perhaps because they were not the standard ones they were accustomed to.

I had several enquiries relating to them beforehand: which one would be most suitable for a 16-year-old? Is a 16-year-old yet considered to be an adult? What about people over 50? Understandably they want to come to the session for adults rather than for seniors. This experience illustrated to me why it is important to treat people as unique, rather than as a manifestation of some broader category of their age group. It also demonstrates the need to think carefully about what labels are used. Older people are still adults. Whilst sometimes it may be necessary to label a group or session as aimed at 'over 50s', for example, be aware that as well as including some people who may not normally take part in dance, it may also alienate others who do not wish to be categorised in this way. The advantage of cross-generational dance is clear, as it does not necessarily rely on boxing people in to these categories or familial relationships.

Crossover members have little control over whether the audience will perceive them as a 'family' (certain moments and images are almost bound to have this resonance), but it is significant to them that they are not. Members of the company view themselves simply as a group of differently aged people dancing and creating work together.

Touch in cross-generational dance

Increasingly, cross-generational dance work has political implications, as any adults working with young children are required to be checked by the Criminal Records Bureau. The intimacy and physical contact required of a dance project can disrupt some social boundaries that are not normally crossed outside of the family. Contact work is one of the most powerful tools of cross-generational dance, as I experienced when I ran a project in a hospice for the elderly and terminally ill. In their evaluations they cited touch as one of the most valuable aspects of the project for them. Allowing themselves to be touched and to experience contact when many of them lived alone, or only experienced the instrumental touch of medical care, was very significant for them. In cross-generational work, touch needs careful negotiation – with parental support and transparency in the case of younger people – but it is an important way of connecting, and indeed a useful choreographic tool. The issue of touch can elicit strong views. Whilst outlining her careful practice of open communication amongst the group on what their boundaries are, Macfarlane was also clear that:

> [...] if we get to the point where touch isn't possible when dancing with young people I will stop being a dance artist [...]. The loss of the whole concept of interactive physicality, particularly in intergenerational dance, where improvisation and subsequent choreography emerge out of physical differences, would deprive both the dancers of their inspiration and the audiences of their fun in witnessing this work [...]. The real delight is permission to be physical: this is at the heart of the work.
>
> (Macfarlane, 2007)[19]

Particularly when working outside of the family, it is important for dance artists to be safeguarded, but also not to have to practise in a climate of fear.

In creative dance practices touch and contact can be an integral part of the process. Deane Juhan states:

> We can never touch just one thing; we always touch two at the same instant, an object and ourselves, and it is in the simultaneous interplay between these two contiguities that the internal sense of self [...] is encountered.
>
> (Juhan, 2003, 34)[20]

Working physically in dance we can come to know ourselves and others better, through embodied knowledge. When these other people are all distinct sizes, heights and weights it gives dancers the opportunity to experience different ages from a sensory perspective; building up a more experiential basis for knowing what it might be to embody another age.

Values in action: Relational practice

Being a dance artist faced with a new group of people can be daunting, and when you are used to working with a certain demographic, a mixture of ages can present new challenges – such as how to introduce contact work.

Many of the theories introduced in this chapter present more questions than answers – how to acknowledge difference, without reducing it to binary systems? How to encourage unique, singular responses from dancers whilst creating a coherent piece of choreography (if that is your aim)? How to make a dancer of 73, and one of 14 or 30, feel equally welcome and artistically challenged? This section will look in more depth at how the values and interests of an artist can influence the actual methods or processes they use in the studio. Rosemary Lee articulates her own approach here:

> Fundamentally what I am doing [...] in making a dance or in teaching a workshop is finding ways to best activate that state of the dancer fully inhabiting the dance, or rather is it the dance fully inhabiting the dancer? It is that place of connection that I ultimately seek in anyone I work with in any context [...]. If I am making a work then I am trying to find ways of enabling the dancers to inhabit the piece that I envisage without losing their identity or being dis-empowered in any way. Similarly, in a workshop I try to find a way to help the participants find a state where they can experience the qualities I am interested in sharing with them. Those qualities are found within themselves, not planted

on them from the outside. My constant aim is to find a way to work primarily from the inside out rather than the outside in.

(Lee, 2004)[21]

In the same article, Lee also discusses becoming familiar with her materials as a visual artist might, by responding to the people she is working with and the dynamic between them. These ideas are a far cry from a choreographer teaching a dance 'work' that exists through time and is unaffected by who the performing dancers are. In the latter example they are simply there to learn a part, usually one that is heavily influenced by the stylised movement of the choreographer, an approach that has more in common with the view of a body being inscribed by outside cultural influences.

Dance artists working across generations need to respond in the moment to the individuals they are working with, rather than having too fixed an idea that – in Lee's words – comes from the 'outside in'. Providing structures within which to find qualities and ways of moving is one way of doing this, as is providing common images or props to which participants respond. Lee, for example, will sometimes work with the four elements – how one dancer interprets fire may be extravagant leaps across the studio, whilst for another it may be a flickering of the fingers. This approach to choreography is not exclusive to cross-generational dance, but working in this way with a group of mixed age dancers is essential, allowing people to take things at their own pace and level of interpretation.

These values and approaches, whilst common in community dance, can be discussed using Nicolas Bourriaud's notion of relational art. Bourriaud refers to artists as 'context providers rather than content providers' (2002, 33).[22] Like the community arts movement, the visual art of the 1990s to which he refers sought ways in which the work of art was no longer a static representation of a particular artist's genius. In the case of choreography then: 'original' movement vocabulary directly taught to mute dancers. Instead, art does not exist without the people who take part in it – the audience or spectator is as much a part of the work of art as the artist who conceived it. Similarly, cross-generational dance practice functions best through a participatory ethic, in which members of a group all contribute to the choreography. Richard, a 58-year-old dancer in Crossover's most recent project,[23] commented that:

I liked the pieces that evolved [...] rather than were choreographed. The sequence we learnt was a done deal, the moves had already been set [...] it was just about learning it and doing it so I didn't feel I got a huge amount out of that, but the bits where we were creating something whole as a group I found the most satisfying. and then I felt we were working well as a group.

(English, 2011)[24]

Collective choreographic processes defined as 'relational art practice' provide a useful link to a wider philosophical movement in the arts sector, relinquishing the need for such clear divisions between choreographer and dancer or professional and community. Who after all is the choreographer when everyone has taken part in constructing a piece of work?

According to Sally Gardener, 'the pair of terms "dancer" and "choreographer" distinguish Western Concert Dance from other kinds of social or so-called folk dance for which the notion of an individual author or choreographer is arguably not appropriate' (Gardener, 2007, 36).[25] Cross-generational dance is often associated with forms of dance such as folk or social dance, in part due to the nostalgic notions of communities dancing together in a more organic way than the often carefully constructed projects of today. Reflecting on her work in 2000, Lee commented that:

I am ready to take on the fact that maybe what I do is folk. I do not feel the nudge of 'that's not art' grasp my shoulder any more because I don't care. Where does that leave me, where is my home then? This idea makes me understand more clearly the dilemma I always feel between experiential work with which I am most familiar and making work to view.

(Lee, 2000)[26]

Largely a matter of language, how dance artists describes themselves and their roles is also reflective of the nature of the work – as Lee indicates. It may be appropriate to consider choreography as a widening field that includes the dance artist in the role of facilitator or director, amongst other things, such as a fellow participant or collaborator. A dance artist's role needs to be flexible depending on the agenda of the particular project or needs of the group.

Putting values into action means not only responding to the outside agendas for the practice, though, but also looking at one's own personal values as an artist. What is it that you want to create and put out into the world?

Bourriaud states that:

the role of artworks is no longer to form imaginary and utopian realities, but to actually be ways of living and models of action within the existing real, whatever scale chosen by the artist.

(Bourriaud, 2002, 12)

This view is clearly reflected by the following quotation from a participant in Lee's 2009 piece 'Common Dance', who said it was '[...] a kind of lived philosophy of community gathered around a personal artistic vision [...] both as a work of art and a function of human interaction'.[27]

The notion of a 'lived philosophy' does not mean that people are acting out an idea, but rather that they are engaged in acts of relating in the here and now. In phenomenological[28] terms, then, this participant had an experience of community through participating in Common Dance.

Whilst community remains a contentious word, it is one that is continually referred to as defining the sector that most cross-generational work appears in,[29] and as Burt Feintuch puts it '[...] we all seem to want community, even if we don't quite know what it is' (2001, 157).[30] Participants in much cross-generational work illustrate that it is possible to have an experience of community when they dance, create work and perform together. Simply the experience of a group of dancers of different ages performing together in a room is already a relational encounter that does not happen often in contemporary culture. Community then is no longer a static notion fixed to a particular time and place.

If the aim of community dance is to get communities dancing then cross-generational practice could not be a better example. It can – as Common Dance exemplified – literally, physically, *become* that community dancing – however temporarily. It can be seen as *both* cross-generational dance and communities dancing.

Conclusion

Demographic changes mean that generational difference is accentuated in the current political climate, a powerful imperative to bring people of different ages together in the creation of something new. Cross-generational dance provides a way to do this, and as a result can be used as a tool to encourage positive perceptions of age groups working together and of the ageing process in general.

This chapter has illustrated that age is not irrelevant or something to be dismissed as people meld to become 'ageless'. Age should be celebrated as a source of inspiration through similarity *and* difference. The failure to find an operationally functioning equivalent to age-based systems in practice must be acknowledged. I still refer to people by their ages as a useful way to identify them, particularly in cross-generational work. Age, as we use it in society, is both necessary *and* available for critique and questioning.

Through an inclusive, person-centred approach to dance – enabling uniqueness to be valued – artists can encourage generational experience to be positive. Dance can surprise people's expectations of what is possible or appropriate at certain ages. It can also be a place to express fears and limitations that come with advancing age, and for these to be witnessed and shared by those of other generations so that they ceases to be something 'other' or 'different'.

Notes

1. Chandler, K. 1993. *Ribbons, Bells and Squeaking Fiddles: The Social History of Morris Dancing in the English South Midlands*, 1st edn, London: Hissarlik Press.
2. See Baudrillard, J. 1998. *Consumer Society: Myths and Structures*. Sage: London; Lyotard, J. 1984. *Postmodern Condition: A Report on Knowledge*. Manchester University Press: Manchester; Hebdige, D. 1979. *Subculture: The Meaning of Style*. Methuen: London and New York.
3. Beckett, C. 2002. *Human Growth and Development*, 6th edn, Sage: London.
4. Baby boomers is a term often used to describe people born after World War II and is associated with certain cultural trends such as increased participation in higher education and growing up through the 1960s, a period of intense change. They are often associated with a lack of planning for future life stages such as retirement. See Beckett, F. 2010. *What Did the Baby Boomers Ever Do for Us?* Biteback Books: London; Willetts, D. 2011. *The Pinch; How the Baby Boomers Took their Children's Future and Why They Should Give it Back*. Atlantic Books: London; Howker, E. and Malik, S. 2010. *Jilted Generation; How Britain Bankrupted Its Youth*. Icon Books: London.
5. Crossover are based in Oxford and in 2003 featured dancers aged between 7 and 69. They are currently working with some of the original members as well as additional cast depending on the project. You can find out more at www.crossoverdance.co.uk.
6. Jordan, S. 1992. *Striding Out, Aspects of Contemporary and New Dance in Britain*. Dance Books: London.
7. Kelly, O. 1984. *Community Art and the State: Storming the Citadels*. Comedia: London and New York.

8. See Foucault, M. and Sheridan, A. 1977. *Discipline and Punish: The Birth of the Prison*. Penguin: Harmondsworth; Bourdieu, P. 1977. *Outline of a Theory of Practice*. Cambridge University Press: Cambridge; Thomas, H. 2003. *The Body, Dance and Cultural Theory*. Palgrave Macmillan: Hampshire.

9. Social constructionism has also been criticised for failing to account for lived experience and vulnerability but it is still a useful school of thought to be aware of in debating notions of age. It calls into question the reliance on chronological age by pointing out how much of it is defined by institutions and power structures.

10. Frith, S. 2005. 'Generation', in *New Keywords: A Revised Vocabulary of Culture and Society*, ed. T. Bennet, L. Grossberg and M. Morris, 2nd edn, Blackwell Publishing: Oxford, pp. 144–146.

11. Bridge, S. 2010. Interview, conducted by Ruth Pethybridge [written response to email] Oxford, September.

12. Ang, I. 2003. 'Together in Difference', *Asian Studies Review*, vol. 27, no. 2, pp. 141–154.

13. Davis-Basting, A. 1998. *The Stages of Age: Performing Age in Contemporary American Society*. University of Michigan Press: Michigan.

14. Ibid.

15. Volf, M. 1996. *Exclusion and Embrace: A Theological Exploration of Identity, Otherness, and Reconciliation*. Abingdon Press: Nashville.

16. Parry, M. 2010. Interview, conducted by Ruth Pethybridge, [written response to email] Cornwall, May 8.

17. Carline, R. 2009. Crossover Interviews, conducted by Ruth Pethybridge [face to face, audio recorded] Oxford, September 2.

18. Spafford, J. 2006. Reflection on working with Crossover [written in email] Oxford, March.

19. Macfarlane, C. 2009. Interview, conducted by Ruth Pethybridge [face to face, audio recorded] Oxford, 27 July 2009.

20. Juhan, D. 2003. *Job's Body: A Handbook for Bodywork*, Station Hill Press, Barrytown, NY.

21. Lee, R. 2004. 'The Possibilities Are Endless', *Animated the Community Dance Magazine*, Spring 2004, DC Publications, Suffolk.

22. Bourriaud, N. 2002. *Relational Aesthetics*; Les Presses du Reel.

23. 'Gifted', a dance piece choreographed by Ruth Pethybridge, looked at the nature of giving and receiving, and what it might mean to be a 'gifted' dancer as it is manifested in each unique dancer of Crossover. Premiered at Pegasus Theatre, Oxford, October 2011.

24. English, R. 2011. Interview, conducted by Ruth Pethybridge [by telephone, audio recorded] November 3.

25. Gardener, S. 2007. 'The Dancer, the Choreographer and Modern Dance Scholarship: A Critical Reading', *Dance Research Journal*, vol. 25, no. 1, pp. 35–53.

26. Lee, R. 2000. Last update, Fragments [Homepage of Rescen Middlesex University], [Online] available at: http://www.rescen.net/Rosemary_Lee/rlwritings3.html [Accessed 23 September, 2010].

27. Le Quesne, L. 2010. 'Uncommon Perspectives', *Animated*, Spring 2010, Foundation for Community Dance.

28. Phenomenology refers to a branch of philosophy that takes experience as a starting point. Rather than using the concept of an external, objective reality, phenomenology takes it that we construct our reality through our experiences.

29. There are exceptions to this such as 'Peeping Tom'/Pina Bausch who work with dancers over the usual retirement age in some of their performance work, but these would not usually be referred to as explicitly 'cross-generational'.

30. Feintuch, B. 2001. 'Longing for Community', *Western Folklore, Communities of Practice: Traditional Music and Dance*, vol. 60, no. 2/3, Western States Folklore Society, Spring–Summer, pp. 149–161.

Part Two
Practical Considerations

9   What Happens When
We Age?

Elizabeth Coleman

Elizabeth Coleman outlines the process of ageing and some of the medical conditions that may affect older people. Chapters 9 and 10 give dance artists valuable information about the effects of ageing and include suggestions for measures that will help to keep participants safe. Although these two chapters are more factual and less discursive than the rest of the book, understanding ageing is an important element of duty of care when a dance artist is working with older adults. We need this information in order to manage the balance between a participant's expectations of what they are capable of and their body's ability to meet those expectations.

This is not a definitive clinical guide – but it will help participatory dance workers to plan and lead activities that are appropriate for mature movers. If you are not yet an older person the exercise at the end of this chapter should make it easier for you to understand the content.

Introduction

Ageing is generally defined as 'the process whereby the structures and functions of the body change after we reach reproductive maturity'[1] (Hawker, 1985). There are changes that begin to affect our ability to adapt to our environment as we become older. The changes may relate to our reaction times, our ability to carry out physical activities, our ability to retain and learn new skills or a reduction in flexibility, muscle strength and stamina. Ageing may also have an effect on our balance and dexterity.

The process is gradual and, often, we are not aware of these small changes taking place. We may be able to delay its onset or slow down its progress, but ageing is an inevitable process. Some of the changes that people notice as they become a little older include struggling to thread a needle, becoming less flexible when dancing and taking longer to recover after physical activity. The differences will be there for us all, as adults. There are, however, some very positive effects of getting older, which will be looked later in this chapter.

The physiological process of ageing does not mean that older people cannot function at a good level; it means that normal ageing of the systems of the body results in a gradual reduction of function over many years. Added to this, some older people may have specific conditions that limit their ability to participate or necessitate some precautions and adaptations to enable them to get the most from movement. Dance can be a fun way to slow this process and gain confidence and enjoyment from moving; experiencing what the body *can* do rather than focusing on things the body finds more difficult.

Ageing is, however, much more than a purely physical process. There are also changes in a person's emotional and social needs and abilities. The way we see the world and our place in it changes as we go through life. Events that may seem of great importance and relevance when we are young may be seen very differently as we grow older. For example, a change in role from being a wage-earner to being retired may be seen as a hugely positive development for someone who is aged 30 and will not be retiring for at least another 35 years. For some people entering retirement the loss of their role as a 'worker' may feel very negative and they may be anxious about how they will fill their time with meaningful activities. For others the freedom to pursue new and exciting opportunities without the stresses of work may feel like the beginning of a new, positive adventure.

This chapter explores the physical, social and emotional aspects of the ageing process – of what it is to be an older human being. It emphasises that the majority of people feel the same inside their head throughout life, despite the changes in outward appearance of the body. Its aim is to enable dancers to think about how they can tap into this feeling inside and engage with the creative movement of the older, more mature body in safe and positive ways.

The physical process of ageing

The effect of ageing means that most systems of the body will, over time, undergo changes of wastage (atrophy), reduction in nourishment of cells (dystrophy) or swelling within the cells (oedema). This may be accompanied by decreased pliability and elasticity, and some destruction of the sheaths surrounding the nerve fibres. The natural physiological functions of the body, which vary in a regular cycle (biorhythms), become less regular as the body ages. There are greater swings throughout the day, which may affect energy levels, concentration, mood and motivation.[2] Dancers planning activities, especially for more frail older old people may be able to take this into account when planning their movement sessions.

Heart, lungs and circulation – During normal ageing the heart gradually becomes less efficient in the way it pumps blood to the lungs and around the body. The heart is a muscular pump, receiving blood, rich in carbon dioxide and reduced in oxygen, from all parts of the body. This blood is then sent to the lungs to release some carbon dioxide and pick up oxygen, before the oxygenated blood is pumped around the body to supply all its organs and systems. The heart becomes less able to accommodate activity with increasing age and takes longer to recover after exercise. The artery walls, taking blood away from the heart, become stiffer, resulting in more pumping effort being needed to circulate the blood. There could also be reduced circulation around the body, which means that frailer older people feel the cold more easily and may be more prone to swelling (oedema), especially around the lower legs. Swollen legs may be more vulnerable to injury, may result in less flexible ankle movement and may have overall reduced mobility. Any movement that encourages ankle, knee and foot movements will help to maintain joint range and improve circulation.

Breathing may be affected by ageing as the lungs become less pliable and have reduced elasticity. There are degenerative changes in the vertebral discs and decreased strength of the respiratory muscles (which expand the ribcage when breathing in). This may lead to a reduction in the amount of air that can be breathed in and out in one breath.

Joints and bones – As people age there will probably be a decrease in elasticity in the connective tissue surrounding their joints (connective tissue is the material produced around and through the organs and tissues of the body giving it support). This reduction is thought to be due to the ageing process itself or the fact that people take part in less physical activity. The cartilage, which is connective tissue covering the surfaces of bones at joints, yellows with age and may become pitted, worn and less elastic. This results in what is known as 'wear and tear' of the joints, especially those that have been worked hard during life. The cartilage over the joint surfaces is maintained by intermittent compression and release, for example, weight-bearing movement.

As we age, the calcium levels in our bones reduce, especially in post-menopausal women, but there may be increased calcium levels in other areas of the body. Reduction in calcium may lead to bones becoming more brittle with a greater risk of fractures in older people, especially in the femur (thigh bone), and the wrist following a fall. Increased calcium levels may occur in the thyroid cartilage in the neck (altering the voice) or in the cartilage joining each rib to the breast bone, which may result in a reduction in the amount of air breathed in and out at each breath.

Muscles, tendons and stamina – As we age our muscles begin to reduce in both their endurance and strength; this gradually leads to a reduction in muscle bulk, which may be very noticeable in frail older people. It is interesting to note that older people have a greater ratio of fat to muscle and may, therefore, appear to be fitter than they are. The tendons (the part of the muscle that attaches to the bone) lose elasticity resulting in shortening of their length, which also contributes to a change in a person's flexibility. Reduced muscle bulk is directly proportional to reduced strength – this is worth noting if you are facilitating movement with older people. The fine movements of the fingers may be altered by reduction in both the strength and range of movement of the finger joints. The ability of muscles to work efficiently is dependent on homeostasis (the process whereby the internal systems of the body, for example, blood pressure and body temperature, are maintained constant, despite variations in external conditions). Homeostasis involves adequate hydration and mineral balance of cells in many organs and systems of the body. Maintaining good nutrition and adequate hydration in frail older people is always a priority for carers. This is an important consideration when working with older adults; think about the timing of sessions and the availability of a drink.

As already described there is a decrease in cardiac, respiratory and circulatory function as we get older. Coupled with less muscle strength and flexibility there is a reduction in stamina. People gradually become aware of small changes; an activity that was once very easy may now need more effort to achieve the same result. Tasks may take slightly longer to achieve; perhaps a longer rest period is needed after physical activity. These changes are all related to our level of stamina. Another factor is the rate at which impulses are carried along nerve fibres to the brain. With ageing, nerve impulses take longer to reach the brain, resulting in slower reaction times. In terms of a movement session, going at a gentle pace, with more time for the older person to process and respond to information, takes into account both the slower reaction time and reduced stamina. Many fitter mature people can move in gloriously active ways, but for others a slower pace is needed to enable them to participate safely and enjoyably.

Brain, pain, senses and skin – Most of the brain's cognitive functions are not affected by the normal process of ageing – despite myths about the brain shrinking. There may be some decline in memory and processing speed but these are usually offset by improvements in coping strategies.

Deterioration of brain function results from either a reduction of the circulation through the brain or some abnormal pathology within the brain itself. These changes may affect short-term memory (long-term memory is often much better) or may reduce our ability to learn new things.

Pain is described as 'an unpleasant sensory and emotional experience associated with actual or potential tissue damage, or described in terms of such damage'.[3] Much research has been undertaken looking at the effect of ageing on the pain threshold – the point at which we become aware of pain. Some studies suggest that older people have a higher threshold.[4] Older people may also have an altered perception of pain,[5] meaning that they may not be aware of their pain to the same extent as a younger person. Again, this is a point to be aware of in movement sessions. A person who has experienced chronic pain over many years may believe that an increase in that pain when participating in an enjoyable activity is acceptable, and may be reluctant to disclose this in a session. Being aware that many older people may have pain, and taking careful notes of changes in non-verbal communication, may enable the dancer to keep participants safe.

From the age of 40 the lens of the eye begins to lose its elasticity, resulting in a reduction in its ability to adapt to changes between light and dark. Many older people become long-sighted, needing glasses, and some will develop cataracts (opacity of the cornea) leading to blurred vision. By age 60 there may be a reduction in the ability to register high-frequency sounds, and this often results in deafness. Normal speech is low frequency (higher in small children), but a participant with a hearing deficit may benefit from being able to see the face of the person speaking.

The skin of those in older old age will have reduced elasticity, with the body no longer producing elastin (a protein similar to albumin) in the outer layer of the skin. This, together with reduced action of the sebaceous glands, may cause very dry skin, which is more prone to damage and may be slower to heal. Weakening of the walls of blood vessels close to the surface of the skin often leads to bruising and skin damage. In frail older and oldest old members of dance sessions there needs to be extra care and vigilance taken to reduce the risk of knocking into or injuring the skin, especially on the shins, which have a poor blood supply.

Social and emotional effects of ageing

For many people there are numerous positive aspects of maturing and growing older. They talk about opportunities to take on new hobbies and challenges following retirement. There is a wealth of leisure activities targeted at this age group. 'University of the Third Age' and 'Silver Surfers' are two examples of organisations offering educational, creative and leisure opportunities for those no longer in full-time employment. There may be less desire to progress within work as we get older, and there may be a desire to relinquish some responsibility to younger colleagues. Part-time work may take the place of full-time working, thus freeing up more leisure time. Many who no longer have parental responsibilities may delight in the joy of grandchildren. For some, retirement may bring financial security, with time to relax and possibly travel and explore. There may also be a realisation that issues that once seemed very important are now seen from a different perspective.

Ageing may also have other, less positive effects on our lives. Bereavement, loneliness and isolation are a reality for many. Bereavement, especially the loss of a partner, involves a huge change in one's way of life. It may be accompanied by changes in financial situation and reduced social contacts. This in turn may lead to emotional distress, physical illness and depression. Being alone does not always equate to loneliness, however the reasons for loneliness may increase with age. Contributory factors include loss of friends, hearing and visual deficits and difficulties in going out. Those who have previously had their own transport may no longer be able to drive, access public transport or visit friends. In these cases isolation becomes increasingly likely. Frail older people and the oldest old often need help in personal and household tasks or personal care, leading to feelings of frustration and reduced self-esteem. For many of these people there may be a very real fear of what their future might be. Anxiety can be a serious problem for those who have a sense of loss of control over their own destiny. Adaptations and loss of roles might be gradual, but for some these changes may be sudden and life changing. With changes in expectations and abilities there may be a reduction in motivation. Involvement in even the most menial of tasks may be difficult and this can lead to a spiral of inactivity.

Conclusion

Despite the rather negative aspects of ageing outlined above, dance offers exciting possibilities for promoting wellbeing – regardless of age or health status. In addition to the physical benefits of maintaining strength and flexibility, dance can contribute to social and emotional health. Participants in dance sessions have opportunities to express emotions, take part in group activity and regain a sense of control in their lives. A sensitive dance artist who understands the process of ageing will be able to devise safe activities, which validate and celebrate a person's past, whilst helping them find enjoyment in the present.

Exercise 1

- Interview an older person about their experience of ageing.
- What have they noticed? What are their pleasures and frustrations?
- Have they experienced some of the effects that Elizabeth describes?

Notes

1. Hawker, M. (1985) *The Older Patient and the Role of the Physiotherapist*. London: Faber and Faber.
2. Jackson, O.S. (1989) *Adapting Physical Therapy Interventions for the Elderly. Manual of Physical Therapy*. New York: Churchill Livingstone.
3. Bonicca, J.J. (1979) The need of a taxonomy. *Pain* 6(3): 247–252.
4. McCleane, G. (2006) "Pain and the Elderly Patient", in McCleane, G. and Smith, H. eds, *Clinical Management of the Elderly Patient in Pain*. New York: The Hawthorn Medical Press, pp. 1–9.
5. Lautenbacher, S., Kunz, M., Strate, P., Nielson, J. and Arendt-Nielson, L. (2005) Age effects on pain thresholds, temporal summation and spatial summation of heat and pressure pain. *Pain* 115: 410–418.

Further Reading

Juhan, D. (2003) *Job's Body*. New York: Barrytown/Station Hill Press.
Sidell, M. (1995) *Health in Old Age*. Buckingham: Open University Press.
Todd, M. (1997) *The Thinking Body*. London: Dance Books.

10   Conditions That May Affect Older People

Elizabeth Coleman

. . . .

As Elizabeth discussed in the previous chapter, getting older does not necessarily mean a significant reduction in mobility and activity, despite the inevitable changes that take place in the body. However, there are some conditions that may affect the participants attending dance sessions. This chapter is aimed at giving the dance practitioner general information about these conditions and suggestions for ways in which activities can be adapted to keep people safe.

. . . .

Conditions affecting joints and bones

- Osteoarthritis
- Rheumatoid arthritis
- Osteoporosis
- Fractured neck of femur
- Total hip replacement

Osteoarthritis is also known as Degenerative Joint Disease or 'wear and tear' of joints. The joints affected may be any that have undertaken hard work during life. These might be the hips or knees of those who have spent an active physical life over many years, or those who have carried a considerable amount of body weight. People whose jobs have involved lifting may have problems with their neck or lower back. Others experience pain and stiffness in fingers and thumbs, which can be a result of doing extensive household or DIY tasks. The condition results from wearing down of the cartilage covering the ends of the bones within joints. This causes the cartilage to become roughened and pitted. Cartilage has a very limited ability to heal once damaged.

Osteoarthritis can start at any age, especially if there has been an injury to the joint earlier in life, but the risk increases with age. Sometimes spurs of bone are formed within the joint, causing pain and restriction of movement. If this pain is very acute and severe, the person may be advised to rest the joint for a period of time; however, there is no generalised inflammation, and regular movement helps to strengthen the muscles supporting the joint. It also maintains joint range of movement. Taking part in dance activities can play a significant part in enabling older people with this condition to move more freely and gain confidence in their physical ability.

Rheumatoid arthritis, on the other hand, is a condition that affects the whole body. It usually starts between the age of 20 and 60, but the effects are often more marked in older people. Although the cause is not fully known it is classified as an autoimmune disease, meaning that the immune system attacks healthy body tissue resulting in damage to joints. This causes inflammation of the lining of the affected joints (the synovial membranes), leading to erosion of the cartilage covering the joint surfaces. There is pain – often constant – even at rest, and also decreased range of movement, instability of the joints, muscle weakness and reduced stamina. There are acute and chronic components to the condition. In acute phases the joints may be swollen and hot and the person may feel tired and generally unwell. In the chronic phase of the condition pain will still be present but of lower intensity. Both sides of the body are involved, commonly the wrists, ankles, knuckles, feet, elbows and the neck. Treatment is individual to the person concerned and may involve a combination of medications, rest, the use of splints to support joints and very carefully managed exercise to limit stiffness. Whilst dancers will want to be able to include as many older people in their sessions as possible, it is important to remember that this may not be appropriate with a person with rheumatoid arthritis if acute pain is present. It may be useful to think of other ways to include people who are not able to participate in movement on a particular day. Choosing music, being a centrepiece to enable the movement to happen around the person or just being able to watch are all valid reasons to be in a group.

Points to be aware of

- **Osteoarthritis** is wear and tear affecting particular joints.
- Movement within a person's own limits may help maintain mobility.
- **Rheumatoid arthritis** affects the whole body and many joints.
- Rest is important in the acute phases of rheumatoid arthritis.
- An older person with rheumatoid arthritis may well have considerable understanding of their own capabilities.

Osteoporosis is a condition where the density of the bones is decreased. We all, both men and women, have our greatest bone mass (density) in our

20s, following which time the density gradually decreases. During pregnancy and lactation a woman's bone density will temporarily decrease if her diet is not calcium rich; immediately after the menopause the level decreases again. Other contributory factors are smoking, excessive alcohol intake and a sedentary lifestyle. Osteoporosis is more common in women than in men and causes the bones to become thinner and weaker, increasing the risk of fractures, especially of the thighbone (fractured neck of femur), wrist (Colles fracture) and spine (crush fracture). It may give rise to pain especially in the back and the weight-bearing leg bones, but many people do not experience any pain. Other symptoms may be loss of height, especially if several vertebrae are involved, and curvature of the spine (Dowager's hump). For those severely affected there may be general reduction in mobility and function, including breathlessness, difficulty holding the head up and difficulty sitting or standing for extended periods. Regular exercise during life, especially weight-bearing exercise, helps to maintain healthy bone density by limiting calcium loss as we get older. Dancing is an ideal way to participate in enjoyable weight-bearing movement for people of all ages, but especially as bodies mature.

Points to be aware of

- There are reasons for concern when working with people with severe osteoporosis.
- Risk of fracture is markedly increased.
- Movement should avoid jarring or twisting on the weight-bearing limb.
- Increase in pain on movement, in this context, is an indication of the need for care and advice from a health colleague.
- If a kyphosis (Dowager's Hump) is present, avoid movement that puts pressure on the back, for example, bending forward to touch the toes.
- Any movement that increases back pain should be avoided.

Fractured neck of femur (thigh bone). The top of the femur has a 'neck', a narrow part pointing inwards and upwards towards the 'head', which fits into the ball and socket hip joint. To pinpoint the hip joint on yourself, it can be felt on the front of the groin, half way along, in the skin fold. Most fractures of the neck of the femur occur as the result of a fall, often from stumbling. The fracture occurs at the narrowest point and may be related to osteoporotic changes in the bone. At the time of the fracture the lower end of the femur will rotate outwards, which results in the outside of the foot resting on the ground. Seventy-five percent of fractures occur in people aged over 75, and 80% of these are in women. Older people tend to lean slightly backwards and sideways when standing and walking, and this makes it more likely that, if they fall, they will land on the top, outside part of the thigh. Frail older people may be less able to protect themselves as they fall. This injury is, understandably, very painful and requires surgery to stabilise the fracture. The procedure either involves pinning a plate across the fracture or replacing the fractured portion with an artificial joint. Either type of surgery will necessitate a stay in hospital, and rehabilitation is aimed at helping the person become mobile as soon as possible. This rehabilitation needs to be undertaken by a health professional in the first weeks following surgery, and permission needs to be sought before joining or rejoining any dance activities.

Total hip replacement is offered to people either following a fracture of the neck of the femur or when the joint is severely affected by osteoarthritis. The benefits are reduced pain, improved range of movement and better function as muscles get stronger. It may enable a return to a more active lifestyle and an improvement in confidence and well-being. Surgery consists firstly of an incision along the outside of the thigh. The replacement may be just the damaged head of the femur or may involve both the ball and the socket parts of the joint. Following surgery the person will have active rehabilitation and advice prior to returning home. They will be given clear instructions about what to avoid in the early post-operative weeks, and these guidelines will be helpful for the dance practitioner wishing to include the person in movement sessions. Once again permission needs to be sought prior to taking part in any dance activities.

Points to be aware of in the early weeks following hip replacement

- When sitting do not allow the knees to be higher than the hips – this relates to the height of chairs and activities.
- Have seats that enable the person to sit in an upright position with the knees level or lower than the hips.
- Do not let the affected leg cross the mid-line of the body, that is, do not sit cross-legged or do activities that take the foot across the body (such as a grapevine step).
- When sitting, have the feet flat on the floor with the knees 15 cm (6 inches) apart.
- Do not stand and rotate the affected leg inwards. For example, when walking and needing to change direction, turn by taking small steps to walk round rather than twisting on the feet.
- Do not bend all the way over from the waist.
- Use a long handled 'grab' to pick up things from the floor.
- On the stairs, lead with the 'good' leg going up and the affected leg coming down.

• Before including the person in dance activities take advice from the appropriate health professional and ask the person to get permission from their GP.

Conditions affecting the heart, lungs and circulation[1]

• Ischaemic heart disease
• Chronic obstructive pulmonary disease
• Asthma
• Deep vein thrombosis

Ischaemic heart disease (also referred to as coronary heart disease), together with stroke, is the most common cause of death in the western world. In the Resources section of this book, there are details of ischaemia and angina, together with brief details of some of the heart surgery treatments available (angioplasty and coronary bypass). Whilst ischaemic heart disease may reduce a person's ability to exercise, once treatment has stabilised or corrected the condition, enjoyable exercise and dance may be a beneficial way of maintaining better health. Advice regarding participation in dance sessions must be at the discretion of health professionals, prior to inclusion in any activity,

Points to be aware of and reasons for concern with people with heart conditions

• Find out about the people attending your sessions and ask for information about their medical conditions. If you have concerns, seek advice from a qualified professional.
• Take note of any changes in participants, when they arrive, during or at the end of the session.
• Be aware of signs of heart disease, that is, chest pain, breathlessness or difficulty breathing, dizziness and blueness of the skin (cyanosis), especially around the lips.
• Reduce stress during the sessions, and be aware of people with anxiety.
• Avoid extremes of temperature, either too hot or too cold.
• Limit the amount of movement with the arms above the head, especially bilateral movement, as this may put pressure on the pumping action of the heart.
• Time sessions so that they do not start immediately following a meal. Allow at least one hour, ideally two, before starting activity.

- Enable participants to work at their own pace, take breaks when needed and be able to opt out of any activity.
- If anyone has medication to take for angina, check that they have it with them.

NB: WITH ALL PEOPLE WITH HEART CONDITIONS, IF IN DOUBT STOP THE ACTIVITY AND SEEK ADVICE FROM HEALTH COLLEAGUES.

Never ignore signs of change or your own concerns

Chronic obstructive pulmonary disease is the most common respiratory disease in the UK, caused by chronic bronchitis and emphysema. Both conditions result in a decrease in the ability to get air into the lungs. **Bronchitis** is inflammation of the main airways into the lungs (the bronchi). **Emphysema** is reduction in the elasticity of the lungs, reducing the degree to which they are able to recoil after each breath in, and resulting in the need for the person to use extra muscle power to force the air out. Both conditions are exhausting.

Asthma is a common condition caused by narrowing of the small airways of the lungs (bronchioles), and production of excess fluid in these airways. The effect is to make breathing more difficult and is characterised by wheezing. The severity of the symptoms varies considerably and may be associated with an allergic response, for example, to pollen, food, feathers and dust. Emotions often play a significant role for those with asthma, both as a trigger or by increasing symptoms. Cold air, especially when moving from warmth into cold, may increase the symptoms, or may induce an asthmatic attack. Some forms of exercise are also linked to asthma attacks. These are thought to be related to the temperature in the airways as the breathing rate rises during exercise, and the drying effect of air passing along the airways. This is especially true in a cold, dry atmosphere.

The symptoms of asthma are

- Shortness of breath, causing great fear and distress.
- Coughing, particularly during the winter when the air is cold.
- Wheezing related to air being forced through the narrow, mucous-filled airways.
- People who have lived with asthma over a long period of time may hold their shoulders high and have thickened muscles around their shoulders.

Treatments for asthma include medication aimed at opening the narrowed airways, for example, inhalers, or steroids that are effective in reducing inflammation in the airways. Oxygen may be helpful during an acute attack. Eliminating some of the triggers, such as allergens or stress, may lessen acute attacks, and physiotherapy may be aimed at teaching effective breathing patterns and clearing secretions.

Points to be aware of and reasons for concern with people with chest conditions

- Inclusion of people with serious chest conditions may involve asking permission from a health professional. In any case, you should discuss their condition with the individual concerned or their carers
- Most people with long-standing respiratory problems have in-depth knowledge of their condition and any changes to it.
- Know the people who are coming to your sessions and understand any chest conditions they may have.
- Check that participants have inhalers and medication if required and that they know when they need to take them.
- Movement and dance may need to be adapted to reduce the aerobic elements of the session.
- Gentle movement may be of benefit in maintaining flexibility in the arms and shoulder girdle, but may need to be done in a sitting position and with great attention to rest periods.
- Avoid doing too many repetitions of movements
- Create an atmosphere that encourages participants to work within their own capabilities and to take rests when needed or desired.
- Changes in the person's condition, before, during or at the end of the dance session may give rise to concern.
- Look for signs of increased breathlessness; change of colour, especially blueness around the lips; sweating not accompanied by increased activity; pallor; pain, particularly in the chest; distress or lack of enjoyment.

NB: NEVER IGNORE SIGNS OF CHANGE, OR YOUR OWN CONCERNS. IF IN DOUBT STOP THE ACTIVITY AND SEEK ADVICE.

Deep vein thrombosis (DVT) is a blood clot in the deep veins of the leg, usually in the calf. During exercise and activity there is a high flow of blood through these veins, but during illness or reduced activity this blood flow reduces significantly. This may be particularly true with frail older people or in those with physical conditions that reduce mobility.

The risk factors are

- Prolonged rest or inactivity, or following surgery.
- The contraceptive pill (this may not be a huge issue with older people!).
- Long journeys without moving the lower legs. This is the reason for exercise on long-haul flights, but may also relate to the frailer older person who has travelled to your session in a bus or taxi.
- The people most at risk are obese older people or those with a previous history of DVT.

The symptoms of DVT are pain and swelling in the calf. There may be tenderness and the calf may be red or feel hot to the touch. The danger to the person is the risk of the clot dislodging and travelling along the increasingly larger veins, through the heart and ending in the smaller arteries in the lungs. This is known as a pulmonary embolism and is a life-threatening condition.

Treatment of DVT is by way of anticoagulant medication (anti-blood clotting).

NB: IF DVT IS SUSPECTED DISCONTINUE EXERCISE IMMEDIATELY AND SEEK ADVICE. AVOID THE PERSON WALKING.

Neurological conditions

This section will look at some of the conditions that result from damage to or deterioration of brain cells, or their ability to transmit signals to the areas and organs of the body. It will include:

- Stroke
- Parkinson's disease
- Dementia

A stroke occurs when the blood supply and, therefore, the oxygen supply to a part of the brain is blocked or restricted. The brain is a complex organ with a network of cells that send and receive messages from all areas and organs of the body. It is rather like a large telephone exchange, routing incoming messages to the right area and sending outgoing messages to all parts of the body. When a stroke occurs some of the network is damaged and the area of the body relating to that part of the brain can no longer send or receive these messages. If the blood supply to a part of the brain is compromised for any length of time brain cells die and disability results. The most common causes are blockage or haemorrhage. Each half of the brain (hemisphere) controls the opposite side of the body, although the two sides do share responsibility for some functions. A stroke on the right side of the brain will result in loss of movement in the left side of the body and vice versa. The Resources section of this book contains further information about the damage caused by stroke and risk factors for the condition.

Points to be aware of and reasons for concern with stroke

- Physical activity and dance can reduce the risk of stroke, lowering blood pressure and cholesterol levels.
- People who have had a stroke may be able to participate in dance sessions, which may need to be adapted in order to keep people safe.
- Concerns relate to anyone who may be showing adverse signs of headache, altered movement ability, changes in speech, dizziness or who appear unwell or different on a particular day.
- Those group members with a previous history of stroke should be monitored carefully.
- Make sure there are sufficient co-workers or carers, including people who know the members, to enable participants to be closely observed and any problems identified.
- Once again, it is important to create an environment where people can work within their real capabilities, feel able to take breaks and have a choice about participation.

NB: NEVER IGNORE SIGNS OF CHANGE, OR YOUR OWN CONCERNS. IF IN DOUBT STOP THE ACTIVITY AND SEEK ADVICE.

Parkinson's disease affects 1–2% of people aged over 65. It is a chronic progressive neurological condition characterised by problems with movement, co-ordination and posture. It is caused by the loss of brain cells that produce dopamine in the brain. This results in a lower level of dopamine, a chemical messenger (neurotransmitter) that transmits impulses across nerve pathways in the brain. The condition may progress slowly and many people function at a high level for many years.

The symptoms of the condition include

- Tremor, which is usually seen at rest, involves the thumb and index finger, and is known as 'pill rolling'.
- Rigidity, which limits the range of movement in the joints, especially the hips, knees, shoulders and neck. The movements are often jerky and may be described as 'cogwheel'.

- Posture is often with the head and shoulders forward and most joints in a flexed or bent position.
- Balance may be difficult to maintain, with leaning either forwards or backwards, increasing the risk of falls.
- Walking is usually slow and shuffling. There may be difficulty picking up the feet to take a step, with a reduced arm swing and short steps. Also, many people with Parkinson's disease have great difficulty initiating walking, stopping or changing direction. Getting in and out of a car can also present problems
- Facial expression may be greatly reduced, with decreased blinking. This is not an indication of decreased emotions and it is useful to note this point when dancing and moving with people with Parkinson's disease.
- Dexterity and co-ordination may affect handwriting the use of cutlery, and activities such as dressing, toileting, and so on.
- Depression is a feature for many, as a result of the condition or as part of the disease. Some people may have memory problems and loss of motivation.
- The 'on–off phenomenon' relates to the fluctuation of symptoms, from the person being very mobile to being unable to move. There may be great differences throughout the day, either as part of the condition itself or due to the timing of medication.

Treatment involves the use of medication to manage the symptoms, by replacing dopamine.

Points to be aware of and reasons to be concerned with Parkinson's disease

- Group movement activities may be very beneficial to people with Parkinson's disease.
- Music often gives a rhythmical background, which is helpful.
- Gentle, rhythmical, repetitive movements may help reduce the difficulty in initiating movement.
- Tiredness can be a real difficulty for these people, so factoring in time for rests or tea breaks will be necessary.
- Very fast or very slow rhythms are not as helpful as moderate paces.
- Enjoyment or distress may not be revealed in facial expression.
- There is a greater risk of falls, necessitating adequate staffing levels, especially with people who know the person and their capabilities.

Chapter 12 has information about Dance for Parkinson's research and the growing network of practitioners specialising in this work.

Dementia is a condition that results in an ongoing decline of the brain and its function. It affects over 750,000 people in the UK, most of whom are older people. Dementia is not a specific disease but a group of symptoms that may be caused by a number of disorders or medical conditions. Two of the most common types are vascular dementia and Alzheimer's disease, though dementia symptoms can be caused by other factors such as infection, nutritional deficiencies and reactions to medications. Although it is most common in elderly people, dementia is not a normal part of the ageing process and may occur in younger people.

Vascular dementia is often caused by a series of minor strokes, and the brain deterioration is due to impaired blood supply. Alzheimer's disease results in a steady and gradual loss of nerve fibres and 'shrinkage' of the brain itself. In vascular dementia there may be sudden changes in function followed by a 'plateau' of symptoms, whereas in Alzheimer's disease the changes are more likely to be slow and steady. In general terms, dementia is said to be mild if the person is able to manage independently, moderate if they need some help in performing general tasks of living and severe if continual help and support are needed.[2]

People with dementia experience difficulties with memory, problem solving, language and attention. Eventually, impaired cognitive functioning affects a person's ability to carry out normal daily living activities (bathing, dressing and feeding). There are often personality changes – individuals may become confused or agitated and have difficulty controlling their emotions. In the later stages of dementia there is also a deterioration in mobility and physical function, and an increased risk of falls.

Drugs are available to treat some of the diseases, specifically progressive dementias such as Alzheimer's. The drugs are not a cure and will not reverse brain damage, but they can slow down the advance of the disease and improve symptoms. As well as resulting in a better quality of life this may delay the need for admitting an individual to a care home.

Chapter 11 outlines ways in which the culture of care for those with dementia has changed in recent years and offers guidelines for dance artists working with people in dementia care settings.

Other conditions that may affect older people

These other conditions do not sit within specific groupings but, nevertheless, are important to look at within this chapter. They include diabetes, obesity, depression and falls.

Diabetes is a condition related to the production and use of insulin in the body. Type 1 diabetes is insulin dependent, where cells in the pancreas do not produce enough insulin. This type most commonly develops in children and young adults and may be known as juvenile or primary diabetes. It is treated by administration of insulin, often by injection. Type 2 diabetes is caused by the cells of the body failing to respond to the insulin it produces. The pancreas produces insulin but body cells become less sensitive to insulin levels. Type 2 diabetes is also known as secondary or late-onset diabetes, and usually occurs later on in life. In both types the person is unable to store glucose in organs such as the liver and muscles. Under normal circumstances, when carbohydrates such as starch and sugar are eaten they are converted to glucose. This raises the blood sugar level, stimulating the pancreas to release insulin into the bloodstream. The liver and muscles store the excess glucose, preventing the blood sugar level from becoming too high. The stored glucose is then released slowly, as it is needed, between meals, maintaining a relatively level blood sugar throughout the day. In diabetes there is an inability to store sugar and the level rises, especially after a meal containing large amounts of carbohydrate and sugar. The kidneys cannot reabsorb all this glucose and it is passed out of the body in the urine. This means that the person with diabetes is unable to make use of stored glucose between meals, and the level drops. Diabetics may also experience problems with eyesight, poor circulation – especially in the extremities – and reduced healing capacity. Symptoms include thirst, weight loss and excessive production of urine. Late onset diabetes is often controlled by diet, with regular meals and snacks and limited intake of carbohydrates.

Points to be aware of and reasons to be concerned with diabetes

- People with diabetes usually know how to manage their condition.
- Talk to the person about what they do if their blood sugar drops to a low level – they may carry sugar or a biscuit with them at all times.
- Ensure they have this available at each session.
- Remember that more glucose is used during exercise and the timing of dance sessions may be significant.
- Remember that people with diabetes have a reduced healing capacity so care needs to be taken, especially with frail older people. Be careful with footplates on wheelchairs, for example.
- Have sufficient support from people who know your group members.

Obesity may be a problem for older adults as it is in any other age group, with around 60% of adults being either overweight or obese in the

UK. It can be measured using the body mass index (BMI), which can be calculated by dividing the weight of a person (in kilograms) by the square of their height (in metres). For example, a person of weight 70 kilograms and height 1.75 metres will have a BMI of 22.9, calculated as 70 divided by 3.06 (1.75 × 1.75). BMI scores are classified as

- Less than 18.5 = underweight.
- 18.5–24.9 = ideal healthy weight.
- 25–29.9 = overweight.
- 30–39.9 = obese.
- 40 and over = very obese.

Health risks increase for those in the overweight and obese categories, although there are also health risks to being underweight. Some of the risks of being overweight include diabetes, heart problems, high blood pressure, strokes and wear and tear in the joints. Increasing age sees an increase in the prevalence of obesity up until the age of 64, after which the prevalence begins to reduce.[3] Losing weight requires a reduction in calorie intake and an increase in calorific expenditure, in other words fewer calories in and more energy used, although there are many reasons and factors involved in a person putting on weight. These factors may be the amount a person eats, the amount of activity they have, their family lifestyle and habits and, in 1% of obese people, a medical problem, together with many psychological factors.

For older, obese people, some of the difficulties may relate to their weight distribution, which may affect circulation, in particular the blood returning to the heart from all areas of the body. If the person is carrying a lot of weight around their middle, this may press on the thigh when sitting, and restrict the flow of blood in the legs. Similarly, pressure of the back of the calf against the back of the knee may restrict the flow of blood from the lower leg. This increases the risk of DVT in a person who has limited mobility or who spends extended periods of the day sitting down. Reducing weight by increasing exercise may be unrealistic for this age group, but experiencing creative ways of moving may give people with weight problems an opportunity to express themselves and participate in a supportive environment.

Points to be aware of and reasons for concern with people with obesity

- Participating in dance movement may be an enjoyable experience. Health benefits will be a bonus.
- Losing weight through exercise may be unrealistic for this age group.

- People with obesity are at greater risk of other conditions.
- Plan for rest periods and for a pace that suits the individual.

NB: OBESITY IS ONE OF THE RISK FACTORS FOR HEART DISEASE, SO ANYONE WHO IS OVERWEIGHT NEEDS TO CHECK WITH THEIR GP BEFORE JOINING AN EXERCISE OR DANCE PROGRAMME.

Depression is a condition of the mood with possible symptoms of sadness, low self-esteem, loss of interest, sleep and eating pattern disturbances, irritability, reduced concentration and motivation, feelings of hopelessness and worthlessness, low energy levels and, for some, thoughts about suicide. In older people there is often a high anxiety rate in those with depression, and many people find their mood changes at different times during the day; for example, their mood is low first thing in the morning but better later in the day. This is a point to note when setting times for dance and movement sessions. Some people may believe that depression is an inevitable part of growing old but many older people feel very content with their life. Depression, however, is a widespread problem in this age group and, for some, may be related to past episodes of depression. For others, the loss of a spouse, reduced physical ability, isolation, loss of role and fear about their future may be huge contributory factors. Depression is the most common mental health issue for older people and is often either unreported, or just accepted by those who believe it is inevitable. Dancers may have a great role to play in working with older people with mild to moderate depression, as exercise and physical activity are known to have a positive effect on mood. You may be aware of the wonderful feelings achieved when you dance and move yourself and this may be true for group members too. In severe depression the person's mood may be too low to be able to access what the dancer has to offer.

  Points to be aware of and reasons for concern with depression

- Older people with depression may not report it to their doctor.
- Movement and dance may need to go at a slower pace to allow for reduced concentration, motivation and energy levels.
- Mood may vary during the day and it may be possible to time sessions to take this into account.
- Dance and movement activities have a positive effect on mood for those with mild to moderate depression.
- Those with severe depression may find it difficult to attend dance sessions, but may be able to access them as their mood changes.
- Once again, having support from those who know the person may help to monitor mood.

- Be aware of changes in the person from session to session and pass information on to a health professional if there are concerns.
- Never ignore signs of change or your own concerns.

Falls and frail older people. Older people have an increased risk of falling for a variety of reasons, including dizziness, low blood sugar, balance disturbances, tripping hazards in the environment, fear and a previous history of a fall. Imagine that you have never fallen. You may believe that you won't fall. If you have a fall, that belief has been shattered and your belief may now be that you will continue to fall. The anxiety this creates actually increases the risk of falling again. Within a movement or dance activity with older people, especially frail older people, there needs to be assessment in relation to both the individuals within the group, the group as a whole, the environment and the support available. People in this category have just as much need and desire to move and be included in activities as any other participants. Precautions will need to be in place to enable them to participate in a safe way.

Points to be aware of and reasons to be concerned with frail older people

- Once again, adequate support, especially from those who know the participants and their needs, can help to ensure that frail, at-risk group members can be closely observed and protected.
- Ideally, participants will have similar levels of frailty or energy. If you are working with a mixed-ability group you will need to manage the pace to ensure that the more frail members of the group do not become over tired.
- Choose activities that are well within the capabilities of the participants.
- Be aware that some group members' expectations of their own, or others' abilities may not be based on reality.
- Establish clear, safe boundaries on the behaviour and activities of the group.
- Ensure a range of activities is available so that adaptation and change of pace, intensity or content can take place if necessary.

Conclusion

It is important to remember that dance artists are not qualified to give advice about medical conditions. This chapter offers a general overview of a range of conditions and includes information that may help dance artists to keep people safe. The Resources section includes further guidance on cautions and precautions relating to leading dance activities with older people who may have some of the conditions described in this chapter. When there is any doubt in the dance practitioner's mind regarding a particular person, or medical condition, it is the responsibility of the dancer to seek information in order to be able to make an informed decision about whether that person is able to join in.

Exercise and discussion points

Would you allow the following people to take part in your dance session? Yes? No? Don't know? What factors would determine whether you say yes or no?

- Jenny – who is experiencing an asthma attack
- Errol – who has had a heart attack
- Sheila – who easily becomes breathless, even though she is only 45 and seems fairly fit
- Kath – who has dementia
- Assad – who has diabetes
- Lionel – who has Parkinson's disease
- Jessie – who had a fall last week
- George – who has unpredictable behaviour
- Anne – who is on medication for depression

If you decide that they can take part, would you need to adapt the session to meet their needs?

Notes

1. The Resources section of this book contains additional information about heart disease, stroke and chronic obstructive pulmonary disease.
2. Kitwood, T. (1997) *Dementia Reconsidered: The Person Comes First.* Buckingham: Oxford University Press.
3. Avenell, A., Broom, J., Brown, T.J. et al. (2004) Systematic review of the long-term effects and economic consequences of treatment for obesity and implications for health improvement. *Health Technology Assessment* 8(21): pp. 1–194. Health Services Unit, University of Aberdeen, UK.

11   Dance and Dementia

Diane Amans

The previous chapter outlined the different types of dementia and how these affect people. Recent developments in non-pharmacological approaches to treating people living with dementia offer opportunities for dancers to contribute to creative arts initiatives.

This chapter explains how dance can be a valuable element in person-centred practice – giving the reader links with current theory and examples of case studies that translate theory into practice.

Changes in the culture of care for people with dementia have challenged some of the perceptions of their being helpless patients who are losing their skills and becoming increasingly difficult to manage. Rather than a focus on what people can no longer do, caregivers are encouraged to look at what they still can do and plan accordingly.

Dancers and other artists are involved with people living with dementia and promoting enjoyable interaction, which has nothing to do with medical approaches.

> [...] engaging the creative arts can activate pathways that release thoughts and words previously held captive by broken circuitry. There are millions of 'back doors' to communication that can be opened with a non-traditional approach, be it art, music, visual stimulus, tactile sensation, humour or strong emotion.[1]

Increasingly, there is acknowledgement that the person living with dementia is still the same person inside. Tom Kitwood's writings on 'personhood' and dementia are often referred to in the dementia care field. He argues the importance of seeing the *person* with dementia rather than the disease, and he highlights elements of positive interactions with dementia patients. These include:

– recognition
– negotiation

- collaboration
- timalation (direct engagement of the senses)
- celebration
- relaxation
- play[2]

Many of the above elements are present in community dance sessions.

Richard Coaten talks of the importance of being in the moment – 'creatively alert' to what happens and emotionally open.[3] If dancers are able to create a safe emotional environment, where spontaneity is encouraged, participants who feel anxious and depressed may develop a greater sense of positive well-being. When I first began working with people with dementia I began to look more closely at what is most likely to result in a *positive* experience – and I believe a positive experience in dance is one that includes playfulness.

Dance and playfulness

There are a number of theoretical models of play and playfulness; the educationalist Lieberman studied the impact that playful qualities in teachers have in engendering playfulness in students. She argues for the nurturing of the playful spirit in individuals from infancy to old age, believing that the truly playful 'childlike' person has a rich resource of coping strategies.[4]

Sandy Crichton, a dancer who worked for many years with the charity JABADAO, writes:

a capacity to play is my greatest strength [...]. This is no random skill; this professional playing is serious work [...] hard work [...] exhausting work. I use it to build relationships, to entice people into moving, to *be with* people.

[...] in this way I can emphasise personhood, not pathology – focusing on the person not the condition. I can work in a way that values embodied experience and the wisdom of the body.[5]

Lucinda Jarrett is artistic director of Rosetta Life, a charity that engages frail and vulnerable people in arts projects. She refers to play in describing her dance work.

> It's about enabling people to play [...]
> Movement is about playing [...] people who best know how to play are people with dementia.[6]

Dance artist as playful practitioner

Occupational therapists Tessa Perrin and Hazel May have written about links between well-being and playful encounter.[7] This notion of playful encounter – creating situations that include spontaneity and joy – is embedded in some artists' approaches to participatory dance. I believe it to be a significant element in my own practice.

Perrin and May describe what they mean by a 'playful practitioner':

> [...] we believe that there is a certain disposition, a certain personality type, that has a greater facility than most to engage people who have dementia. The person who is able to engage in playful encounter is essentially the person whose own 'inner child' is free and accessible; who is confident and at ease with the way they use their body and voice and emotions; who is spontaneous and immediate and able intuitively to adopt a stance of openness, unconditional acceptance and receptivity to whatever the person with dementia wishes to bring to the encounter. We have all seen such people in action: the care assistant who notices a tapping foot and turns it into a shared and enjoyable dance; the hairdresser who engages freely and authentically in a rich two way stream of inconsequential small talk; the domestic who hears the humming and joins in with her own voice and the rhythm of her dusting. These, we believe, are the qualities of true playfulness [...] qualities that have real potential to enrich the wellbeing of people with dementia [...][8]

Here are three examples of playful encounters in my own dance experience with people who have dementia:

Example 1 Balloon in bed

10 am on a hospital ward. I've been booked to do a dance session and, as some patients are still getting dressed, I put on a CD with some gentle music and begin a leisurely dance with a giant balloon. I gradually move around the ward; keeping my distance, noticing responses. Ethel catches my eye – she looks interested. I move closer and she reaches out her hand. I pat the balloon towards her and

she hits it. I react with an exaggerated jump backwards as I catch it. She laughs and leans forward for another go.

Out of the corner of my eye I notice Jack shuffling over for a look. I ask one of the nurses to go and stand with him:

– 'It's OK,' she says, 'he's quite steady'.
– 'I'd rather you stayed with him,' I respond.

As the balloon comes towards him he 'heads' it and the nurse supports him as he scores his imaginary goal. (Men will often kick or head the balloon and this move takes them off balance so it is worth being ready to offer support if needed.)

Example 2 – What you need is a pint of milk on your head!

In the day centre for people with dementia, Terence joins me in a partner dance to some waltz music. Suddenly he stops, looks at me and smiles, saying, 'What you need is a pint of milk on your head.'

> I burst out laughing and ask, 'In a bottle or a jug?'
> He laughs with me and says, 'Never mind.'
> We carry on dancing.

In both of the above examples I was aiming to generate the right conditions for positive experiences where people feel able to engage with me, in the moment, on their terms.

I don't always manage to do that, though.

In some sessions it is really difficult to generate an atmosphere where playful encounters are likely to occur.

Example 3 – It's not all 'magic moments'

Six care home residents are accompanied into the lounge, where four people have been sitting for some time. This is *their* lounge; the others have come to join them because the activity organiser has decided that this new initiative – a dance project – will take place in the front lounge, rather than the conservatory lounge (the usual venue for activities). The organiser is trying to integrate residents and discourage territorial behaviour (think 'towels on sunbeds' and replace them with 'newspapers on chairs').

This is a rather diverse group. Some are very mobile, others have limited movement and use walking aids and wheelchairs. Some are alert, others are fairly confused. Some are eagerly looking forward to a new activity, others resent their peaceful afternoon being interrupted by 'people who belong in the other lounge'.

I try the usual icebreakers – name games and passing a ball around.

'Bugger off,' says Doris. 'It's daft, this. Does she think we're children?'

The 'follow me' warm up activities get a mixed response.

The most successful part of this difficult initial session is the improvisation with scarves. Additional staff members join us and, for a few brief moments, there is a feeling of playfulness.

Doris didn't feel playful, though; her afternoon had been disrupted.

Sometimes we just have to accept that playful encounters are going to be in short supply – if not entirely absent. When this happens it is important to reflect on any lessons to be learned, think about any changes that need to be made and accept that occasionally a session does not go as well as we would like it to. Incidentally, subsequent sessions at the above home went fairly well. Doris tolerated the 'intrusion', smiled from time to time and did join in some of the activities.

My approach was more or less the same, but more staff joined in and this definitely helped to generate a playful atmosphere. Naturally, staff needed the chance to see what is likely to be expected of them before they can take part. Wherever possible I try to arrange an introductory session with staff beforehand to explain my approach and give them an opportunity to play together with some of the materials.

Methods

When working with people who have dementia I use what Ken Bartlett[9] calls a 'lure' to invite people to respond – and the focus is on the 'here and now' experience. I do have a planned structure to come back to if necessary but it is more important to go along with what emerges in the session.

In her book *Invitation to the Dance*, Heather Hill, a dance therapist, highlights the importance of being flexible. Her guidelines for leaders who are new to this work recommend:

a fairly detailed plan [...]. However, be prepared to let go (with experience will come the courage to do this) and follow where the group takes you. [...]. It's a much more equal situation to be working creatively ALONGSIDE the older people in your group. They have a lot to offer – use it![10]

The activities I initiate are intended to be *'failure free'* movement – not dependent on memory or understanding verbal instructions. Neither do they involve learning steps or 'getting it right'. Occasionally someone wants to do a square tango or a jive – to revisit a known dance – and I'm happy to oblige, when it is their agenda.

I don't mind them correcting my moves but I'm not going to correct theirs.

Getting the 'fit' right

I try hard to 'get the fit right' between what I offer and what is likely to result in a positive experience – assessing how best to engage with each individual. This involves careful observation, reading facial expressions and making a real effort to understand the changing nature of each individual's world. If we're working in groups it is quite a challenge to 'get the fit right' for everyone simultaneously.

Sometimes it just isn't possible – but what we can do is manage our own responses. We can be aware of our own non-verbal communication and do our best to maintain a relaxed, friendly, encouraging manner.

Non-verbal communication

The dance activities most likely to result in a playful encounter do not rely on verbal skills and memory – in fact there are times when words can complicate communication. Verbal language and speech are often disrupted and destroyed as dementia advances so, in my dance sessions, I often try to engage with people non-verbally, and I encourage my support workers to do the same.

Some carers (and dancers) find this quite difficult but are often pleasantly surprised by the extent to which they can have a rich, pleasurable, meaningful, non-verbal dialogue. There is a particular quality to this interaction – which involves tuning in to another person's body. I have witnessed the most exquisite improvised dances where two people are 'in the moment'. Sometimes the person who has dementia is initiating the movement and their partner is going along with the flow.

Going with the flow

This is an expression we hear quite often – it has particular significance in the context of interaction in dementia care. Dr Mihalyi Csikszentmihalyi has written about the critical importance of flow to human experience.

In his research into human behaviour he has studied the experiences of people who are in a 'state of complete involvement' in an activity for its own sake. He noticed that

> [...] the challenges were in balance with the skills. And when those conditions were present you began to forget the things that bothered you in everyday life.[11]

Csikszentmihalyi's theories about children and flow give food for thought:

> What children do most of the time is interact with the environment on a level at which their skills match opportunities. Left to themselves children seek out flow with the inevitability of a natural law [...].[12]

Interacting with the environment on a level at which people's skills match opportunities is another way of 'getting the fit right'. A dance artist who is delivering sessions in dementia care settings will be able to assess how best to engage with each individual and help them experience 'flow'.

Evaluating the impact of dance work in dementia care settings

As well as taking part in playful encounters, dance practitioners are constantly assessing the effectiveness of their dance work – looking for ways of measuring its impact. In reflecting on our practice we need to understand what we've done to contribute to a positive experience and what we can do to improve on situations where things haven't gone so well.

When I was working at Stockport NHS trust we devised an observation checklist based on the methods used in Dementia Care Mapping.[13] For each session an observer noted participants' behaviour in the ten minutes before each session and then during it. Body posture, movement, eye contact, tracking, verbal and non-verbal communication and facial expression were noted. After each session, the observer, at least one of the therapy assistants and I discussed what we had observed – sharing some of the 'special moments' and noting individual responses. We had some interesting debates about how we know what we think we know about participants' experiences.[14]

Some guidelines for working with people who have dementia

Dance artists have a valuable role to play in both helping to maintain mobility and sharing meaningful and joyful interaction with the whole person. The following are useful guidelines for practitioners working with people living with dementia:

- Lead as non-verbally as you can.
- Agree with their version of how they see things – avoid unnecessary conflict.
- Take your lead from the person rather than giving instructions they won't understand.
- Try to avoid asking questions – it can cause confusion.
- Use language that is familiar to the person – carers or family may be able to help with this.
- Think carefully about what you say and how you say it.
- Adapt your approach to suit the individual person (in this case 'one size does not fit all!').
- Approach the person from the front.
- Address the person by name and remind them who you are – keep reminding them when appropriate.
- Use positive statements rather than negative ones, for example, "let's sit down" rather than "don't stand up".
- Use gestures to reinforce what you want to achieve, for example, using a sweeping gesture with an arm or patting the seat when saying "let's sit down".
- Model movements to give information, but avoid overwhelming the person with too much, too soon.
- Give the person time to try to understand what is happening – remember their ability to process information may be reduced.
- Try to have fun – an enjoyable few minutes may be a real joy for the person and for you. Capture moments.

Notes

1. Allen Power, G. (2011) in Lee, H. and Adams, T. (eds) *Creative Approaches in Dementia Care*. Basingstoke: Palgrave Macmillan.
2. Kitwood, T. (1997) *Dementia Reconsidered: The Person Comes First.* Buckingham: Oxford University Press.

3. Coaten, R. (2001) Exploring Reminiscence through Dance and Movement. *Journal of Dementia Care* 9(5), September/October 2001, 19–22.

4. Lieberman, J. in Perrin, T. and May, H. (2000) *Wellbeing in Dementia: An Occupational Approach for Therapists and Carers.* Oxford, UK: Churchill Livingstone.

5. Crichton, S. (2000) Donkey at a Horse Fair. In: *What dancers do that other health workers don't* ed. Greenland, P. Leeds: JABADAO.

6. Lucinda Jarrett. *Dance and Movement at the End of Life*, presentation at Arts and Dementia Conference, Oxford University, 22 June 2011.

7. Perrin, T. and May, H. (2000) *Wellbeing in Dementia.*

8. Ibid.

9. Diane Amans interview with Ken Bartlett, July 2011.

10. Hill, H. (2001) Invitation to the Dance: Dance for People with Dementia and Their Carers. Stirling, Scotland: Dementia Services Centre University of Stirling.

11. Csikszentmihalyi, M. In Debold, E. *Flow with Soul.* An Interview with Dr Mihalyi Csikszentmihalyi. Reproduced in *Enlighten Next magazine*, Spring–Summer 2002.

12. Csikszentmihalyi, M. (1975) *Beyond Boredom and Anxiety: Experiencing Flow in Work and Play.* San Francisco: Jossey-Bass.

13. For information on Dementia Care Mapping visit the website of the Bradford Dementia Group www.brad.ac.uk.

14. See the Resources section of this book for the observation checklist used during dance sessions in dementia care hospital wards.

Further reading

Killick, J. and Craig, C. (2012) *Creativity and Communications in People with Dementia.* London: Jessica Kingsley.

12 Dance and Parkinson's Disease

Diane Amans

In Chapter 10 Elizabeth Coleman outlined the symptoms of Parkinson's Disease and suggests some general points to be aware of when working with people living with the disease. This chapter includes information on Dance for Parkinson's research, and contributions from some of the practitioners working in this field.

Dancing with people who have Parkinson's disease is an expanding area of practice, with many dance artists and movement specialists developing their own approach to the work. In the UK there is a growing number of practitioners delivering different dance forms, including creative dance, ballet, Argentine Tango and aspects of somatic practice combined with dance. In the United States, dancers from the Mark Morris Dance Group (MMDG) have been delivering dance sessions with the Brooklyn Parkinson Group for many years. There has been effective international collaboration with dancers from MMDG, who have visited the UK to share their experience.

Tony Beazley, Executive Director of Dance Umbrella, initially set up a day of Dance for Parkinson's at the English National Ballet Studios in 2008. Since then there have been a number of events to progress the work and there is now a network of dancers involved in Dance for Parkinson's.

UK network

The first UK network meeting was held in 2011. Members come from a range of different backgrounds; there are dancers, teachers, health workers, therapists, community dance practitioners and musicians. They share ideas and experience and have a strong commitment to common aims. David Leventhal, Program Manager for Dance for PD® in the United States, is impressed with the network's collaborative spirit.

It's been a great pleasure working with the talented, innovative teachers who are part of a growing network of dance professionals dedicated to sharing knowledge and skills with the Parkinson's population. Whenever my colleagues from Brooklyn and I work with the UK teachers, we remark on the terrific camaraderie and energy this network shares [...]. It's rewarding to see these teachers coalesce into a unified team. In many ways this process serves as a model for the development of a closer-knit network of Dance for Parkinson's teachers here in the USA.[1]

English National Ballet: Dance for Parkinson's research

In 2010 English National Ballet commissioned Roehampton University to carry out research into Dance and Parkinson's during the company's pilot project. During the period from October 2010 to February 2011 there were 12 sessions based on the ballet *Romeo and Juliet.* The project, which combined creative movement with structured exercises, was accompanied by live music.

The aims of the research were:

- To examine how the dance affects participants, their carers and other stakeholders
- To assess participants' ongoing motivation to attend sessions
- To assess the value of community to participants within the group
- To assess the creative and aesthetic value of dancing with music for the participants
- To evaluate the physiological impact on participants of dancing, specifically in the areas of postural alignment, balance and stability, and motor control[2]

The study concluded that there were various ways in which taking part in dance activities affected people with Parkinson's.

[...] it was a project that enabled people to achieve more physically and helped them to rise above some of the limitations of their neurological condition. It created an event where people relished the social interaction and, in some, it encouraged a more positive outlook on their lives.

The artistic content, both the *Romeo & Juliet* ballet and score, played an important role in attracting people who were not interested in coming to a Parkinson's support group. Dancing to the music as a group also provided an interesting way for participants to exercise, particularly for those who were not keen on exercising alone. Most dramatically, dancing to the musical score enabled participants to increase fluidity of movement. The opportunity for freedom of expression through movement creation stimulated imaginations and allowed participants to expand beyond their habitual ways of moving.

Researchers, fellow participants, carers and some medical professionals all observed positive changes in participants either during sessions, or afterwards. The study did not detect long-term changes in mobility, but short-term gains in mobility were observed particularly in the latter half of the project. Well-being, positive attitude and other beneficial emotional feelings were consistently documented.[3]

In the Resources section of this book there is an executive summary of the English National Ballet/Roehampton University study on Dance for Parkinson's.

Dance practitioners describe their work with people who have Parkinson's disease

Amanda Fogg has many years' experience of running dance sessions for people with Parkinson's disease. Like several other UK practitioners, she has attended training with the MMDG and has developed her own approach to helping participants maintain fitness and deal with the challenges of the disease.

> My groups and their partners have taught me at least as much as I have taught them. They are truly in the front line and often come up with solutions of their own which help them with their individual problems – solutions which are then tried and adopted or adapted by other group members where appropriate. Sessions combine elements of general keep fit, Tai Chi, Yoga, Pilates, Conductive Education, dance, and exercises recommended by physiotherapists that are specific to Parkinson's Disease. We also do vocal and facial exercises.

> Many elements in the session would apply to any fitness class, but they become even more critical in prolonging well-being with reference to Parkinson's. We work on posture throughout the session, aiming to correct the pitched forward stance characteristic of the disease, and where

such posture has already become habitual we work to restore mobility in the upper spine and to re-align focus. There is a lot of work with the breath, using Pilates breathing as a model, aiming to increase lung capacity and mobility of the inter-costal muscles. This leads to seated Tai Chi warm-up exercises, again using the breath and including gentle but powerful arm movements to open the chest, improve posture and allow full tidal breathing, without strain. Some of the participants may choose to stand during the Tai Chi section of movements, but they may choose to sit at any time, and are encouraged to adapt their practice to how they are feeling.

We do general exercise, seated and standing, taking all the joints through as full a range of movement as is individually possible, using the large, then small muscle groups and where necessary the exercise is differentiated to suit each person's needs on that particular day. We work particularly to strengthen the quadriceps, maintain flexibility in the hamstrings, calves, ankles and feet, whilst aiming for freedom of movement in the upper body, with oppositional arm swing and erect, well-supported head.

In standing, initially we work between chairs, holding on to the backs of heavy chairs, so that there is support on both sides. Many specific problems of Parkinson's are addressed in this section as we practise heel strike, changes of weight from one foot to the other, shifts of centre of gravity towards different sides of the foot, gentle knee bends, hip circles, and low leg swings to keep hip joints free and loose. This work also has the benefit of strengthening both the supporting and working legs, and of course, the importance of good posture and eye focus is also stressed. The use of chairs assists work on balance, which is monitored so that it is appropriate to the needs of each individual on that particular day.

We continue the work on balance and posture in the centre of the space, individuals being gently supported by their partners where necessary. Props are sometimes used here as batons, for example, may take the focus outside the body, enabling freer, less inhibited movement.[4]

Gemma Coldicott is another dance practitioner, and is one of the founder members of the UK Network of Dance and Parkinson's. Like many of the other members she has attended training with the MMDG. She runs a weekly session for a group that was set up as part of Croydon Council's Healthy Living Programme.

The approach of my work with people with Parkinson's includes using ballet, contemporary and creative dance, ballroom, salsa and tango dance technique. We use a combination of seated exercises, circle dances, barre exercises, traveling sequences and creative tasks. I give the group lots of coordination, balance, postural alignment and visualisation exercises to ease the symptoms of Parkinson's including freezing and tremors.

However a large part of the session is to forget about the disease, to release the body and mind and above all to have fun. Many people attend with their carer, who is usually their wife, and we all dance together. I have a pianist who plays for us and brings another level of joy and celebration to the class.

Daphne Cushnie and Melanie Brierley work in partnership to offer dance sessions to people with Parkinson's. Together they have formed The Cumbria Parkinson's Disease Dance Collective.

Our particular approach is underpinned by some of the key principles used in both dance and neurological physiotherapy to address the complex functional, relational and spatial problems commonly experienced by people affected by PD.

It relies on a subtle understanding of the components of normal movement including the role of perception, intention, and sensation. We use strategies and frameworks to promote effective, fluid and expressive movement, and improve balance, poise and confidence.

We have been influenced by the field of somatic practice, which is based on the principle that without awareness of sensation, movement can become impoverished and truncated. In PD this disconnection to self and the environment is magnified by the disease process. For this reason, emphasis is placed on conscious relaxed control of movement, deepening felt connections within the moving body and in relationship to others in the group.

Humour, respect, camaraderie and open-heartedness are vital elements in enabling group members to rekindle joy in movement, and fostering a sense of optimism about the future, despite having a diagnosis of PD.

Marina Benini, Joanne Duff and Anna Gillespie are three practitioners who have joined together to create the group Musical Moving. Based in London, they offer dance sessions designed specially for people living with

Parkinson's disease. The classes have live musical accompaniment, which can bring a particular dynamic and energy to the group.

I love moving to music. It makes you feel so good.

This session I really felt the benefit of moving to music. Things I could not do without music became possible if I listened hard to the beat – if I let myself be focused and freed by the melody.

I like being made to move and moving to music ... I tend to become very stiff and every joint hurts. I like the pleasure of moving to music. I like classical music.[5]

Anna Gillespie, musician with Musical Moving, describes how she supports dancers in engaging with both the movement and the music.

Young or old, professional or otherwise, music can profoundly affect the experience of moving and, as an accompanist, it is a joy to feel part of this. The sounds and silences that comprise music only become meaningful when an active mind is attending to them and this applies to both dancer and accompanist.

It is through this shared, reciprocal and yet personal experience that my musical meeting with dancers occurs. A class never sounds exactly the same because we are all constantly responding to each other. This is particularly useful in a Parkinson's dance class. I'm free to 'personalise' moments in music, following and/or encouraging the movement of a particular dancer. I can change tempo and quality at will, shifting the 'sense of motion', or try to oblige requests.[6]

Conclusion

In the above quote Anna Gillespie refers to dance sessions where 'we are all constantly responding to each other'. This is a clear illustration of person-centred practice – which characterises the approach of many community dance artists, including the Dance for Parkinson's practitioners. They have each developed their own unique style, influenced by their journeys and experiences, but all work hard to ensure that participants engage in life-affirming movement, which acknowledges their individual needs and preferences.

Notes

1. Leventhal, D. In Fogg, A. *Our Network* (2011) in Animated Magazine Foundation for Community Dance Autumn.
2. Houston, S. and McGill, A. (2011) *English National Ballet, Dance for Parkinson's: An Investigative Study.* London: Roehampton University.
3. Ibid.
4. Fogg, A. In Tufnell, M. (2010) *Dance, Health and Wellbeing; Pathway to Practice for Dance Leaders working in Health and Care Settings.* Leicester: Foundation for Community Dance.
5. Houston and McGill, *English National Ballet, Dance for Parkinson's.*
6. Gillespie, A. *Reflections of a Dance Accompanist* (2011) in Animated Magazine Foundation for Community Dance Autumn.

13   Duty of Care: Keeping Older Bodies Safe

Diane Amans

....

What does duty of care mean? To whom do we have a duty of care? This chapter outlines ways in which dance artists can take reasonable care to keep people safe. It includes:

- a duty of care checklist
- practical examples of ways to adapt activities
- leadership behaviour
- working with support staff
- documenting duty of care practice

There is a section on issues and dilemmas in relation to duty of care and a consideration of duty of care in performance projects.
....

An introduction to duty of care in community dance

Dance artists who are involved in creating opportunities for people to participate in dance activities have a duty of care to those participants. Regardless of the age of the people taking part in participatory arts sessions, the practitioner responsible for leading the sessions must ensure people's safety and keep their best interests at heart.

Community dance practitioners owe a duty of care to:

- participants in the dance sessions
- colleagues, support workers and volunteers
- themselves

In practice this means using professional skills, knowledge and understanding to protect people from harm when they take part in dance activities. As dance artists we need to think about duty of care and how it relates to all areas of our work. We are accustomed to carrying out risk assessments of venues, but there are many other factors involved in taking reasonable care to protect people from harm.

Duty of care checklist

Venue – where will the session take place? What is in the space? Does any furniture need moving? Who will do this? Are there any hazards? (For example, columns, sharp corners, low light fittings that may cause a problem with some props.) Is the space too cold? Too hot? Is it easily accessible for your participants? Have you carried out a risk assessment? Is this documented?

Equipment – will you bring this or is it provided? Is electrical equipment in good working order? Has it been portable appliance tested (PAT tested)?[1] Will you be using props? If you are working with people who are ill have you thought about infection control for shared props? (Passing round scarves and feathers is not a good idea in some settings where people are ill.) Does anyone have any allergies or phobias? (Fear of feathers and fear of balloons are common phobias, for instance.)

Participants – what information do you need in order to plan appropriate activities and keep people safe? What do you know about the health status of the participants? Is there anyone with a medical condition that needs special consideration? How will you find out and store this information? Are there any people you would not want to take part? How will you manage this?

Co-leaders – do you need one or more co-leaders working with you? Is there sufficient budget for a paid co-leader? Will there be support workers or carers in the session? What will their role be and how will you brief them?

Dance activities – what sort of dance? What are participants expecting? Have you thought about the pace of activities? Do you need to build in time for a break? Are your proposed activities reliant on memory? How will you deal with a range of abilities and energy levels? Will you be using music?

Duty of care and older people dancing

Whilst much of the above applies to participants of any age, there are specific duty of care considerations relating to older dancers. Chapters 9 and 10 include information about what happens to bodies as they age. We also need to know what happens to bodies as they exercise and whether there are any particular precautions that need to be taken when dealing with older bodies.

Active older people dancing

What do you need to be aware of if you are leading dance activities for active mature movers – people in their fifties, sixties and older? Even if these participants seem fairly fit there are a number of factors to be taken into account. As with any group of adults it is useful to know how long it is since individuals last took part in physical activity. If people have had a period of inactivity, exercise needs to be gradual and not too strenuous, otherwise there is a risk of injury and fatigue.

The elements of warm up exercises for older dancers are no different from those with any other group – but there are some small changes that will probably need to be made. Certainly there should be a period of adjustment from rest to physical activity, and this may need to be a little longer than in a warm-up for younger people. Allowing time to focus is a significant factor in preventing accidents. Dancers who are concentrating are less likely to become distracted and injure themselves.

The sample sessions plans in the Resources section include activities for effective warm-ups, which:

– raise the body temperature
– increase heart and breathing rate
– stretch muscles
– extend range of movement at joints

One key point to remember is to avoid too many repetitions of any activity – build these up gradually and alternate between different sides and parts of the body. For example, in a balance exercise that involves standing on one leg (such as making circular movements with the ankle), it is safer if the supporting leg changes. So two sets of four repetitions on each leg is preferable to one set of eight repetitions each side.

In creative activities, where there are opportunities to experience playful spontaneous movement, it is important to make sure that enthusiasm does not outstrip capacity. Also, in open ended activities, such as group or paired improvisation, it is worth thinking about which dancers work together. If you have a new member of the group do you pair them with a more experienced participant? Or do you put two relative newcomers together? From a duty of care perspective there may be good reasons for taking either approach. It will depend on the individuals involved and the improvisation structure. You may decide *not* to determine who dances with whom; what matters is that you have thought about it before making your decision.

Where there is a range of ability and experience the dance leader has to take a number of factors into consideration to ensure the physical and psychological well-being of the individuals in the group. Whilst it is good practice to encourage people to work at their own pace and take a break when they need one, some individuals do not realise they are becoming tired; others are reluctant to admit they need a rest. It is important to *observe* the dancers and find a way of introducing a pause or change of pace if you feel it is necessary. There are occasions when dancers' expectations of their own or other people's abilities are not based on reality. This is when an observant dance leader can intervene and adapt the task to ensure that people are working within their capabilities.

Practical example

Linda is an active 60-year-old who enjoys taking part in performance projects. She acknowledges that the experience will be challenging, as choreographers sometimes ask them to move in a way that is uncomfortable or difficult, but she is reluctant to admit defeat.

> ... we enter into these things knowing damn well our knees are knackered and we'll have aches and pains, but I like a challenge. The choreographers are really good about it if we have any difficulties but it's hard to put your hand up and say 'actually I can't do it.'

Linda describes warm-up activities where they are performing leaps. She is determined to jump like she did when she was much younger. Linda recognises that she puts pressure on herself; the choreographers are happy to adapt activities to suit participants but they are not very good at seeing when dancers are struggling with a move.

Linda believes that choreographers who are younger and physically stronger do not understand what they are asking of people who are 20 or 30 years older. She has few complaints and is happy to take responsibility for her own safety, but her experiences highlight the fact that duty of care is much more than saying 'take care of yourself and rest when you need to'. In dance projects where participants have different stamina levels and a range of physical abilities the dance artist or choreographer leading the sessions needs to find imaginative ways to manage these differences.[2]

Practical example

Harry is a dance artist working with an intergenerational group to choreograph a piece for Big Dance. Participants are very enthusiastic and are keen to attend full day rehearsals on Saturdays and Sundays.

Harry has noticed that some of the adults are eager to show they can keep up with the young people, but he is aware that he has a responsibility to make sure that people do not push themselves too much. Two of the men in their 50s look red-faced and breathless by the morning break and, rather than draw attention to this, he divides the participants into small groups for costume making and for rehearsing duets and trio dances.

This way he is taking care of individuals and managing the different needs and energy levels without drawing attention to the fact that some dancers look like they need a break.

Dance with less active older people – including chair-based sessions

Participants in this group are likely to include individuals who have some of the conditions described in Chapter 10. Ideally you would have had the opportunity to find out about people's medical circumstances beforehand,

Figure 13.1   Freedom in Dance Class, Lincolnshire
Source: Mark Hurd

but even if you do not have this information, you can plan a session that takes account of the likelihood of conditions such as arthritis and heart disease. The guidelines outlined under 'points to be aware of' (see Chapter 10) are helpful duty of care principles for any group of older people.

Once again, the dance leader's observation skills are a critical element of safe working practice. Paying attention to individuals as they enter the space and during the session will mean you are more likely to notice any changes. How do they usually move? What is their normal skin colour? Are they often breathless? Do they normally smile and look cheerful? Are they quite talkative? Do they join in most of the time?

Duty of care: Leadership behaviour

As part of a recent research inquiry,[3] I carried out interviews with participants in dance classes for active older people. I asked what made them trust a dance artist; what made them feel safer with some practitioners and less safe with others?

What makes participants feel safe?

- Pre-session chat with a leader who asks about any medical conditions
- A leader who keeps an eye on the group and adjusts the activity or offers alternatives when necessary
- A non-competitive atmosphere
- A chance to express and share feelings about the session content
- A pace that suits energy levels
- Flexibility in incorporating and valuing members' reactions and suggestions
- The freedom to opt out and take a rest
- An environment that fosters support amongst participants and is welcoming to newcomers

What makes participants feel unsafe?

- Being asked to do activities that are too challenging
- Leaders who join in most of the time and 'lose themselves' in the dance
- Being asked to demonstrate in front of the group without any chance to opt out
- Lack of flexibility on the part of dance artists who do not adapt activities when people struggle to achieve the task

In every group interviewed there were similar comments relating to leadership behaviour that makes dancers feel unsafe. Some participants will happily give feedback to the dance leader – others, like Linda in the above example, would feel embarrassed to admit that she was experiencing difficulties.

Safe practice: Adapting or translating dance activities[4]

Any community dance artist who is working inclusively will already be used to adapting activities to suit the individuals taking part. Working inclusively with older people is the same as working inclusively with people of all ages. We do what we can to remove barriers and allow people to take part. Sometimes that means making changes to a planned dance activity to take account of individual needs.

For example, some circle dances include a grapevine step, which could cause problems for participants who have had a hip replacement, as they are advised to avoid movements where the leg crosses the midline of the body. It is easy to replace the grapevine step with a side step.

Managing different physical abilities

Most dance activities can be modified to include dancers who need to remain in chairs alongside more active participants. If dancers are moving together in a line or a circle, the dancers either side of a seated participant can adjust their steps. (I have seen this done successfully with a double amputee who was able to lift his stumps in time to the music.) In improvisation work the inclusion of seated performers offers some interesting choreographic possibilities.

Creating a safe way for participants to watch each other dance

It can be rather intimidating to 'perform' for other people – even if the audience is just other members of the dance session. Yet there is much to be gained from observing how other people interpret a creative task or perform their dance. This is one of the ways in which dancers develop their movement vocabulary and performance skills.

It may not be a problem for individuals or small groups if they are asked to dance with their peers watching. There have been occasions, though, when a newcomer, who is just beginning to gain confidence, feels embarrassed and exposed if they are expected to perform for the rest of the group. A sensitive practitioner can devise ways for participants to show their work and view the dance, without this being a stressful experience.

- Divide the group in half and have half the participants observing the others
- Invite people one by one to just step out and watch for half a minute and then rejoin the group
- Ask individuals discreetly if they are happy to perform with the rest of the class watching
- Set up a structure where people perform a small motif in canon (one after the other); when they are not actually moving they can watch other people dance

Duty of care to self

Dance artists are responsible for making sure they take reasonable care of themselves. This duty of care includes:

- Making time for professional development activities to help the artists gain skills and confidence
- Being clear about what is expected of them and being prepared to say 'no' when asked to take on work for which they do not have the appropriate qualifications or experience
- Negotiating a realistic fee for their work – to take into account preparation, documentation and evaluation
- Carrying out risk assessments and taking steps to control possible hazards
- Knowing what to do when something unexpected occurs
- Keeping written records – these do not need to be complicated or time consuming. They just need to be brief documented evidence of duty of care

Litigious society

The main reason for paying attention to duty of care is that it is good practice. However, in a world where there are increasing numbers of people seeking compensation, it makes sense to make sure that we can demonstrate the measures we take to keep participants as safe as possible.

Documenting our duty of care practice is one way of protecting ourselves from accusations of negligence.

Documentary evidence of a dance artist's duty of care practice

- Written risk assessment of the venue
- Risk assessment of all the dance activities
- Briefing paper given to co-leaders and support workers outlining their roles and responsibilities
- Project diary containing brief notes on participants
- Health and safety questionnaires completed by all participants
- Record of leader's continuing professional development
- Leader's qualifications and experience

This list of evidence looks quite daunting if you're not used to it, but once you have systems in place, it does not take long to do and it gives you confidence, credibility and protection if things go wrong (Amans 2006).[5]

Other aspects of duty of care: Colleagues and support workers

Duty of care in dance extends to everyone who is present. This is usually fairly straightforward and just involves thinking through all aspects of the sessions – from organising the space and planning the activities to considering the needs of the participants and other people involved.

Dance artists working with colleagues are responsible for taking reasonable care to ensure their safety. A simple example is making sure your co-leader has assistance with carrying heavy equipment or moving furniture to prepare the space. Another practical element concerns roles and responsibilities before, during and after the sessions. Whether the support staff are dancers or care workers it will be helpful to all concerned if the lead artist has thought about what people will actually *do* during the session.

I used to be reluctant to allocate tasks to support staff who are part of a host organisation, for example, a day centre. However, I have learned through experience that some 'helper behaviour' can be very disruptive. It is difficult to lead a dance session when there are self-appointed 'co-leaders' making well-intentioned interventions that distract and confuse participants. It is in everyone's best interests if roles are clearly defined and understood.

Ideally there will be a chance to meet with support staff beforehand and clarify what will happen during the session – occasionally projects include a brief training session beforehand so that staff have a chance to experience the dance activities. However, if there is no time for a proper briefing, it is worth taking a few minutes at the beginning of the session to explain what will be happening and ask if there is any specific information you need to be aware of to keep people safe. I usually ask staff and volunteers to just participate, keeping verbal prompts to a minimum and watching for anyone who seems to be in difficulty.

Duty of care: Some issues and dilemmas

Despite clear policies and procedures there are still ambiguities about best practice in this field. Here are some questions for you:

- Can you keep people safe if they choose not to tell you about their health problems?[6]
- How much do we need to know about participants' medical conditions? How would you find out?
- One of the participants tells you she has had a pain in her back since last week's class. What would you say? What would you do?
- When working with active older people is it enough to say 'look after yourself... work within your limits... take a rest when you need one'?
- Would you let some people dance in shoes and others in bare feet?
- If it was cold would you let barefoot dancers warm up in socks?
- Would you feel able to ask a 70-year-old to remove her chewing gum?

If you find any of the above questions difficult to answer it is worth discussing them with other practitioners. There are no simple 'one size fits all' answers to these questions. This is a complex area and community dance professionals sometimes have different views about duty of care issues.

Some situations are more straightforward than others. For example, I would definitely ask a dancer of any age to remove chewing gum – most people realise immediately that there are good reasons for the request. I either have a quiet word with the individual or make a general announcement reminding people to finish chewing sweets or gum before we start.

The question of whether or not to allow participants to dance in socks seems to divide dance leaders. Some people allow participants to choose but make sure they warn people that socks may cause accidents if dancers are moving quickly on a slippery surface. Others (including me) ask people to remove socks or roll back the heel so they are less likely to slip. I do sometimes run classes where some people wear shoes and others dance barefoot. Naturally I point out that participants need to take extra care.

With regard to the participant who has back pain – whilst it is important to find out whether the pain occurred as a result of taking part in the dance class, the person should seek advice from a doctor. As dance practitioners we are not qualified to give advice, and the pain may be a symptom of a condition that needs medical treatment.

The first two questions invite you to consider how much information you need to have about the people in your group. You need to know enough to keep people safe, and this really does differ from project to project, depending on the extent to which participants are able to take responsibility for their own safety and well-being. When working with active older people I usually say 'look after yourself... work within your limits... take a rest when you need one...' – but I still see it as part of my duty of care responsibility to observe them as they move and to do what I can to ensure they avoid injury. I also encourage participants to let me know if there is anything I need to be aware of – for example, if they have had a fall or have a particular medical condition. Many dance practitioners ask participants to complete a questionnaire giving details of health conditions: this is very useful – provided we understand how to use this knowledge. Whilst dance leaders are not expected to be medical experts, the information outlined in chapters 9 and 10 will give you an idea of some of the more common conditions associated with ageing.

As I have already indicated, when you are working with less active individuals with support needs, it may be necessary to ask them and their care workers to let you know about any significant causes for concern. It can be rather daunting if you encounter someone with a condition that is unfamiliar to you. If this happens, take advice from someone who is medically qualified. If I have doubts or cause for concern I ask the person to just watch on this occasion and check that their doctor is happy for them to take part in future.

Duty of care and performance projects

There are additional duty of care considerations to be taken into account when working with a group who are preparing to perform for an audience.

If the performance is to take place at an unfamiliar venue this will require a risk assessment to be carried out. On the day of the performance there is likely to be a technical rehearsal, which can be very demanding in terms of stamina and stress management. It may be the first time some people have ever been on a stage and, when the lights go down, older eyes take longer to adjust to blackout conditions.

Other considerations, which are sometimes overlooked, are the distance from the changing room to the performance area and whether this involves climbing several flights of stairs. Also – what are the arrangements if participants wish to keep their personal belongings (such as handbags) with them? This may seem a trivial point to mention but, if handbags contain inhalers or other medication, people are often reluctant to have them locked away for a few hours. The above points are all taken from an evaluation report following a dance showcase event where several participants felt uncomfortable and stressed. Dance artists working with groups need to ensure they have carefully thought through all stages of the performance experience and factored in opportunities for rest and refreshment.

Conclusion

The duty of care guidelines suggested in this chapter apply to dance work with people of any age. The dance practitioner is responsible for creating an atmosphere that encourages participants to work within their own capabilities and take rests when needed or desired. The feedback from participants – about what makes them feel safe and unsafe – is useful information for younger practitioners who have not yet experienced dancing in an older body.

The Resources section of this book includes additional material that is relevant to duty of care: an example of a completed risk assessment form, further details of conditions affecting older people and information about safeguarding vulnerable adults. These guidelines will help dancers to fulfil their duty of care to their individual participants, other group members, co-workers and themselves.

Exercise 1

Test your duty of care knowledge by completing the health and safety quiz in the Resources section.

Exercise 2

Your local dance agency has asked you to run eight weekly sessions in a nearby residential home for older people. This is a new project and the manager is keen to support an ongoing project if these initial sessions are successful.

As part of your preparation you will visit the venue and have a meeting with the manager.

With duty of care in mind what information do you need to find out during this visit? Make a list of questions and points to discuss with the manager, and anything you need to check out about the venue.

Are there any people you would not involve in a dance session?

Give reasons for your answer.

Exercise 3

- Rita is a new member of the group. She tells you she has high blood pressure and sometimes she has angina.
  What else would you need to know about Rita?
  What would you watch out for during the session?
- Gordon has had several falls but is keen to join in your class. What will you do to keep him safe?

Exercise 4

- You are invited to lead sessions with a group of older adults in a day centre. They are a mixed ability group and include a few members who seem rather frail, and one who is sometimes confused.
- During your first session one of the support workers is very patronising towards the less able members of the group and tends to repeat your instructions in a loud voice – 'She wants you to lift your arms up, Alan. Come on now show us what you can do!'
- What are the issues here?
- How would you handle them?

Notes

1. The *Electricity at Work Regulations 1989* require employers and self-employed practitioners to make sure that all electrical systems (including portable equipment) are maintained to prevent danger. Further information is available at http://www.pat-testing.info/.

2. The Foundation for Community Dance code of practice requires professional community dance artists to commit to working in a way that creates 'an inclusive and supportive environment in which individual experiences, abilities and interests are acknowledged and given space to be shared', available at www.communitydance.org.uk/member-services/professional-code-of-conduct.html.

3. Amans, D. Interviews conducted with older performers during 2011 as part of the research for this book.

4. Leading dance practitioner, Cecilia Macfarlane, prefers to use the term 'translate' rather than 'adapt' – a term Cecilia finds patronising. I see her point and now often refer to 'translating' activities as part of an inclusive approach.

5. Amans, D. (2010) *Passport to Practice; An Induction to Professional Practice in Community Dance*. Leicester: Foundation for Community Dance.

6. If people choose not to share health details with you that is their choice: the important point is that you make it clear you take duty of care seriously and you welcome any information that will help with this. The Guidelines for Exercise and Health and Safety questionnaire in Resources asks the participant to sign the following statement: 'I have read the guidelines for dance exercise and agree to advise the dance leader of any changes in my health condition which may affect my ability to exercise.'

14 Continuing Professional Development, Training Opportunities, Gaining Skills and Qualifications

Diane Amans

. . . .

When and how do dance practitioners acquire the skills, knowledge and understanding to keep ageing bodies safe? Should training for community dance practitioners equip them to facilitate sessions for participants of all ages? Is it necessary to treat older people as a separate specialist area? This chapter examines these issues and offers information about professional development opportunities, training courses and more informal ways of gaining skills and experience.

A commitment to regular continuing professional development (CPD) activity is an essential part of our professional practice. As community dance practitioners we need to be able to provide evidence of our experience and learning. The various activities described in this chapter can all be included in a CPD portfolio together with notes and reflections on some of the discussion points included throughout the book.

Many of the examples given are UK specific, but the issues discussed will have relevance in other countries where dance artists are working in community settings.

. . . .

– Is it necessary to have specialist training to lead dance activities with older people? I've been teaching adult classes for years and in some of my groups there are people over 60.
– You don't need to do a course to lead dance with older people – they're just like us only a bit slower.
– Maybe – if they're fairly fit... but if I were working with frail older people I wouldn't know where to start when planning a session for them. I'd worry about how much they can do without hurting themselves.
– Yes – I don't know much about older bodies. We didn't learn much about anatomy and physiology when I was studying so I feel I don't know a lot about bodies – young or old.

These comments came during a discussion with community dance practitioners who were interested in working with older people. They raise some interesting questions. What is so special about leading dance with older people? Surely if dance artists have an inclusive approach to their work they will be able to offer experiences that are suited to the individuals in their group, whatever their age.

When I first delivered dance projects with older people – some of whom were frail and in their 80s and 90s – I hadn't had any specialist training for this work. There were few courses for community dance artists in the 1980s and any specialist training for working with older people was limited to courses in exercise to music, such as the EXTEND course[1] run in the UK by the Women's League of Health and Beauty. I developed skills and gained experience by running creative dance classes in a wide range of settings, sometimes working alongside care professionals who could give me information about some of the health conditions that were new to me.

I subsequently attended specialised training courses in falls prevention, chair-based exercise and postural stability. This was an important part of my CPD as it helped me to develop a greater understanding of the ageing process – a critical element in exercising duty of care. Dance practitioners working with mature movers need to understand what it feels like to be 60, 70 or older. Whilst the content of the dance session – the actual activities – may be more or less the same for different age groups, it will probably be necessary to adapt the pace. We all know what it feels like to be a child, a teenager and a young adult. However, there are relatively few community dance practitioners who know how it feels to be an older dancer.

This may change in the future, as there are a number of initiatives to train older people to work as co-leaders alongside dance practitioners or to run their own sessions. For example, Age and Opportunity and the Irish Sports Council have delivered several peer leadership programmes, helping older people develop the skills and confidence to lead group activities.

In Lincolnshire, the training delivered by Freedom in Dance illustrates how a new learning experience can open up exciting opportunities for an older person. At the age of 61 Jacky Simpson decided to enrol on the training course, and she now leads several groups and accepts invitations to share her experiences both locally and outside the UK. In her case study in the Resources section of this book, Jacky shares her delight in her new role.[2]

Specialist training or specialist knowledge?

Several of the practitioners who took part in the discussion quoted at the beginning of this chapter subsequently attended an accredited training course and were surprised how much they learned – particularly as the course had a comprehensive input on specific conditions affecting older people. Ideally dance artists working with older groups would understand the physiological, social and emotional aspects of ageing and know about the contexts in which the work might take place. So perhaps what we need is specialist *knowledge* rather than specialist training. This is certainly the view of Ken Bartlett, who argues:

> If your pedagogy is right then all you need is specialist knowledge.

> We need to know the impact of ageing on the body. If we understand that, then our pedagogy can remain the same.[3]

Ken believes that community dance artists need to be genuinely person centred and good at reading bodies – 'good at reading what it is that people are doing when they are doing dance'.[4]

He has a point. If we understand the individuals in our group and make sure we provide appropriate movement opportunities, then our approach is likely to work in any community context. As I mention in Chapter 11, effective dance practitioners have the skills and knowledge to get the right 'fit' – between what they offer and what participants want. In this respect working with older people is no different from working with any other individuals. However, the Foundation for Community Dance's *Charter for the Older Dancer* includes the following recommendation:

> Those who work with older dancers should recognise that adults learn differently from younger dancers and should therefore acquaint themselves with models of adult learning.[5]

Continuing professional development: Acquiring specialist knowledge

There are various routes open to practitioners who want to learn more about dance with older people. Some dance organisations run one-day courses that provide practical ideas and an introduction to health and safety issues. Longer accredited programmes (see below) offer a more in-depth study and sometimes include a placement with older people. The Foundation for Community Dance has set up a National College for Community Dance and runs a summer school that includes a module on Age Inclusive Practice.

It is also worth looking outside the dance profession for relevant training. Falls prevention courses run by health care professionals contain excellent input on physiology and postural stability.

You might want to put together your own programme of CPD to complement your current interests and past experience. Here are some possible starting places:

- Specialist dance courses
- Training in exercise for older people
- Online learning resources
- Falls prevention and postural stability courses
- Dementia care training
- One-day introductory events
- Shadowing dance artists
- Co-leading in exercise classes
- Volunteering on dance projects with older people
- Spending time with individuals to gain insight into the mindset of older people

If you are devising your own programme of CPD you may find it useful to look at the national occupational standards in community dance. These professional standards, developed by the Dance Training and Accreditation Partnership, were launched in 2011. They help practitioners evaluate their practice and identify areas where they need further experience or skills development.[6]

Courses run by dance organisations

Accredited training programmes usually include a study of the ageing process, benefits of dance, practical sessions and placements with older people. Two such courses are the Lincolnshire Dance *Leading Dance with Older People* programme, and the *Older People Dancing* course run by Green Candle Dance Company. Both are accredited by the Open College Network at Level 3.

There are occasional short courses or one-day introductory events focusing on older people dancing. These may be run by individual dance companies or charities such as Age UK. Sometimes an event is set up by the arts services department of a council such as West Lothian in Scotland.

These opportunities change from year to year. Up-to-date information is available from local and regional dance agencies and the Foundation for Community Dance website.[7]

Partnership working

Some dance companies link up with organisations that provide services for older people. An example of collaborative working with combined training is the project initiated by Powys Dance in 2011. They ran a course that set up learning partnerships between dance practitioners and activities officers in local residential and day care settings. In addition to the taught sessions each pair worked together to plan, deliver and evaluate sessions in their setting, putting into practice what they had learnt.

This professional development initiative was supported with funding from the Local Authority Partnership Agreement, Powys.[8] It was part of a national initiative prompted by the Welsh Assembly Government's strategy document *Climbing Higher: Creating an Active Wales*.

Higher education

There are increasing numbers of undergraduate programmes in dance studies, which offer the opportunity to specialise in community dance. Some of these courses include specialist knowledge relating to different sections of the community, such as older people and intergenerational groups. The Foundation for Community Dance website has information about UK colleges and universities offering degree courses that include community dance.

Organisations offering training in exercise for older people

Dance artists who want an intensive training in strength and balance exercise together with input on anatomy and physiology may find it helpful to look at courses run by Later Life Training and EXTEND. Although they do not offer professional development in dance, both organisations offer detailed and rigorous study of older bodies and specific conditions related to ageing. Their programmes are aimed at chair-based exercise leaders and instructors in postural stability and falls prevention.

The Later Life Training website[9] offers free home exercise booklets on

- postural stability, strength and balance
- Otago strength and balance
- chair-based strength and flexibility

Roles, relationships and boundary management

The specialist knowledge gained from these exercise courses is invaluable for the dance artist working with older dancers. However, in contrast to community dance practice, the training in exercise model is one based on *instruction* rather than facilitation. Participants in an exercise class will usually expect to be following a leader who will show them the correct way to move. In a community dance class participants will often have a more collaborative relationship with the leader.

I mentioned in Chapter 1 that, as dance artists, we need to be clear about our role, what our aims are and what we are qualified to do. An important element of CPD is taking time to reflect on our practice: this will help us to clarify the boundaries between our practice and that of other professionals. The following exercise invites you to look in more detail at the questions posed in Chapter 1.

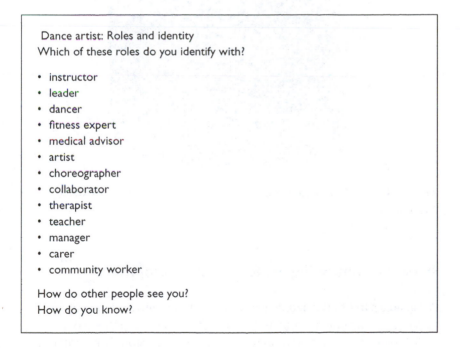

Dance artist: Roles and identity
Which of these roles do you identify with?

- instructor
- leader
- dancer
- fitness expert
- medical advisor
- artist
- choreographer
- collaborator
- therapist
- teacher
- manager
- carer
- community worker

How do other people see you?
How do you know?

Most dance practitioners probably identify with several of these roles. The extent to which they can answer the final two questions will depend on whether they receive feedback about their work.

Figure 14.1   Rebecca Seymour: Movement for the Mind, Wiltshire
Source: Stephany Bardzil

Informal continuing professional development

A valuable part of my ongoing professional development is the opportunity to reflect on my practice and discuss it with other practitioners. Where possible I work with co-leaders and make time for discussion with participants. These feedback sessions are just as important to my skills development as taking part in more structured activities, such as training courses. Dance artists who work independently in community settings have few formal opportunities for reviewing our practice. It is worth joining or setting up a peer mentoring network; observing other people's dance sessions and being observed by a fellow practitioner provide great potential for personal development.

Shadowing opportunities

Some dance companies offer the chance to work on a project with older people. They often employ support workers or co-leaders to work alongside experienced artists. Even if there are no paid vacancies there may be scope for working as a volunteer on these projects to gain valuable experience. Dance practitioners often welcome additional help when they are running sessions with community groups. Shadowing an experienced dance leader, who can also offer time to discuss the session, is an ideal way to build a body of knowledge and awareness. It is possible to negotiate such opportunities without incurring too many costs, but mentors should be paid for their time. How do dance practitioners fund these informal activities that are such an important part of their professional development?

Funding – some suggestions in the UK

A number of the professional development options mentioned above – shadowing and volunteering, for example – will cost very little. Also, some training courses are subsidised – and costs for attending training are tax deductible. Occasionally dance artists manage to persuade an agency such as a housing association or a charitable trust to pay for them to attend training. In return the dance artist offers a number of free sessions once training is completed.

Whether you choose to attend an accredited training course or devise your own professional development programme, you could submit an application for an Arts Council grant. There is always competition for the limited funds available but many individual artists have been successful in receiving awards for their CPD. One of the key elements in a successful application is being able to demonstrate how this financial support will contribute to your development.

Conclusion

This chapter began by raising the question of whether or not it is necessary to have specialist training to lead dance activities with older people. It may not be necessary to attend a specialist course, but I would suggest that dance artists who work with older adults should:

- Know about the effects of ageing, including some specific conditions affecting older people.
- Understand how to keep older dancers safe.
- Be able to communicate with older people in an appropriate, non-patronising way.
- Have an awareness of some of the stereotypes of older people and how these might be challenged.
- Be prepared to learn from participants

Notes

1. EXTEND is a charity that runs training courses in leading gentle exercise to music. http://www.extend.org.uk.
2. Jacky's experiences are described in Resources – see Case Study: Jacky Simpson.
3. Amans, D. Interview with Ken Bartlett, 28 March 2011.
4. Ibid.
5. Foundation for Community Dance, *A Charter for the Older Dancer.* First published in January 1997, revised 2009. The charter is a useful reference point for evaluation and reflecting on dance practice with older people. It is reproduced in full in Resources section.
6. Dance Training and Accreditation Partnership (DTAP) is a consortium of UK national dance organisations. The development of National Occupational Standards for dance leadership was led by the Foundation for Community Dance, which works closely with the sector skills council Creative and Cultural Skills. Further information is available from www.dtap.org.uk, www.ccskills.org.uk and www.communitydance.org.uk.
7. Foundation for Community Dance website: www.communitydance.org.uk.
8. For further information on the Powys Dance Leading Dance with Older Adults partnership see the Case Study in Resources section.
9. Later Life Training website: www.laterlifetraining.co.uk.

15   Evaluation

Sara Houston

....

How do we evaluate dance sessions with older people? Regardless of the age of the participants, we need to be clear what we are looking for and how we can best measure the effects of our work. Sara Houston examines the complexities of deciding what is meant by success and challenges us to think creatively about the way we evaluate our dance practices. She highlights the need to clarify terms such as 'impact' and 'successful', and to ensure that we select appropriate evaluation tools to help us make judgements about the quality of our work.
....

The sister companion to this book, *An Introduction to Community Dance Practice*,[1] gives some useful examples of practitioner-led evaluation forms. In a different vein, this chapter will look at particular challenges with evaluation, and at some of the other, more unconventional, methods of evaluation that dance practitioners may wish to use, particularly with older people. Let us start with a challenging situation.

Chrissie is looking for her bag. She can't bend very well and is having trouble picking her bag up. Eventually she finds it. She then gets into conversation with Audrey, who is talking about her troublesome niece. 'Now then,' says Chrissie, 'where are my specs?' She fumbles with the zip on her bag. Audrey asks what all the sheets of paper are for. The evaluator tells her, again, that it's a questionnaire about how you liked the dancing. 'Oh yes,' says Audrey, 'the dancing is doing me good.' She makes no attempt at taking the paper to write this down, preferring instead just to talk. The evaluator panics as she realises she needs a pen and paper to write down what Audrey is saying. Audrey digresses onto how she likes playing bingo too. George and Peter join in. Oh yes, bingo is fun. 'Now just where did I put my glasses?' asks Chrissie. George asks, 'Do you need these filling in?' The evaluator eagerly nods. 'Give one here. I'll do it,' he volunteers. 'Now, you'll have to fill it in for me as I can't write now with my condition.' Peter also takes a sheet and gesticulates towards George. 'He's got Parkinson's, you know.' The evaluator bites her lip. She hadn't realised the connection. Audrey starts talking about her niece again. George and Peter make suitably sympathetic remarks to Audrey instead of filling in the paper and Chrissie puts down her newly found glasses case to pick up a cup of tea given to her by an orderly. Just then the manager in charge of the community centre walks in. 'Come on now,' she calls, 'the bus is waiting to take you back home.' The evaluator is left with a pile of empty papers.

Evaluating older people dancing, as with any group, is fraught with pitfalls, not only in how one makes sense of what is going on, but also in the choice of tools one uses to evaluate. The example above illustrates how particular evaluation tools, such as a questionnaire given out at the end of a session, may not be suitable for the context.

Evaluating older people dancing brings some particular challenges, but there are a number of things to bear in mind when evaluating dance, no matter what group one is working with. Evaluation, where one is making a judgement based on certain criteria, is used within dance workshops, sessions and projects for a variety of reasons.

- To help dance practitioners become aware of what worked and what did not work, and how things worked or did not work, whether the project was liked or was not liked, whether it was successful or not. This in turn can aid development of the practitioners' delivery and professional practice if further reflection is undertaken.
- To satisfy funders that grant money has been used wisely.
- To help bid for future funds.
- To be accountable to stakeholders (funders, the organisation that recruited you, participants, other interested parties).
- To be responsible for, and accountable to, current and future participants. Honest and productive evaluation can help steer dance practitioners in delivering high quality work and can give participants a way of getting to know the standard of the work with which they are involved.
- To give dance practitioners a tangible way of communicating to potential employers how their work is received by the general public.
- To enhance understanding of how dance can be experienced, how it can be facilitated and how dance can make an impact on people.

These reasons for evaluation throw up several issues that one needs to consider when evaluating dance for older people, or indeed any group. Let's take the idea of a project being successful. Here are some questions that show what a complicated entity success is.

What do you consider a successful project? Is this the same as your funder's idea of success, or that of your local press office or politician? What makes a successful project? Is it that everyone goes away smiling? Is it that the audience loved the show? Is it when one of your participants, for the first time with you, manages to stretch out her arms and meet your eyes? Is it when participants' carers decide to join in too as individual participants in their own right? Is it when everyone in the room can touch their toes? Is it when people have said they were challenged? Is it that visits to the doctor by participants decrease by 10%? Is it that two participants take up another arts-based activity in addition to yours?

Success has many guises and may be intrinsic or extrinsic to the dancing – in other words, it can be seen within the dancing session (touching toes), or noted outside of the dancing session (visits to the doctor) – but if you want to evaluate the success of a project, then you need to decide what success means. Success in your specific context will also depend on the reasons why you are doing the evaluation and on who the evaluation is for.

As these questions testify, success is a concept that needs clarification. Moreover, although evaluation is about making judgements against criteria, you may not know what success is within your project until something surprising happens that makes you aware that some kind of achievement has happened. All of the situations within the questions above may indicate success, but there may be some situations that one might hesitate to put down as criteria before the project began. It is worth thinking about which questions would easily fit into a plan for evaluation and which might be the surprising, unforeseen elements that make the evaluation even richer.

'Impact' is another slippery word, like 'success'. Dancing may have an effect (impact) on people in many ways; for example, fewer visits to the doctor, or an increased ability to get dressed on one's own. The impact of dancing might be seen in the social integration of a participant, or in their propensity to smile and laugh with others. The impact might be in cognitive or artistic stimulation. It might be seen in the collective decisions that people make to form action groups, stimulated by their time together dancing, such as a residents' forum, a dance group to continue on from yours, a cultural activity group, an ecology group. There may be a negative impact too, which ought to be noted as part of the learning process for project leaders. The problem with impact is that it is often difficult to evaluate in relation to dance alone. How will you know that it is the dancing that has made a difference? Often it is important to qualify our statements as to the impact of our work because it might very well be the bingo that has stimulated the creation of the ecology group, not the dancing, unless you can determine otherwise.

In addition, some of these effects mentioned above need measuring. How will you know how visits to the doctor have decreased unless you know the number of visits before the project began? From how long ago will you measure? How will you know whether people are more flexible now than before? How reliable is your source of information?

Some impact, such as social integration, cannot be measured precisely. Such impact calls for a different way of collating the information, which relies on an understanding of what loneliness means to the individual in question, and what it is about the dance sessions that has made him or her feel less lonely. Note my emphasis on the individual. Impact is rarely the same for all participants.

Impact and success are examples of tricky concepts that any person evaluating will have to be aware of and take a stance on. The tools one uses to evaluate also need careful appraisal. There are various tools one can use, but not all will elicit the same information. Evaluation tools (research methods) come broadly in two categories: quantitative and qualitative.

Quantitative evaluation tools are for looking at quantity. In order to use these effectively, then you need to have something to measure. For example, the evaluation of the visits to the doctor produces two numbers (quantity); one before the project and one at the end. Perhaps you wanted to see how dancing makes an impact on physical flexibility. The evaluation could include measuring how far someone can bend down to the floor (if that was the type of flexibility you feel your dance classes would encourage). This again would produce two numbers, if you measured before the project began and afterwards. The use of a statistical method could then give you something even more meaningful from the numbers, but if you aren't any good with statistics, you can still use numbers simply. For example, look at how many people return to your classes. That in itself says something about whether people enjoy your classes or find them useful.

If you would like to evaluate the value that the class brings, then a selection of qualitative tools would be useful. These indicate the quality of the experience. Interviewing (not one-liners) is one method to ascertain the quality of the experience. Qualitative tools do not produce numbers and are not measurements. Instead, this type of evaluation is about coming to a greater understanding of, in this case, the participants' experiences. It deals with people, rather than quantities. The data will be rich, complex and interesting because one is dealing with people, but it may be more difficult to analyse because the data will not give you a straightforward answer.

If you are lucky enough to be able to afford a professional researcher to come into your project for the evaluation, he or she could bring a variety of research methods, depending on what you wanted to evaluate, and his or her expertise. Some of these methods (tools) might include, for instance, interviewing techniques, special physiological or psychological tests, questionnaires (numerical or discursive) and Laban analysis, amongst others. The researcher, or research team, would also conduct substantial research into the relevant literature surrounding the context of older people, and their lives, issues and dancing (if a qualitative researcher), and other research in the field (for both qualitative and quantitative analysis).

However, not many dance projects can afford that luxury and some practitioners feel wary about entrusting data collection to someone else, who may or may not understand the sensitivities of community dance work. More often than not practitioners will complete the evaluation themselves. This might feel daunting if you haven't had any training or your time is limited. However, there are a number of easy and creative ways in which you might obtain evidence to support your intuition in how successful the project has been (or to counteract that intuition).

As the example at the beginning of the chapter indicates, evaluation is not something that can always be done well by having a questionnaire with a number of set questions, to be filled in at the end of the project or workshop. Indeed, in working through an artistic medium, it may be useful to think more creatively about how to get the information needed.

Bisakha Sarker is a dance practitioner who has worked for many years with older people dancing. Sarker is a trained statistician but remains convinced that arts projects need creative evaluation, rather than numbers. She argues that evaluation works well as an extension of the artistic process. As such, evaluation need not disrupt the mood set by the dancing and might be more accessible to participants. Sarker has worked with many people in hospital waiting rooms where anxiety and distress can be high. Simple, creative ideas can offer people fun and non-taxing ways to respond. Sarker uses colours in the form of coloured pipe cleaners, feathers, sand in cups, paperclips or sticky dots. Choices of colour are given to participants. The colour is then associated by the individual participant with one of the three choices of response: 'I liked it', 'it wasn't for me', 'I liked it and would like to do it again'. People also can respond by creating something out of a malleable coloured object, such as a pipe cleaner, or by tying a coloured ribbon with the appropriate phrase onto a cut-out tree. In giving colours rather than numbers, Sarker maintains that it reduces the hierarchy of good and bad; more befitting for a community dance project that attempts to value every person's achievements, rather than creating value structures around

159

good or bad dancing. In addition, the phrase 'not for me' sounds more constructive than 'I didn't like it', and so it is easier for people to pick this option.

Other ways of retrieving evaluation data from participants include making up songs or poems and drawing pictures. In documenting this creative output, the evaluation will generate interesting qualitative data that express the thoughts and feelings of participants. Posters of artwork hung up on the wall can be productive too. Which picture do people identify with at the beginning of the session and why; which picture do they identify with at the end and why. This method allows for a before and after snapshot of how people are feeling. This could take the form of verbal thoughts recorded, or written thoughts on Post-it notes stuck to the posters. It also allows different responses to be documented despite the use of the same pictures. As with the coloured objects, the posters highlight the complexity of art, where there are multiple interpretations and responses that open out the discussion, rather than closing it down.

The ways listed above ask participants for a reaction through choosing options ('I liked it', 'it wasn't for me', I liked it and would like to do it again'), choosing a particular object that resonates with them (the green stone, the rainbow poster), so they can use it as a prop to think about the dancing, choosing creative ways of communicating how they feel about the experience (the ribbon on the tree) and creating art by channelling their experiences and emotions. The particular examples given above can certainly be adapted. Can you think of other creative ways of asking people about the project? Use your experience as a creative person and your knowledge of your group to invent other ways based around similar structures to those listed above.

Technology also provides tools for evaluation. Perhaps you want to make a video diary of the project, collecting comments, interviews and dancing throughout a number of sessions. Perhaps some participants could keep a diary for you. Some may like to do this on a computer if they have access to one, others might like to handwrite or speak into a camera or voice recorder. Don't forget that diaries need time afterwards so that you can go through all the data and analyse it. Do not pick these ways of evaluating if your time is limited!

As noted above, one of the uses of evaluation is to get feedback on your work. This can be helpful to dance professionals who would like to think about how to do things better or differently, and to obtain feedback during the creative process. Participants may not always be able to tell you about this in the ways listed above for evaluating the project in general. You yourself may not always be aware of how to move forward with ideas and ways of facilitating. Different ways of evaluating are needed. Liz Lerman is a dance practitioner living in the United States who has invented her own way of obtaining feedback by asking questions. She calls it the Critical Response Process.[2] Questions are posed to and made by the dance artist (the practitioner) and a group of 'responders', as well as by a facilitator who guides the process. Responders could be made up of people who know you professionally or personally, or they could be people with whom you are not familiar; they could be dance experts or not.

The Critical Response Process consists of four steps. The first step is to produce 'statements of meaning'. These statements should be anchored around questions concerning the communicative power of the work. Lerman argues that saying 'I liked it because...' is not enough for the artist to understand that there are other ways in which observers and participants are stimulated. She lists useful adjectives such as 'challenging, compelling, delightful, different, unique' as being more productive ways of giving feedback rather than talking about like or dislike. In highlighting statements of meaning, practitioners may uncover what people value and what social and aesthetic values people bring to the experience.

The second stage is focusing on the artist as questioner. In asking questions of those who observed the work, the artist can begin to work out how he or she would like to proceed. Step three involves neutral questions from the responders, where questions are asked in a way that does not involve judgement. Lerman offers some useful examples of neutral questions put together with opinionated questions, so that the reader can see the difference. Some of these are worth repeating here[3]:

Opinionated question	Embedded opinion	Neutral question
Why is the video so long?	The video is too long.	How are you thinking about time in relation to the viewer's experience?
What made you put the entire cast in green costumes?	The green costumes don't work. OR There are too many green costumes.	What's the significance of the colour green to your concept? OR Talk about your costuming choices.
Why do you think you need to tell the moral of the story at the end?	The moral is obvious, you don't need to tell it.	Where do you want your listeners [or viewers] to be at the end of the story?

Again, these questions can aid the artist in thinking about the most fruitful course of action in a constructive way. The fourth step is to offer 'permissioned opinions'. The artist may choose whether or not to hear an opinion about a certain element of his or her work and this, Lerman argues, is the way to a really challenging but useful dialogue. Lerman's Critical Response Process is like that used by Action Learning Sets to stimulate reflection and then action. One member of the group talks about a situation and the others then ask non-judgemental questions to that member, in order that he or she may see a way forward from the situation by him- or herself. It is a very powerful reflective tool that is used by some professionals in many different industry sectors, including dance. One of the fundamental steps attached to evaluation, if it is to work properly, is the process of reflection and further action after the evaluation is done. After the judgements, how can we, as reflective dance practitioners, move on and develop from what we have accomplished already?

Notes

1. Amans, Diane (ed.) (2008) *An Introduction to Community Dance Practice*, Basingstoke: Palgrave Macmillan.
2. Lerman, Liz and John Borstel (2003) *Liz Lerman's Critical Response Process: A Method for Getting Useful Feedback on Anything You Make, from Dance to Dessert*, Takoma Park, MD: Liz Lerman Dance Exchange.
3. Lerman (2003: 23).

16   Choreography and Performance with Older People

Diane Amans

....

In this chapter choreographers and community dancers share their experiences of performance projects. Interviews with older performers and dance artists of all ages reveal some thought-provoking tension lines. Subjects discussed include:

- Movement memory – challenges and strategies for helping dancers remember material.
- Facilitating improvisation or teaching set material – does it have to be one or the other?
- The extent to which participants contribute to the choreographic process.
- Do choreographers adapt their methods when working with older dancers?
- Who are the audience and what do we want them to see?
- Some alternative approaches to performance.

There are suggestions for different ways of presenting performance work and influencing how this is described by the media. Finally, this chapter shows how some choreographers develop performance qualities in their older dancers.

....

A choreographer working with older people can expect to work in a range of different contexts. There are companies that focus exclusively on creating work to perform, and other groups that meet for regular weekly sessions and take part in occasional performance projects. Many of the community groups for older dancers are led by dance artists who also choreograph the performance pieces.

What do older dancers say about their choreographers?

Interviews with older performers reveal some interesting feedback for choreographers. Here is a selection of comments from older dancers who took part in performance projects during 2011:

> You need to have more than just a good piece – you need to have confidence in the choreographer's confidence in you.

> A good choreographer will know when to stop trying – when some of us are struggling and just can't get it. They need to adapt the dance.

> I don't like it when the choreographer is clearly nervous about whether or not we're going to make it.

> What we struggle with is change. Once it gets into an older person's muscle memory it takes longer to get it out and put something else in its place.

> I agree – especially if it's a small change – subtle differences are more difficult to accommodate.[1]

Movement memory

Both choreographers and participants highlight memory as one of the more challenging aspects of working towards a performance. Dancers acknowledge the difficulties in remembering material and many feel that an intensive block of rehearsals works well – though only if they perform immediately after creating the work. Weekly rehearsals can be too far apart for people to remember the material, and there often needs to be a substantial period of time at the beginning of sessions for recapping what was learned the previous week. For this reason, Glen Murray, artistic director of the Tasmania-based company 'MADE' (Mature Artists Dance Experience), schedules creative development or rehearsal sessions three times a week. When the group was first set up, in 2005, they used to meet once a week, but they requested more frequent rehearsals to help them remember what they had done.

Glen's performance projects with MADE usually last for 12 months, and participants have the option of attending up to three sessions a week. The classes are delivered on Mondays, Tuesdays and Thursdays during school terms. On Mondays and Thursdays the first hour is an open class followed by a creative development class.

> Each term I run the class and each night of the week. Once they're familiar with an exercise, and they know *what* they're doing, we can start working on *how* they're doing it.[2]

Glen finds that this constant repetition helps the group to remember the material and develop more embodied movement.

Other companies have their own strategies for helping dancers remember the movement material. Simona Scotto, rehearsal director for the London-based Company of Elders, makes a DVD of rehearsals and gives participants a copy of the music so they can practise between rehearsals.

To what extent are participants involved in choreographing a dance piece?

Some dancers find it easier to remember the dance if they have played a part in developing the choreography. I posed the above question to choreographer Rosemary Lee, who works with dancers of all ages.

> In as much as they are involved in interpreting a task and their interpretation being used – they are involved. Happy accidents or suggestions might be incorporated. For example, in *Common Dance* one whole section was sparked by a cha cha solo danced by the 84-year-old during break time. We developed a group improvisation around him as he danced. However, initial concept, structuring and themes are usually just me. I haven't found a way of successfully avoiding that. So the vocabulary might often be theirs and hopefully they feel as if they own the dance because it's so much about their presence in the work.[3]

Stephen Kirkham, a choreographer who has worked with the Company of Elders, also finds ways of helping the group generate some of the dance vocabulary whilst he takes responsibility for structures and themes:

> ... It's about tuning in to them. It's got to be a compromise – choreography on them and moves they've made up ... I've tried lots of things that just didn't work. You just have to let go of that.[4]

Company members seem to appreciate the compromise:

> Structure is helpful but I do like to improvise as well.

> I like pieces which are a combination of given work and our own moves... You feel like you've been part of the creativity of the work...

> ... If there's a bit of me in it, it gives me stuff to hang onto. I remember it better.[5]

Teaching set material – or facilitating improvisation?

There is sometimes a tension line between teaching set material and developing a more free improvised approach to making a dance piece. Dance practitioners working with older people in community groups sometimes find that participants are reluctant to take part in creative activities, particularly when they are used to learning steps from the teacher or dance leader. Here are some of the views expressed by dance artists during a research project in 2011.[6]

First of all, practitioners who are confident that their participants do not want to create their own dance movement said:

- Why introduce improvisation when the group are perfectly happy following a dance artist?
- My group wouldn't like it – they like to learn steps that have names. Otherwise they think it's not 'proper dance'.
- I've tried creative work – they don't like it. They're happier following me.
- I get around 40 people coming to my class. They like learning routines. Why would I want to change it?

Then there are dance artists who feel that participants in their sessions are missing out; that they have not made an informed choice.

- They might enjoy improvising – how will they know if they've never tried?

Practitioners who really value creative work may become frustrated if their participants only want to learn set movements.

- How do I get dancers to feel more comfortable about being creative? How do we get someone who has never experienced that instinctive, free movement to do it without angst?

166

The dance artists' own preferences, experiences and skills are going to impact on the ways in which they run sessions and the choices they offer to participants. If we consider both ends of the tension line we have classes with leaders teaching set steps and classes that are mostly improvisation. This need not be an either/or decision though. There are many points along the line, and flexible practitioners are able to move between these points.

Frameworks and structures

Anna Halprin, renowned dancer, choreographer and teacher (still teaching in her nineties) has written about the need for structure within improvisation. She has voiced her concerns about creating movement material that did not really lead anywhere.

> It wasn't enough to have a momentary movement image feeling. What do you do with it? Where does it go?[7]

Halprin uses scores – similar to the scores a musician might use – and she devised a system of open and closed scoring to shape improvisation when she is creating work. Together with her husband Lawrence she developed a scoring continuum ranging from 1 (open) to 10 (closed). At the open end of the scale participants have few instructions and are free to move in whatever way they choose. A closed score is much more prescriptive, with participants being given comprehensive instructions and little opportunity to develop their own ideas.

> [...] Halprin recommended aiming for about 5 on the scale to ensure sufficient stimulus and focus for performers while retaining a reasonable degree of space for individual creative response. However... scores at either end of the scale have their own distinct functions and Halprin uses almost the full range when appropriate in her teaching and performance.[8]

Halprin's inspirational work has made a significant contribution to community performance. Her scores offer valuable structures for collaborative group work and developing heightened awareness of self and others.[9]

Another teacher, whose research is very relevant to any study of choreographic processes, is Jo Butterworth, a lecturer who has developed a framework model to help dance artist–practitioners reflect on the relationships between dancer and choreographer. In her Didactic–Democratic framework Butterworth looks at 'dance-devising' processes and examines the varying roles taken by choreographer and dance participants.

At one end of the continuum is the traditional 'choreographer as expert' process, where dancers are 'instruments'. At the other end is a more collaborative relationship where both choreographer and dancers may share ownership of the material created. In the middle of the continuum the roles are referred to as 'choreographer as pilot' and 'dancer as contributor'.[10]

The above paragraphs offer a brief introduction to the work of two very different specialists. Suggestions for further reading on the work of Halprin and Butterworth are included at the end of this chapter.

Do choreographers adapt their methods when they work with older dancers?

In many ways choreographing dance with older adults is no different from choreography with any group or individual. Some choreographers use the same approach and methods regardless of the age of the group.

> My methods do not change at all. To the extent that I work with imagery, task-based generation of material and simple motifs – the presence I might be after will be the same. However, the physicality of the work has to be different in the areas of speed, balance, aerial work and getting on and off the floor. I try to make the work allow for all the ages present if it's intergenerational.[11]

Cecilia Macfarlane makes a similar point

> I'm aware of making sure all work is inclusive and translatable. The same task will need translating both for the 5-year-old and the 95-year-old.[12]

Both Cecilia and Rosemary think carefully about avoiding or challenging stereotypes of older people:

> My interest is in difference; not in stereotyping.... Personally I have a real objection as an artist to the idea that older people can only do less, in terms of technique. That our dance is about a growing process of what we can't do.

> ...As we get older our vocabulary changes, but it's not about lessening...it's about honesty and intention that's cellular and owned.

> ...and I expect no less from any dancer I work with.[13]

Since my aim is to find a way for people to look empowered when they perform, not weakened, I try to avoid older dancers ever looking as if they are struggling to be like anyone else or to keep up. On the one occasion I created a work for an over 60s group I found myself wanting to subvert the tendencies I had seen in choreography for older dancers. Work that was loosely folk based with circles and group configurations that really didn't show off the various personalities and differing qualities of the women. So I purposefully had them performing with sections of absolute stillness focused on the audience and other times sections of fast-paced crossings where they moved with power, speed and strength sweeping and swiping the air. Rather than wafting in, neither here nor there – a quality that you often see with older people in dance works. I wanted to help them to either be bold or very delicate, fast or slow, still or busy.[14]

How should we present dance performance by older dancers? Can we influence media coverage?

At an *Older People Dancing* conference in England,[15] one of the overseas delegates asked why people in the UK make a particular feature of the fact that the dancers are older people. Why is this noteworthy? Do we really need to separate out older adults from other adults? Why do we do it? The speaker referred to watching dance in other countries – he often went to see dance performances in India, for example, but never considered the age of the performers. He was just interested in seeing high quality performing arts; the age of the performers was immaterial.

What do we want people to see when they see older dancers performing? Do we actually *want* to highlight the fact that the group is an older dance group? Does this not invite certain stereotyped expectations? Who are the audiences for this work? Could choreographers and performers be proactive in liaising with journalists and giving them some interesting angles so that they present the work in a way that is consistent with the group's values and avoids patronising coverage?

Some dance companies make sure that everyone who is interviewed as part of a feature has the same points to make – and these are repeated so that the message is conveyed without ambiguity. This may seem rather defensive but it is worth being clear about what you want (or don't want) and making sure journalists know this. If you would rather not see an article with the headline 'Go Go Grannies get in the Groove', then think about how you would like to see your work described. There is no guarantee that

Figure 16.1   Time to Dance, Stockport
Source: Moira Dickens

the media will take any notice but at least you will have thought about the coverage you would prefer to have.

'What is the dancing about?'

This is a question posed by American choreographer, Liz Lerman, in her collection of essays – *Hiking the Horizontal*.[16] I have also been asked similar questions by dancers in my performance projects. Does the dance *have* to have a narrative content? Does it need to have an explicit meaning or is it an abstract piece? Does it have to be one or the other?

Lerman challenges the 'reality/abstraction dichotomy and the representational/"dance-for-itself" dichotomy'. She argues that 'so-called reality and abstraction are ever-present and that most of us move frequently between these poles. [...] Each requires the other in order to be experienced.'

To what extent should choreographers and performers take responsibility for the way the audience reads the dance? Lerman acknowledges the challenge of including sufficient contextual information for an audience to follow her ideas.

A problem with this kind of art-making is that sometimes we are living in abstractions and sometimes in concrete imagery and sometimes in the many places in between. Thus our audiences must be able to constantly shift their positions along the spectrum to meet us where we are. One of my earliest understandings of this dilemma of now-it-means-something, now-it-doesn't came through my use of older people on stage. Sometimes I asked an audience to see the older dancers as old people, whereas at other times I asked them just to see moving bodies. How was an audience member supposed to know which I intended? I knew of course, but the knowledge was embedded in my hidden intentions and wilfulness. What clues could I set out for an audience so that it could also follow along?[17]

It takes time to develop accessible choreography that has meaning for both performers and the audience. In making dances we need to decide when it is important to communicate a clear idea and then find ways of achieving this.

When I have observed choreographers working with groups I have been impressed by the methods they use to ensure that certain moments in the dance are performed in a particular way so that the meaning is clear. Some choreographers combine structured improvisation with sections of set material – thus reducing the amount of material that has to be memorised. One effective strategy is to link moments in the dance to a very clear musical cue or to have the performers follow a dancer or dancers who can be relied on to remember key moments and lead the group. Sometimes it is the dance artist or choreographer who takes this role – a controversial issue that is discussed below.

Should the dance artist or choreographer perform as part of the group?

In conducting interviews with dance artists who choreograph work with community groups, I asked them about whether or not they take part in the performance. There was an interesting range of views on the question of whether or not dance artists *should* perform as part of the group they have been working with. Those in favour say:

- Participants feel more confident with a leader taking part.
- I have done this on a number of occasions to help with 'on the night' nerves – it doesn't distract from older dancers
- Yes – it gives the group reassurance and a memory aid.

Dance artists who would not dance with their groups say:

- It's not a showcase for the dance artist.
- No – I think the focus is then centred on that person (the leader).
- Depending on the performers, the project, the timescale to perform work dance artists should give performers material that is achievable and therefore gives them the confidence to perform on their own.
- Key word here is achievable movement. The dance artist need not perform if they've done the job of creating movement that people can perform.
- If a group lacks confidence should they be performing? Or does performing create confidence?

Amongst the dance artists who perform alongside their groups there are a variety of ways in which they do this. One artist positions herself at the edge of the performance space close to the least confident member of the group. In other dance performances the dance artist who has choreographed the work is centre stage at the front of the group so that participants have someone to follow.

The above examples are taken from projects where the dance artist has choreographed work with a group with whom they have regular contact. On projects where a guest choreographer creates a piece with a group and then moves on to other projects, it is rare to find them performing with the group.

Performance – some alternative approaches

In the above discussion some of the reasons given for dance artists performing alongside participants are to give the group confidence. Should we be looking at other ways to give people performance experiences? First of all we need to be clear about why we are putting on a performance and who the audience will be.

Community artist Petra Kuppers suggests the following possible audiences for performance work:

- the actual group
- a small pre-selected audience where everybody knows everybody else
- an audience that might include people who hold power over participants, for instance social workers, doctors and other medical personnel
- a general audience in a live setting
- a general audience in contact with the group through media such as videos and photographs
- a wider specialised audience, reached through material generated as part of the workshops (such as politicians to whom postcards are sent)[18]

If the primary reason is to give participants the opportunity to be seen and to show others what they have done, this could perhaps be achieved by letting the audience see a 'class on stage'. This approach reduces the need for the participants to remember the dance and they can focus on enjoyment and the performance quality. It also means that the dance leader need not be the centre of the audience's attention. However, some groups feel this is not real performance – particularly if they are sharing the bill with other community groups who are presenting work in a more traditional way.

An alternative to live performance is to film work and show an edited video. When working with physically frail participants, or people with significant memory difficulties, I sometimes create a video that can be shown in lieu of a live performance. This has been an ideal solution for people who do not have the stamina to cope with technical rehearsals but who want to enjoy a sense of achievement and their moment in the spotlight.

Performance work with older people: Some issues and dilemmas

The challenge of creating accessible opportunities for dancers to perform for an audience can give rise to a number of issues. First of all, there are groups where some members want to develop dance pieces for an audience to view whilst others just want weekly sessions without an end product. Certainly, when a group is working towards a performance it changes the dynamic and focus of the sessions. This can be an exciting and positive experience; or it may take away the fun of a relaxing, playful dance class. There is no 'right way' in such situations. Participants are all individuals and people enjoy different experiences.

One solution is to have rehearsals scheduled after regular sessions. This avoids the cost of booking a venue for additional sessions and means that those members who do not want to perform can leave before the rehearsal starts. However, the dance artist leading the sessions needs to make a clear shift in emphasis from a recreational class to a focussed performance group in rehearsal. Also, it may be too tiring for dancers to take part in a class followed by a rehearsal.

Another, related, tension line occurs when the impending performance date results in an emphasis on the quality of the end product rather than the quality of the process experienced by the dancers. Some of the dancers I interviewed said that, whilst they enjoyed performing to an audience, they did not always enjoy the rehearsals. This was particularly noticeable in groups where the social contact was an important element of weekly meetings.

How do choreographers support participants to develop their performance skills? Some choreographers feel they are letting a group down if they do not push them to achieve a high standard of performance. However, there have been instances of participants feeling stressed and leaving the group because they are no longer enjoying themselves.

The challenge here is to help dancers develop confidence and ownership of the material without becoming too anxious about 'getting it right'. Embodied performance is achieved when this balance is successfully managed.

**Figure 16.2   Freedom in Dance Performers at Big Dance –
Commissioned by Dance Initiative Greater Manchester 2006**
Source: Brian Slater

I have observed skilled choreographers working with groups and noticed some aspects of practice that are common to many of them:

- they use humour to relieve tension
- they are able to see where the difficulties are and suggest alternatives or adapt the choreography
- they are selective about which aspects of the dance need to be done in a certain way – for example, a moment of stillness or a phrase performed in unison
- they allow dancers the freedom to find their own way of performing other elements of the piece
- they give positive feedback and a good deal of encouragement

Here is a short section from a rehearsal with Ruth Tyson Jones, working with the Time to Dance group in Stockport:

> ...let's try and run the piece as though everyone is here – if your partner isn't here, do it with an imaginary partner

> ...all we're going to do is calmly go through each section – we need those freezes to be a little bit longer. It may seem like ages but for the audience it's interesting...

> ...it doesn't matter what your feet are doing, as long as you slot in with your partner.

> ...this shouldn't be a serious moment – I dare you to smile.[19]

Several choreographers described the difficulties of preparing a group for a performance when attendance at rehearsals is erratic, possibly due to health problems of the participants. One solution is to make a work in sections – which can be performed independently of each other. As a result, rehearsals are easier to manage and the more unreliable attendees are included in fewer sections. This has provided useful flexibility when a group wants to tour a dance piece and some members of the company are unavailable to perform.

Conclusion

This chapter has illustrated some of the ways in which choreographers create dance with and for older people. In the Resources section there are suggestions for choreographic structures that have been used successfully with both active performers and more frail, seated groups. Most of the ideas are not heavily dependent on memory. Emerging practitioners have found these structures very useful and relevant for their work in a range of different community settings – not just those with older people.

Discussion points

– What is the purpose of performance work with community groups?
– Do you think that performers, dance artists, audience members and funders have the same expectations of a dance performance?
– How would you manage a situation in a community dance group where some members want to perform and others just want to attend a regular weekly class?
– Can you think of more ways of sharing work with an audience?

Notes

1. Amans, D. Interviews conducted with dance practitioners and older performers during 2011 as part of the research for this book.
2. Glen Murray. Interview for this book, 2012.
3. Rosemary Lee. Interview for this book, 2011.
4. Stephen Kirkham. Interview for this book, 2011.
5. Amans.
6. Amans, D. (2011) Twenty dance artists took part in one of two seminar days to discuss a range of issues relating to community dance.
7. Halprin, A. (1995) in Worth, L. and Poynor, H. (2004) *Anna Halprin*, London: Routledge.
8. Worth, L. and Poynor, H.(2004) *Anna Halprin*, London: Routledge.
9. Ibid, for more information about Anna Halprin's work and examples of her scores.
10. Butterworth, J. and Wildschut, L. (eds) (2009) *Contemporary Choreography: A Critical Reader*, London: Routledge.
11. Lee.
12. Cecilia Macfarlane. Interview for this book, 2011.
13. Ibid.
14. Lee.
15. *Older People Dancing* (2009) Taunton, Somerset. Conference hosted by Take Art on 9 and 10 July 2009.
16. Lerman, L. (2011) *Hiking the Horizontal; Field Notes from a Choreographer*, Connecticut: Wesleyan University Press.
17. Ibid.
18. Kuppers, P. (2007) *Community Performance: An Introduction*, London: Routledge.
19. Tyson Jones, R. (2011) Transcript of guidelines given during rehearsal with the Time to Dance performance group in Stockport.

Further reading

Butterworth, J. (2012) *Dance Studies: The Basics*, London: Routledge.

Halprin, A. (2002) *Returning to Health: With Dance, Movement and Imagery.* Mendocino, CA: LifeRhythm.

Tuffnell, M. and Crickmay, C. (1990) *Body Space Image: Notes towards Improvisation and Performance*, London: Virago.

Conclusion

This book has examined themes relating to ageing and older people dancing, together with a reflection on the experiences of older professional dancers.

In setting out to write this book I did question whether or not I wanted to contribute to the development of a branch of dance practice that is seen as somehow separate. The issue about whether older people dancing should be seen as different from other people dancing has emerged as a theme in several chapters. In Chapter 14, for example, which deals with professional development, there is a discussion about whether dance artists need any specialist skills to work with older people. Chapter 13 points out that many aspects of duty of care – having a flexible, person-centred approach to facilitating safe dance practices – apply to working with dancers of any age. So why write a book about *Older People Dancing?*

The main reason is because I believe there *are* some specific differences: some considerations that are particular to older people. In the chapter on duty of care I outline a few areas where dance practitioners may need to make adjustments to warm-up activities and be aware of age-related conditions that affect an individual's stamina or flexibility. Similarly, Sara Houston's chapter on evaluation and my chapter on choreography and performance highlight issues and aspects of practice that are common to working with people of all ages, but they also include some specific differences in older people dancing. In these respects dance with older people is only separate in the sense that dance with children or teenagers is separate. Some aspects of the practice will need to be adapted but it is all part of the rich diversity of practice that comes under the umbrella of community dance.

However, I am aware of a number of tension lines here. On the one hand I argue that this is not a discrete field within dance practice, yet I am happy to contribute to conferences, books and professional development events that focus exclusively on older people. I choreograph dance pieces with mature movers who perform at showcases for older people dancing; I apply for funding streams that target healthy ageing.

François Matarasso, a leading researcher on the role of the arts in society, cautions against allowing the emergence of something that is seen to be separate. He argues that using the arts to make things better for older people is condescending and reinforces loss of autonomy.

> Ageing concerns us all...this is an experience that we are all going to have. I struggle with the lack of imagination that we have in thinking that older people are somehow 'other' – they're just us in 20 years' time.[1]

I share Matarasso's concerns yet, at the same time, I empathise with those who argue that, without its being defined as a sector, it is often difficult to secure funding for arts with older people.

There are no easy answers here but we can play an important part in ensuring a future where older people are actively involved – not merely passive recipients of dance projects that have been organised without consulting them. There are examples, in a number of chapters in this book, of proactive older people who are involved in shaping policies, raising funds and seeking out opportunities for being artists. (See Chapter 6 on partnership working and Chapter 3 for Pegge Vissicaro's Moving Communities Model in Arizona).

As dance practitioners we need to pay attention to our leadership style and the power relationships within our work. If we are really committed to facilitating creative engagement we should ensure that all aspects of our practice support the right of the individual 'freely to participate in the cultural life of the community'.[2] Several chapters in this book include examples of interventions that strengthen participant autonomy and recognise older people as artists.

This is an evolving area of the arts, and the themes developed here are not presented as a definitive summation of *Older People Dancing*. The field will continue to change and grow as societal change brings new opportunities.

I hope this book has offered food for thought and stimulated the reader to reflect on their practice and ways in which they can influence future directions.

Notes

1. Matarasso, F. (2012) Speaking at the *Creating a New Old* conference as part of the Bealtaine Festival. The conference posed the questions: What kind of old do you want to be? What kind of world do you want to grow up in?
2. This right is enshrined in Article 27 of the Universal Declaration of Human Rights. www.claiminghumanrights.org, accessed 1 June 2012.

Part Three
Resources

A Charter for the Older Dancer: Foundation for Community Dance 183

Sample Constitution for a Community Dance Group 185

Health and Safety Quiz – Older People Dancing 188

Health and Safety Quiz Answers – Older People Dancing 189

Lincolnshire Dance: General Risk Assessment form www.
  lincolnshiredance.com 190

Further Information about Conditions That May Affect Older People 192

Duty of Care: Cautions, Precautions and Reasons for Concern 197

Observation Checklist Used in Dance Sessions in Dementia Care 199

Partnership Questionnaire 202

Powys Dance Case Study 203

Executive Summary: English National Ballet Dance for Parkinson's Report 205

Mind Your Rhetoric: *Animated* Article 207

Case Study: Jacky Simpson, a 61-Year-Old, Who Trained to Be a Dance
  Leader 210

Notes on Ideas for Seated Activities 212

Sample Session Plans 215

  • Example 1: Redholme Memory Care Home 215

  • Example 2: Llys Hafren Residential Home 216

  • Example 3: Let's Tango Fiesta! 217

  • Example 4: Cross-generational Session (Group Aged 3–83 Years) 219

  • Example 5: Marple Movers (Active Group Aged 55–75 Years) 220

Starting Points for Choreography 222

Poetry and Dance 225

Lucky Me 228

Surprise and Delight 230

Props and Other Resources for Dance and Movement Work with Older
  People 232

Useful Contacts (UK) 235

Useful Contacts (Outside the UK) 240

This section contains materials and information to help practitioners lead dance activities with older people. There are sample session plans that include activities for use with both seated and more active groups, together with starting points for choreography and some ideas for introducing an element of 'surprise and delight' to the work.

The health and safety quiz will help the reader to test their understanding of the information covered in chapters 9 and 10, and there is additional information about conditions that may affect older people. Other duty of care resources include a sample risk assessment form, an observation checklist used in dementia care settings, a health and safety questionnaire form, and guidelines on safeguarding vulnerable adults.

In addition this section contains information on where to obtain resources, and some useful contacts in the UK and other countries.

A Charter for the Older Dancer: Foundation for Community Dance

1. Everyone should have equal access to participate, express and enjoy themselves in dance irrespective of age or physical ability.

2. People can begin to dance, train, become choreographers, leaders and critics at any age. People's ability to express themselves and communicate effectively in dance is frequently enhanced by age and experience.

3. A diverse range of dance cultures should be available to older people reflective of those cultures found amongst our population ballroom and modern sequence dancing, classical ballet, tap, contemporary dance, African, Scottish, Welsh, Irish and English folk dance, line dancing, Jamaican quadrilles and folk and classical forms from South East Asia to name but a few.

4. Older people should have the opportunity to express the full range of emotions in dance and movement – not excluding their sensuality and sexuality, as well as anger, joy, grief, fear and so on.

5. A new aesthetic must continue to be encouraged which allows for the real appreciation of older people in movement and dance.

6. Older dancers provide a role model and a positive image of ageing.

7. At a time when the benefits of 'moderate' exercise regimes are widely recognised as having enormous physical and mental health benefits, dance should be accepted as having a central role to play in all health programmes.

8. Dance and exercise classes, creative sessions and performing opportunities should be a consistent part of older people's activity programmes, taking account of the individual needs with regard to health and fitness, and available in arts and community centres, day centres, residential homes, hospitals and other places where older people gather.

9. Professional dance companies should look for consistent opportunities to employ older as well as younger dancers. Choreographers and artistic directors should be encouraged to acknowledge the exciting opportunities that older dancers can bring to dance.

10. Dance companies and choreographers should employ older dancers on an equal footing as younger dancers.

11. It is the responsibility of all sectors of the arts industry to nurture and develop dance artists and choreographers as they mature in age and skill.

12. Dance companies and projects which employ older people should take care to schedule rehearsals, performances and tours, and arrange all working conditions in such a way to take into account the particular needs of older people.

13. Those who work with older dancers should recognise that adults learn differently from younger dancers and should therefore acquaint themselves with models of adult learning.

14. All dance and associated courses in colleges, universities, academies and so on should acknowledge the important role older dancers can play either as students or as part of the faculties.

15. Companies and venues audience development programmes should target older people as well as the young.

16. The dance industry should positively embrace the potential of older people to contribute to a wide variety of professional roles within the industry.

17. The industry should take the opportunity to learn from other cultural traditions, some of which may provide alternative models for valuing and supporting the older dancer.

18. Those organising dance activities and opportunities for older dancers should recognise the importance of intergenerational work which places the older dancer as an equal.

19. Opportunities to debate issues surrounding the older dancer, nationally and internationally, should continue.

20. There should be a review of the language used around the older dancer and how we define 'older'.

21. There should be a central responsibility for ensuring that Dance Agencies and individual artists are kept informed of small pots of funding that can help sustain groups.

22. A national standard of training for dance with older people should be established.

23. A national older people's network of artists, researchers, policy makers, agencies and participants should be established, leading to opportunity for joined up thinking, research and projects.

24. There should be greater research, opportunity and projects for older men dancing.

Sample Constitution for a Community Dance Group

Some community groups have found it helpful to become constituted organisations with their own bank accounts. This is not difficult and can mean that they can access a wider range of funding opportunities. Here is an example of a constitution, which can be adapted to fit your group.

Marple Movers constitution

Marple Movers is a voluntary, constituted non-profit-making organisation, referred to as 'the group' in these rules.

1   Aims

1.1 To create opportunities for older people to join in dance activities.
1.2 To develop members' dance and movement vocabulary.
1.3 To challenge perceptions of older people dancing through performance projects.

2   Powers

To further these aims the group may exercise the following powers:

2.1 To hold a bank account in the name of Marple Movers.
2.2 To raise funds and receive contributions, donations, grants and affiliations.
2.3 To disseminate information affecting the above aims and exchange such information and affiliate with other bodies having similar aims.
2.4 To promote and organise co-operation in the achievement of the above aims and, to that end, work in association with appropriate organisations and individuals engaged in the furtherance of the above aims.
2.5 To arrange and facilitate classes, projects, workshops and performances.
2.6 To produce publicity materials to promote the group's activities.
2.7 To pay the necessary expenses involved in the running of the group.

3   Management of the group

3.1 The group shall appoint a Management Group from its members, consisting of not less than five persons. Meetings should consist of no less than three persons to be quorate. Appropriate persons outside the group may also be co-opted as required to fulfil an elected role.

3.2 From the Management Group, a Chairperson, a Secretary and a Treasurer shall be elected. Other members may be appointed to undertake particular responsibilities within the group, for example, fundraising/marketing/quality assurance.

3.3 The Management Group shall meet not less than four times a year.

4 Quality assurance

4.1 All work undertaken is evaluated using a range of methods and reported to the Management Group meetings.

5 Finances

5.1 All monies raised by, or on behalf of, the group shall be used to further the aims of the group and for no other purpose.

5.2 A bank account will be kept in the name of the group at The Royal Bank of Scotland.

5.3 The Management Group shall authorise the Treasurer and two other members of the group to sign cheques on the group's behalf. (Two signatories out of three to sign any cheque.)

5.4 The Treasurer will report on the group's financial position at the Management Group meetings.

5.5 No money will be paid out in the name of the group without a receipt or invoice being presented with the possible exception of sums under £5.00. A record must be kept of any such items for which no receipt is available.

5.6 The accounts will be audited annually by an external auditor and these audited accounts will be presented at the AGM.

6 Annual General Meeting

6.1 An AGM of the group shall be held each year and all members and associates shall be notified not less than 28 days before the meeting.

7 In addition to the AGM an Open Forum will be held at six monthly intervals when all members will be canvassed on their views on the direction and running of the group

7.1 Amendments to the Constitution: If amendments to the constitution are necessary, members will be informed in writing and given the opportunity to consider and vote on the amendments. The amendments will only be made if there is a two-thirds majority vote of all members.

8 Dissolution

8.1 If the Management Group deem it advisable to dissolve the group it shall call a meeting of all members giving not less than 14 days notice. If such a decision is confirmed by a majority of those present then all assets of the group shall be transferred to another community dance group or nationally recognised body having similar aims to Marple Movers.

November, 2011

Health and Safety Quiz – Older People Dancing

True or false?

1. People with heart conditions should not take part in dance sessions
2. Osteoporosis increases the risk of fractured neck of femur
3. Angioplasty is a form of cosmetic surgery
4. Following a hip replacement always sit on a low chair
5. Rheumatoid arthritis is a condition that affects the whole body
6. People over 90 years old should not take part in dance activities
7. A person with a deep vein thrombosis may dance if they feel up to it, as long as they are seated and just move the upper body
8. An asthma attack may be brought on by cold air
9. Gentle rhythmical movements may be of benefit to those with Parkinson's disease
10. It is important to explain every activity in detail when working with people who have dementia

When you have decided whether the statements are true or false discuss the above conditions with other people.

Have you experience of participants with these conditions? How have you adapted activities for them?

Health and Safety Quiz Answers – Older People Dancing

True or false?

People with heart conditions should not take part in dance sessions
False – but you do need to know more about what the heart condition is and what the person's doctor advises

Osteoporosis increases the risk of fractured neck of femur
True

Angioplasty is a form of cosmetic surgery
False – angioplasty is a procedure for widening a narrowed or blocked blood vessel often in the coronary arteries in the heart

Following a hip replacement always sit on a low chair
False – in the early weeks following a hip replacement patients are advised to make sure the hips are higher than the knees when seated

Rheumatoid arthritis is a condition that affects the whole body
True

People over 90 years old should not take part in dance activities
False

A person with a deep vein thrombosis may dance if they feel up to it as long as they are seated and just move the upper body
False – if a deep vein thrombosis is suspected the person should seek medical advice as soon as possible and definitely not take part in any form of exercise

An asthma attack may be brought on by cold air
True

Gentle rhythmical movements may be of benefit to those with Parkinson's disease
True

It is important to explain every activity in detail when working with people who have dementia
False – lengthy explanations are likely to confuse. Try to lead using more non-verbal communication

Lincolnshire Dance: General Risk Assessment form
www.lincolnshiredance.com

Date of assessment	Location/venue assessed	Class taught	Assessed by
15/11/2011	Boston Conservative Club	Freedom in dance taster session	Lisa Hurst

Description of activities	Scale of Risk Assessment (1–5)
Providing a Freedom in Dance Taster Session for Age UK Boston and South Holland's Fit as a Fiddle Group in Boston. The group meet weekly to try different activities. This is their fourth session, the first dance one	1: Low Risk (No action required) 2: Low to Medium Risk (Adequately controlled) 3: Medium Risk (Action required by event leader) 4: Medium to High Risk (Immediate action required/Inform LD [Lincolnshire Dance] or venue management of action taken before activity begins) 5: High Risk (Consult venue management or LD immediately/Activity cannot run until consultation & action has been taken)

Specific activity	Hazard	Who might be at risk & how	Risk rating	Existing measures to control risk/action taken	Further action required by venue management or LD
Wooden floor to carpet floor	There is a rise in levels between the carpet and the wooden floor	Participants as this could cause injury if not identified to them	3	Mention at the start of the class about taking care in the space including tripping on the floor	N/A
CD player location	The only socket is in the middle of the wall, and intrudes into the space where the group will dance	Participants and Leader as they could trip over the CD player	3	Place the CD player onto a small table. This is raised off the floor minimising risk of trips/falls – mention to class about the obstacle	N/A

Specific activity	Hazard	Who might be at risk & how	Risk rating	Existing measures to control risk/action taken	Further action required by venue management or LD
Bags, coats, walking sticks	Items under chairs, or left around the room	Everyone in the room There is a high risk of trips/falls/ injuries	3	Ask participants to move bags and coats to one side of the room. Walking sticks to be put at the side near with easy access for support worker and participant	N/A

Further Information about Conditions That May Affect Older People

In Chapter 9 Elizabeth Coleman described conditions that affect some older people. Here is further information about:

- heart disease
- chronic obstructive pulmonary disease
- stroke

Ischaemic heart disease (also referred to as coronary heart disease). Ischaemia is inadequate blood supply to a part of the body, caused by constriction or blockage of the blood vessels to the area. In relation to the heart it is restriction of the arteries supplying the heart muscle itself. This may give rise to pain in the chest (angina pectoris). If this restriction is severe it may cause the part of the heart muscle supplied by that artery to have such a reduced blood supply that the segment dies. This is called a myocardial infarction. A coronary thrombosis is the formation of a blood clot in the coronary artery, obstructing the blood flow to part of the heart. In other words, a coronary thrombosis leads to a myocardial infarction. The cause is a build up of fatty deposits in the walls of the blood vessels (atherosclerosis), which may then make it more likely that a blood clot will form in the artery.

Angina pectoris is a transient pain in the centre of the chest, usually brought on by exercise and relieved by rest. People who have angina may describe it as a dull or heavy pain, with tightening of the chest that usually passes off in a few minutes. The pain may spread to the left arm, neck, jaw and back. In this form angina is described as 'stable'. In 'unstable' angina the symptoms may be similar but may come on without any of the triggers, such as exercise or exertion, and may not pass off. In this case emergency treatment may be necessary and urgent medical help is called for.

It is useful to look at some of the following risk factors for coronary heart disease, as understanding the lifestyle of the older people you may be dancing with may enable you to pick out those for whom caution is needed.

- Family history. The risk is increased if either parent has had heart disease under the age of 55. The higher risk may be due to genetic or lifestyle factors.
- Cholesterol levels. Once again this level may be related to inherited risk or may be due to diet. People with a diet low in animal fat and

refined carbohydrate, and high in fibre and fish may tend to have lower cholesterol levels.

- Blood pressure (BP). The higher the BP, the greater the risk.
- Tobacco smoking. The risk increases with the number of cigarettes smoked per day.
- Physical activity. The risk is reduced with activity, at work or leisure.
- Personality. Those with type 'A' personality have increased risk. They may be competitive, aggressive and set strict deadlines – the 'workaholic' type. When looking at the benefits of dance and exercise, the dancer may be able to see ways in which what they have to offer may begin to reduce the risk in some people.
- Stress. Once again the risk increases with increased stress.

For some people with heart disease surgery may be performed to widen narrowed or blocked coronary arteries. **Angioplasty** is the insertion of a balloon or ring (stent) into the coronary artery at the point at which it narrows. The effect is to open the artery, enabling blood to flow to the heart muscle leading to relief of angina. **Coronary bypass grafting** is also used to relieve angina. In this procedure a vein is taken from the front of the leg to use as a graft. Several arteries may be grafted at the same time. The piece of leg vein is placed either side of the blockage in the coronary artery, thus 'bypassing' it and enabling blood to flow. Following surgery many people will undertake rehabilitation under the direction of specialist health professionals.

Whilst ischaemic heart disease may reduce a person's ability to exercise, once treatment has stabilised or corrected the condition enjoyable exercise and dance may be a beneficial way of maintaining better health. Advice regarding participation in dance sessions must be at the discretion of health professionals, prior to inclusion in any activity.

Heart failure occurs when the system of circulation of blood around the heart, lungs and circulatory system becomes insufficient. Blood is moved around the body by the action of the ventricles – muscle pumps. Blood is returned to the heart partly by the massaging effect of the muscles in the limbs. Valves in the veins stop the blood from flowing back down the veins. Heart failure is a failure of this system.

As the heart begins to fail it tries to compensate by:

- Increasing the heart rate. This puts more demand on the heart muscle.
- Increasing the filling pressure of the heart, by retaining fluid. This stretches the heart muscle to increase the force of the contraction. The

result is back pressure and congestion in other organs of the body, for example, the lungs, liver and kidneys.

- Increasing the resistance in the blood vessel walls. This puts more pressure on the heart.

The symptoms experienced as the heart fails are breathlessness, with the person finding it easier to breathe when sitting and more difficult when lying (people with heart failure will often sleep propped up in a sitting position or not go to bed at all), and swelling (oedema), especially in the lower legs around the ankles. Treatment is by medication, aimed at helping the heart to beat more strongly, and reducing swelling-induced congestion in the lungs and other organs and limbs.

Chronic obstructive pulmonary disease (COPD) is the most common respiratory disease in the UK, and is caused by chronic bronchitis and emphysema. Both conditions result in a decrease in the ability to get air into the lungs. **Bronchitis** is inflammation of the main airways into the lungs (the bronchi). **Emphysema** is a reduction in the elasticity of the lungs, reducing the amount by which they are able to recoil after each breath in, and resulting in the need for the person to use extra muscles to force the air out. Both conditions are exhausting.

COPD usually develops over a long period of time and is especially prevalent in smokers. In fact, smoking is by far the biggest cause of the condition. It may start with an acute infection, which may recur many times and eventually lead to severe reduction of mobility and activity.

The symptoms of the condition include an irritating cough that produces sputum; breathlessness, often on exertion, but in the later stages the person may be breathless even when resting; wheezing due to the production of sputum; reduction in both the amount of air breathed in and out in each breath (tidal volume) and the force of the air breathed out (peak flow); and blueness (cyanosis), especially around the lips, indicating reduced oxygenation of the blood.

Treatment is by way of:

- Encouragement to stop smoking.
- Encouragement to lose weight if necessary.
- Antibiotics if a chest infection is present.
- Bronchodilator therapy given by mouth or as an inhaler, to open up the airways. A humidifier enables medication to be administered in a moist atmosphere, which helps to remove secretions.
- Oxygen therapy to increase the proportion of oxygen in the air breathed in, thus improving the oxygen levels in the blood.

- Physiotherapy to teach effective breathing and clearance of secretions.
- Rehabilitation to produce a gradual improvement in activity levels.

A stroke occurs when the blood supply and, therefore, the oxygen supply to a part of the brain is blocked or restricted. The brain is a complex organ with a network of cells that send and receive messages from all areas and organs of the body. It is rather like a large telephone exchange, routing incoming messages to the right area and sending outgoing messages to all parts of the body. When a stroke occurs some of the network is damaged and the area of the body relating to that part of the brain can no longer send or receive these messages. If the blood supply to a part of the brain is compromised for any length of time, brain cells die and disability results. The most common causes are blockage or haemorrhage. Each half of the brain (hemisphere) controls the opposite side of the body, although the two sides do share responsibility for some functions.

Damage to the right side of the brain may cause:

- Reduced movement on the left side of the body.
- Loss or reduced sensation on the left side.
- Reduced perception or spatial awareness.
- Reduced ability to judge distance or size.
- Left-sided neglect, for example, ignoring objects or people on their left side, or not being aware of their own left side.
- A reduced ability to judge their own ability. They may be impulsive and have unrealistic expectations of what they are capable of in a dance session.
- Loss of vision in the left side of each eye (hemianopia), leading to not being able to see things to the left side of the body.

Damage to the left side of the brain may cause:

- Reduced movement on the right side of the body.
- Loss or reduced sensation on the right side.
- Problems with speech, language and swallowing.
- A tendency to be disorganised, slow and cautious.
- Loss of vision in the right side of each eye (hemianopia).

Anyone who has had a stroke may experience changes in their emotional response, often being tearful, or changing from laughter to tears very easily. Depression may also be an understandable problem, resulting from loss of function and mobility and the need for assistance with many activities, where once they were independent.

The degree of severity of a stroke varies according to the area of the brain affected and any resulting symptoms may be temporary or permanent. When the blood flow to one area of the brain is blocked, the body will try to heal itself. Brain tissue does not have the capacity to repair itself, but some of the damage may be from pressure on undamaged brain cells, and these may show some recovery over time. Blood vessels close to the blockage will increase in size and try to take over the work of the damaged vessels.

Risk factors for stroke are:

- High blood pressure (hypertension).
- Fatty build-up in the blood vessels, causing narrowing and increased risk of blood clots (atherosclerosis).
- Heart problems.
- High cholesterol.
- Cigarette smoking.
- Family history of stroke.
- Previous strokes.
- The contraceptive pill (again not a huge risk for older people, but they may have taken the pill for extended times in their younger life).

Duty of Care: Cautions, Precautions and Reasons for Concern

At all stages of planning and running dance and movement sessions, for people of any age and ability, there is a need to look at, and prepare for, health issues of participants, or incidents in the session, which may affect their ability to participate.

- **Caution:** Taking care and paying attention to safety. In dance and movement this relates to having an understanding of the conditions which might give cause for concern in a session, together with relevant information about the individuals attending the session.
- **Precaution:** This is any action taken before a session to prevent accidents and avoid risk. In practical terms this also may relate to having information about the people in the group. It also relates to having procedures in place to be able to deal with incidences or emergencies. For example - what to look for in an individual; who to contact in an emergency; how, and with whom, you share responsibility; plans for action for incidents; who is in charge and when to say **STOP**.
- **Reasons for Concern:** This relates to any worries about participants or the activity. It may involve recognising change and knowing when to take action. The changes may be in group members on arrival, e.g. looking unwell; or may be things which happen during or at the end of the session.

Relating concerns to the cautions and precautions will enable dancers to fulfil their duty of care to their individual participants, other group members, co-workers and themselves.

General Reasons for Concern/Risk to Self When Working with Older People:

- Having an understanding of, and information about, any health issues of those attending dance and movement sessions which may give cause for concern, enables appropriate planning of activities and reduces risk to both participants and workers.
- With any group, precautions need to be in place to reduce the risk to participants, co-workers and themselves. This may be in terms of protection from aggression and/or safety of the environment.
- No-one has the right to be aggressive, no matter how old, frail or poorly they may be, Aggression, either verbal or physical, must not be tolerated and precautions need to be in place, by way of protocols, to ensure this is the case.

- Sharing concerns, regarding risk, with colleagues and being aware of potential risk factors avoids or limits confrontation and conflict.
- Ensuring the venue and environment is safe in terms of space, clutter, temperature etc.
- Having an understanding of "moving and handling" legislation and local policies.
- Being aware of one's own limitations and boundaries regarding movement, touch, level of self-disclosure etc.
- Being able to say **NO** or **STOP** and meaning it.

Elizabeth Coleman (2011)

Observation Checklist Used in Dance Sessions in Dementia Care

Names				
Facial expression				
Little or no change in facial expression				
Smile				
Frown				
Other				
Eye contact/movement				
Asleep				
No eye contact				
Looks at people/watching				
Looks at objects				
Looks towards sound/listening				
Body movement				
No movement/no change in movement				
Body movement increases				
Body movement decreases				
Copying actions				
Tapping/clapping				
Dancing				
Repetitive actions cease				
Touch				
Reaches out/touches person				
Reaches out/touches object				
Examines object (handling/looking)				
Attempts to use object (as shown?)				
Uses object (as shown?)				
Verbalisation				
No vocalisation/communication				
Makes sounds/intonation + or −				
Uses words + or −				

Uses sentences + or −				
Repetitive verbalisations cease				
Laughs				
Sings				
Emotions				
Hard to ascertain				
No emotion expressed				
Happy				
Agitated				
Sad/angry				

© Diane Amans 2008

Safeguarding vulnerable adults

Dance artists working in care settings with older people may have vulnerable adults within their groups. As part of the duty of care to these vulnerable adults, the dance practitioner is responsible for both taking steps to prevent abuse and responding promptly and appropriately where abuse is suspected.

Participatory dance workers have a responsibility to understand what is meant by the terms 'vulnerable adult' and 'abuse'. It is also important to know how to recognise signs of abuse and to whom this should be reported. This will be different in each context and setting.

Vulnerable adults

Vulnerable adults are people 18 or over who may be unable to take care of themselves or protect themselves from harm or exploitation. This may be because of age or illness; or it may be because of a sensory impairment, mental health problem or other disability.

It is important to recognise that there is not a particular age when older people are classified as vulnerable. Many people live their life to old age without being classified as a vulnerable adult; some go through periods when they are vulnerable adults and then they recover.

Abuse

Abuse is a violation of an individual's human rights or dignity. It may consist of a single act or repeated acts. It may be physical, verbal, psychological or sexual.

Neglect and acts of omission are also forms of abuse. These may include ignoring medical or physical care needs, failure to provide access to appropriate health, social care or educational services, and the withholding of the necessities of life, such as medication, adequate nutrition, shelter and heating.

Financial or material abuse includes theft, fraud or exploitation; pressure in connection with property, inheritance or wills or financial transactions; or the misuse or misappropriation of property, possessions or benefits.

Institutional abuse sometimes occurs in residential homes, hospitals or nursing homes and may be a result of neglect or poor practice within the organisation. Sometimes the abuse is not deliberate; rather it occurs because of ignorance or lack of awareness or training. Regardless of whether or not it is intentional, it needs to be reported.

In addition to the brief notes above, further information about safeguarding policies and training is available from local authority social services departments, Age UK (www.ageuk.org.uk) and the Department of Health website, http://www.dh.gov.uk.

Partnership Questionnaire

The following is an example of a questionnaire distributed to people who attended an event to profile the launch of a Freedom in Dance Older People Dancing project. Those attending included health care professionals, housing managers, staff from voluntary agencies and arts development workers. The roadshow included a brief presentation, video showing, live performance and demonstration workshop.

* * *

If you would like us to contact you to discuss how you can be involved in the Older People Dancing project please complete this form and leave it with a **Freedom in Dance** representative.

Name
Contact details
What is your interest in the project? – Please tick

- I'd like to take part in a dance project
- I'm interested in the training course
- I'd like a taster session in my organisation
- My organisation can offer funding
- My organisation can offer support in kind (e.g. venue/transport)
- Other (please specify)

When is the best time for us to contact you?

Powys Dance Case Study

Leading dance with older adults

Case study

Powys Dance has been developing dance activities in community settings and schools across Powys since 1979. Work with older adults has been a component of the programme for the past 15 years including company performance, workshops and intergenerational projects. Leading Dance with Older Adults aimed to share the skills that Powys Dance has developed, and to support others to develop their skills in this area. Powys is a large rural county covering a quarter of the land mass of Wales, making parity of provision across the county a challenge. Developing skills in others is a step towards addressing this issue.

Aims

The course aimed to facilitate professional development through a learning partnership between an activities officer (or equivalent) and a dance practitioner. In addition to the taught sessions each pair would work together to plan, deliver and evaluate sessions in their setting, putting into practice what they had learnt.

Course objectives

- To train ten practitioners (five dance practitioners and five activities officers) in leading safe dance activities with older adults.
- For older people to access an element of their 5×30 (see below) through dance activities led by the above practitioners in their residential or day care settings.
- Legacy: a minimum of ten trained and competent staff who can lead regular weekly dance sessions in their own setting.

Participants

Dance practitioners were drawn from existing Powys Dance staff who wanted to develop this aspect of their work and from a bank of freelance tutors in the county. Activities officers were invited from five residential or day care settings from around the county.

Funding

£3270 was received from the Local Authority Partnership Agreement, Powys. This is part of a national initiative prompted by the Welsh Assembly

203

Government's strategy document *Climbing Higher: Creating an Active Wales*. The Welsh Health Survey (2007) identified that only 30% of adults in Wales were participating in 30 minutes of moderate physical activity five times a week (5×30), the current recommendation for benefiting health. With funding from Sport Wales, local authorities were charged with brokering partnerships with the third sector to help increase opportunities for people to become involved in physical activity.

The funding supported the research and development of the course and its delivery. It also allowed the sourcing of six resources boxes containing props and music, which could be borrowed or purchased by each setting.

Partnerships

During the study, the course discussions were held with Powys Corporate Learning and Development Team. Shelly Jackson, Exercise Referral Coordinating Officer, developed a session on identifying and eliminating risk in movement activity with older adults. Diane Amans facilitated Day 3 of the training and led a course evaluation with all participants. Each setting committed staff time to the programme. Brynhyfryd Bupa Care Home linked the project with My Home Life Cymru, an Age Concern initiative that they are involved in, which considers quality of life in residential care settings.

Outline of course content

- Laban Analysis of movement (body, space, dynamics, relationship)
- structuring and planning a dance session for older adults
- delivery of sessions in your setting
- evaluation of completed sessions in settings
- identifying risk: movement patterns to avoid; tailoring movement for individual needs
- ideas and props to stimulate movement (seated)
- some ideas for standing activities
- reminiscence and intergenerational work: project case study
- preparation for further sessions in your settings

Legacy and future developments

The Young Men's Christian Association (YMCA) Wales Community College will be accrediting participants' learning through the development of a portfolio to evidence their practice in their settings. This will release some funding to support the further delivery of sessions by dance practitioners (in partnership with each setting) and facilitate mentoring visits by course tutors. This partnership with YMCA Wales Community College has provided the resources and the stimulus for the continuation of the work over the next academic year, which it is hoped will lead to longer term continuation of practice.

Executive Summary: English National Ballet Dance for Parkinson's Report

English National Ballet commissioned Roehampton University to conduct research into the effects of dancing with Parkinson's, as seen within the company's pilot project. It was hosted at Markova House, London, between October 2010 and February 2011. The project introduced participants to the ballet *Romeo & Juliet* and provided 12 ability-appropriate dance sessions of structured and creative movement accompanied by live piano and flute music.

The research collected qualitative and quantitative data from the project using interviews, film footage, validated measurement techniques, diaries and observations. The resulting report analysed and documented the findings.

The research study concluded that dancing, as seen within English National Ballet's project:

- Aids people with Parkinson's physically, mentally and socially.
- Does not help with physical development in a uniform or linear fashion, but can help with mobility in the short term, particularly when there is musical accompaniment.
- Gives participants the tools to increase body awareness and to increase confidence in order to use the mobility they have, but may not have had the courage to use.
- Provides tools to help with activities in everyday life.
- Gives participants the opportunity to experience different qualities and ways of moving.
- Can loosen up the spinal area and help with stability and posture.
- Can encourage a greater reach, focus and projection.
- Provides a vehicle for social interaction.
- Precipitates feelings of well-being, determination and achievement.
- Provides opportunities to create movement and stimulate the imagination.
- Provides an event for people with Parkinson's that is about art, rather than about disease.

- Provides opportunities to learn about ballet.
- Provides an enjoyable way for participants to exercise as a group in a structured environment.
- Allows participants to enjoy the excitement of being a part of the goings on of a professional ballet company.

Mind Your Rhetoric: *Animated* Article

This article, first published in the Winter 1996/97 edition of *Animated*, is reproduced by permission of the Foundation for Community Dance. All Rights Reserved. See www.communitydance.org.uk/animated for more information.

Animated, **Winter 1997. Antony Smith** on limited lexicons and the importance of the tea dance.

How much do we limit our vision of the role of older people in dance by the language we use to describe them, however well intentioned our choice of words might be? To mind our language is not just to tackle the negative lexical stereotyping of old age, but also to take on the vague and altogether limited terminology we use when attempting to talk positively. In the context of older people and dance we are almost all guilty of using the same small reference book of platitudes at least once when we are asked for our comments. The words go something like: 'Older people bring a sense of calm/of dignity/of serenity to dance; they bring a lifetime's rich experience'.

There is nothing intrinsically wrong with the words; they are perfectly agreeable. But they are just not enough, and we do an injustice to older dancers by continuing to be limited by them. Taken as part of our usual terms of reference when describing dance they fail even more miserably, and begin to sound as original (and as appropriate) as that apocryphal 'Twilight Lodge' retirement home.

The problem of this limited lexicon is compounded by the fact that it is so difficult to come up with any realistic alternatives, because before we can expand the way we talk about older people in the dance world it is necessary to expand our terms of reference for describing dance generally. One of the leading issues is that there is no continuity. The visible dancer becomes invisible at thirty something with a string of appropriate adjectives attached to his or her work. If she or he reappears at all, it is as something of a novelty several decades later, when those adjectives are simply no longer appropriate. We can celebrate the fact that colleagues in dance are challenging this state of affairs, but we are still left with a major generational divide – lissom young bodies alongside considerably older ones.

It is astonishing to think how much we have had our vision of a dance aesthetic challenged and expanded in the past few decades. A dance culture that speaks for the late 20th century is more in tune with the realities of the world; as a result it reflects all its movements, small as well as expansive, ugly as well as beautiful. And yet we continue to be blinkered in terms of age. Why older people cannot be as expert exponents of this new world of dance as the young is wholly a question of perception rather than ability.

Inevitably, those of us promoting the role of the older dancer fall back at some point on the word 'experience', but how do we honestly translate this word into dance terms? 'Dignity', 'serenity' and 'calm' are at least tangible concepts in movement terminology even though all we may mean when we use them is 'tries hard but moves rather slowly'. In theatre, music, the visual arts, good artists are perceived to grow in stature as they grow in years and experience. Not so in dance. We may respect dancers' past work. We may marvel that they're still dancing at 40, let alone 60, 70 or 80. But we tend to get embarrassed when we actually see them on stage, because the contrast with what we're used to is so immense. Again we have lissom young bodies on one side and almost nothing on the other until we reach the dancer as novelty age. The importance and value of experience are unquestionable. We are, however, in grave need of a set of working references by which we can judge and assess how successfully this 'experience' manifests itself in dance. We must stop our clutching at the term rather desperately and begin to know what we mean. Let's hope the 'Beyond the Tea Dance' debate can help us build a language for older dancers that is honest, in which we believe, and which expands rather than limits our vision.

In defence of the tea dance (and its cousins)

If we were to make a list with tea dance at the top, we could include underneath it all the folk, national, barn, square and disco dances that are related in their 'social' characteristics, that are extremely enjoyable and enjoyed by millions, but which are not quite art. Of course, to take issues forward, to expand horizons, to develop work that is innovative and challenging we must look 'beyond the tea dance', but we must tread very carefully as we do so. Let us please acknowledge its fun and its status and include it in our discussions rather than imply it's time to leave it behind. Again, it seems to be a question of continuity – we classify as social dances or we classify as art, yet they are not poles apart. There can be overlap and there can be shared experiences. Dance forms have borrowed from each other for centuries.

A particular danger is that if we dismiss the tea dance, we dismiss one of the areas of dance in which many older people feel confidence and pride – even feel they have something to give and share with the rest of us. In countries with strong folk or national dance traditions it also tends to be the old who uphold and preserve them. In those countries, however, those older people often have a valued position as 'guardians' of a unique heritage.

Their experience and knowledge give them a status in the dance world that has nothing to do with questions of whether what they're doing is social activity or art.

The ballroom and sequence dances that constitute the classic tea dance can have a similar status if we only learn to value them. If, in doing so, we risk upholding a rather clichéd image of older people dancing, we have only to be sure that they are part of a wider spectrum of opportunities, and that we build on their huge following as a starting point for involvement in many other kinds of dance. [At the time this article was first published Antony Smith was ActivAge Programme Manager for Eurolink Age.]

Case Study: Jacky Simpson, a 61-Year-Old, Who Trained to Be a Dance Leader

I first met Lincolnshire Dance in 2005. I had recently lost my husband to cancer after nursing him for a number of years. By chance, I saw an advert in the local paper about the Freedom in Dance training programme, which Lincolnshire Dance offer. I wasn't a trained dancer but had enjoyed dance as a social activity/hobby all of my life and the possibilities that it offered really captured my imagination. I was 61 years old at the time but both my daughters told me to 'go for it' so I plucked up courage and contacted Lincolnshire Dance.

They were very welcoming and after several telephone conversations I decided to enrol for the course. I still remember that I was very nervous as I arrived for the first session. I couldn't stop thinking how the young people on the course would react to me working alongside them? Would any of them talk to me? I needn't have worried everyone was very friendly and the course led in such a way that everyone was valued as an individual and I soon learned that I had knowledge that others didn't so we all learned from each other!

I completed the course and was very proud of my OCN level 3 qualification. I can truly say that it changed my life. As part of the course everyone has to undertake a ten week placement. I set up a community class in my local church hall and initially asked lots of friends to come as the participants. I like to tell people that my placement never ended as I still run the class which is now attended by over 30 people each week, in fact demand was so great that in 2009 I started another class at the same venue which also attracts over 30 participants each week. We dance to all kinds of music from classical through to Rock and Pop, we laugh a lot and I have made so many new friends!

Since 2007 the group, now known as the 'Magic Mover' has been performing. We started small, taking part in local events including the prestigious Lincolnshire Show. The buzz of performing was amazing and the group wanted to do more and more. We became quite well known locally and after Gillian Merron (MP for Lincoln) saw us on the local news we got a mention in parliament!

In 2009 we were offered the chance to dance at 'The Retirement Show – London Olympia'. Twelve of the class decided they wanted to take up this amazing opportunity so we started planning and set off for London, a rare and exciting treat.

By now we really had the taste for adventure so in 2010 it seemed natural to agree to undertake a small tour of Russia when we were invited! Twelve younger members of the group (no one over 77) spent some time in St Petersburg and performed at a festival in Petrozavodsk. The emotion when the crowd, including children and adults, danced with us in Kirov square was overwhelming and I feel tears welling in my eyes when I remember the event. It was a great chance to share our ideas with our counterparts in Russia.

This year we decided not to travel as a big group, so I travelled to Montreal to lead two dance workshops at an international convention, whilst some other members of the group took part in an intergeneration project which was part of the SO festival in Skegness. We couldn't resist however the offer to take part in two-days filming for the Age UK commercial, or the chance to dance on national television and be interviewed by Gabby Logan as part of The Wright Stuff Extra. Not to mention the Champagne at the Savoy afterwards to celebrate – who'd have thought we would have all of these new experiences at our ages!

If I had my life again I would lead dance rather than anything else. The Magic Movers remain my focus but I lead workshops around Lincoln and not only for those over 50. I have found that my sessions are also a real hit with the under-fives!

I feel very privileged, the Magic Movers are my inspiration and I often reflect how that first telephone call with Keyna* started an amazing journey for me and 1000s of other ladies

Jacky Simpson, December 2011

*Keyna Paul is Director of Lincolnshire Dance

Notes on Ideas for Seated Activities

The following ideas are suitable for seated groups – though many activities can be adapted and used with more active participants. You can adapt activities to suit the energy level and physical needs of the group by varying the speed and number of repetitions.

Name game: Large ball

1. Form a seated circle
2. Going clockwise around the circle everyone calls out their name
3. Repeat going anticlockwise
4. Introduce a large inflatable ball and roll it gently across the circle to another person when they call out their name
5. Introduce humour by 'tossing' a soft toy or beanbag at the same time as the large ball
6. Additional items thrown simultaneously help encourage quick reactions

NB: Make sure everyone is included. It's easy to miss out people with difficult names or those who are fairly new to a group.

Follow me warm up (Music: Rock and roll such as Buddy Holly's 'That'll be the Day')

- Body rub – rub hands together
- Body rub – rub arms briskly
- Brushing movement up and down arms
- Change arms and repeat first movements
- Percussion on thighs, legs and knees, moving slowly down shins and back up again
- Rubbing motion on hips, back, tummy
- Tickle face gently
- Gently pat top of the head
- Freestyle movement
- Move entire body 'in chair' – walking feet backwards and forwards

Seated exercises for the lower body (Music: Regular beat, not too fast. JABADAO's 'Penny on the Water' works well)

- Tap feet slowly (to the half beat)
- Lift heel leaving ball of foot on floor

- Tap toe then heel – change legs
- Roll from toe to heel – change legs
- Marching
- Charlie Chaplin steps
- Tap ball of foot on coloured spot on floor, change to heel. Repeat with other foot
- Lift leg and lower. Repeat with other leg
- Lift leg – then circle foot slowly in both directions. Repeat with other leg
- 'Free style movements' Shake and pat down

Seated exercises for upper body (Music: Java Jive by The Casablanca Steps works well)

- Circle shoulder backwards
- Rock your baby
- Raise folded arms and look through the space
- Stir stew – large movement clockwise and anticlockwise
- Royal wave – change direction – change arms
- Catch 'bubbles' with a clap
- Paint the fence – change arms
- Pinch together finger to thumb – all fingers – then change hands
- Play imaginary piano
- Play your neighbour's imaginary piano

Elastic stretch (Music: 'The Stripper' by Joe Loss, from 'The Full Monty')

All hold a large piece of soft stretchy elastic stretched around the circle.

- Hold and kick legs – changing legs each time
- Hold and kick – stretching out with arms
- Wind the bobbin up – then pull, pull, pull
- Finish freestyle

Try free move to a slower piece of classical music. There is no right or wrong way – the challenge is to get the 'fit' right for your group.

Feathers (Music: Gentle piano music – Einaudi collection)

Seated in circle, a feather is passed round with gentle music playing in the background.

- The leader moves around the room asking individuals to 'blow' the feather off the back or palm of their hand.
- The feather is then blown or caught from person to person around the circle.
- Introduce a second feather going the opposite way around the circle.
- In pairs or threes, people pass the feather back and forth 'playing' and exploring ways of blowing, patting or passing the feather.

Scarves

- Explore different ways of making scarves move
- Make a scarf dance in small groups

Pass the move – with a paper plate (Try Nina Simone, 'Baby Just Cares for Me')

Each participant holds a paper plate and makes up a movement, which everyone copies. Encourage them to find ways of moving the lower body. Reassure people that it is OK to 'pass', and it is OK to repeat a move.

'Strictly Come Dancing'

Start with a quiz to see if participants can 'name that dance' by listening to music that accompanies a range of ballroom dances (waltz, tango, quick-step, cha cha, slow foxtrot). Then ask them to help you make up a seated version of some of these dances.

Hand jive

See how many different hand jive moves participants can remember (rock and roll music works well).

Sample Session Plans

Dance artist: Wendy Thomas, Merseyside Dance Initiative

Warm up (giving the option for sitting or standing). Music ranges from 40s big band songs to Irish folk music

- Breathing and slow circling movements with arms opening out and coming back through the centre line.
- Rubbing and patting the limbs and torso.
- Stretches and circles with limbs, focusing on a contrast of large and small movements with images such as playing the piano, picking fruit off trees. Stretches and circles of lower limbs.
- Pick up on different individuals' movements and all use them in turn.

Main section

- Work with large elastic to connect the group and to explore different levels in space.
- Use arm swings – introduce the feel and idea of swinging the arms and letting the movement take you into turns. Work in pairs to initiate your own ideas – improvise to connect with a free sense of body.
- Use scarves to different styles of music, both quieter and with lyrical movement. (This brought out humour and mischief and well as some beautiful dancing!)
- Playing ballroom rhythms for step dancing that a few of the participants love – time for requests.
- Playing percussion instruments to Fats Waller (some participants danced with hats that we had from last week while others accompanied).
- Parachute – build on running through and swapping places.

Cool down

- Seated stretches
- Rolling down the spine
- Guided relaxation – letting the muscles sink into the chair; breathing and imagery

This group is active and enjoys a full session, often spontaneously initiating dance and song and using the full hour in a dynamic way.

A dance activity that I find good, especially for the less active participants, is one where I look for and reflect a participant's movement back to them, and encourage the whole group to use it. This affirms that person and often leads to more exploration for that person, as well as being a way of including someone with a minimum of movement.

Example 2: Llys Hafren Residential Home

Dance artist: Bethan Smith, Powys Dance

Exercise	*Music*
Warm up	You Are My Sunshine
• Straight back – good posture	(From the soundtrack of *O Brother*
• Tap knees with hands	*Where art thou?*)
• Lift shoulders up & down	
• Roll shoulders back	
(Repeat all)	
• Tap toes	Anything Goes, by Tony Bennett
• Lift legs up and down	
• Tap both hands on knees	
(Repeat all)	
• Sway from side to side	Papa Loves Mambo, by Nat King Cole
• Wave your hand	
• Tap toes	
(Repeat all)	
• Pass the scarf around the circle	Dream a Little Dream, by Dean
• One scarf each and have a play	Martin
• Move the scarf up, down, side to side	
• Create your own dance with the scarf	
(Repeat all)	
• Pose	Jailhouse Rock, by Elvis Presley
• Hand slices	
• Pose	
• Mash potato	
• Pose	
• Hand twirl	
(Repeat all)	
Cool down	When You're Smiling, by Dean Martin
• Straight back	
• Stretch	
• Open/close hands	
• Tap toes	
• Sway from side to side	
(Repeat all)	

Example 3: Let's Tango Fiesta!

Sample session plan from the Tea Time to Move Programme

Dance artist: Rosie Perdikeas Arts for Health, Cornwall

Arts for Health Cornwall has produced a *Dancing for Older People's Health and Wellbeing* toolkit. It contains advice on planning and delivering dance sessions in care settings. In addition to warm-up exercises there are themed activities such as:

- tea dance with a difference
- 1940s jive dance
- old time music hall
- let's tango fiesta!
- creative movement sessions

Display: Red balloons on a white sheet in the centre of the space, tango photographs, red props and other brightly coloured objects.

    Music . . . 'Gotan Project' CD 1 track 4, 'Tango Collection' – CD 1 track 1, 'Tango Collection' – CD 3 track 5, but any tango-based music can be used.

Introduction

Introduce the theme 'tango fiesta!', travelling to South America to learn to dance the Argentine tango! Lots of guided imagery can be used for this session to help stimulate new ideas and to get the feel of a different environment. Explain that the colour red is associated with this dance as it is with the continent; for example, hot climates, temperaments and bright clothing.

Warm-up

(Imagine we wake up and find ourselves in hot South America!)

- Close eyes, take deep lung breathing.
- Bring hands to face and rub gently, slowly stretch out arms to shoulder height and yawn, bring arms into body, repeat stretch a few times to stretch and wake the body up.
- Holding arms out ahead flex hands up and down, then side to side, introduce head turning with movement. Close and open hands and fingers with 'sunshine hands' palms facing away from body.
- 'Putting sun cream on', rub up and down arms and into legs.
- 'Sand between toes', draw toes and feet up, then stretch and relax flat.

Talk about tango dance and how the props make you feel in relation to the dance.

- 'Walking on the beach', gentle walking, jogging, then into water and splashing with both feet.
- 'Diving into the sea', diving action lifting arms and head then diving forwards, open arms to side then bring back into centre of body (repeat three or four times).
- 'Before fiesta lets siesta!' – Imagine lying on beach, taking in sun, breathing deeply from abdomen – rest.

Creative section Props – tango dance photographs, red scarves, hats, clothes, instruments (shakers, tambourines etc.).

- Hand out props, show tango photographs, talk about tango dance and how the props make them feel in relation to the dance ask them to find a simple movement related to the prop or item of clothing, supporting and encouraging ideas. As individuals find a movement ask the group to try the movement out too. Using the movements create a sequence, put this to the music and have the group try it out.

Tango sequence:

- Emphasise that this is a proud dance with the body lifted, head held high.
- Start with clapping, elbows lifted out to the sides ($\times$ 8).
- Two slow claps then three quick.
- Repeat the above with feet joining in to stamp (whilst sitting or standing).
- Using arms only, take tango ballroom hold (left bent in, right extended) with arms, head turned in direction of extended arm. Change direction of arms with head (repeat four times).
- With arms still in ballroom hold introduce leg work, right leg steps away from body to right side, left leg follows with step to right side of body also. Step left leg back to body, right follows. Change arms repeat other side ($\times$ 4).
- Put both the group's sequence and the taught sequence together.
- For the last part of 'fiesta party', have people lift a part of a cloth or sheet, and wave the sheet in the air to float balloons up, and then the group enjoys playing with the balloons!

Cool-down

- Lying on a beach looking up at the stars, warm sand enveloping the body. Stretch each limb out, stretch whole body and yawn as in warm-up but slower.

- Feel seawater lapping at the feet; gently flex feet up and down.
- Focus on breathing deeply and evenly.
- Enjoy listening to music, relax and rest.

The toolkit can be viewed at the website; www.artsforhealthcornwall.org. uk To buy a toolkit contact info@artsforhealthcornwall.org.uk, or call 01326 377772.

Example 4: Cross-generational Session (Group Aged 3–83 Years)

Dance artist: Diane Amans

This was the initial session in a four-day performance project.

Ice-breakers

- Pass the clap. Participants stand or sit in a circle. Leader turns to the next person in the circle and claps. The clap is passed round till it returns to the leader.
- Repeat with each person saying their name after the clap.
- Repeat with everyone saying the person's name after the clap.
- Roll a giant ball across the circle, saying the name of the person who will receive the ball.

Warm-up activities

- Go/stop – a small child calls out 'go' and all participants move around the space. Child calls 'stop' and the movers freeze. Repeat several times.
- Shaky and still. This is another activity where the child can lead. Child shakes tambourine and participants make fast, jerky movements. Movers stop suddenly when the tambourine is banged. Can be adapted to incorporate one child tearing newspaper (dancers make jerky moves), whilst another child bangs on tambourine (everyone stops).
- Heads and shoulders. Following the leader tap a different body part eight times: heads, shoulders, tums, bums, legs, knees, feet, floor. Repeat with four repetitions, then twice and once. Works well to lively music with a clear, rhythmic beat.
- Ribbons – moving with coloured ribbons on sticks. Begin with all moving freely then leader calls out a colour – 'blue' – and all movers with blue ribbons come into the centre and make their ribbons 'dance' together.

Main Section

- 1, 2, 3 statue. In groups of three the first dancer moves for about four counts and holds a shape. The second person moves and attaches to the shape.

Third dancer moves and attaches so there is a three-person sculpture. Repeat several times.

- Unison move (see Starting Points for Choreography below).
- Bookends – free movement in the space with two movers as 'bookends'. When the bookends pause (at some distance from each other) the other dancers find a way of connecting and holding a shape until the whole group is connected between the two bookends. When everyone is still a child crawls through from one end to the other. (Repeat with all small children).

Cool-down

Pizza massage: In pairs – one person working on partner's back. Leader talks the group through – knead the dough, spread tomato paste, add mushrooms, salami and so on, sprinkle with cheese, place in the oven, cheese melts, take out of oven, cut into slices and eat. Change over.

Example 5: Marple Movers (Active Group Aged 55–75 Years)

Dance artist: Diane Amans

Warm-up activities

- Ribbons – free movement using ribbon sticks (music: Odissea Veneziana, Rondo Veneziano).
- Elastic stretch – free move holding onto a giant piece of elastic (music: tango).
- Follow my leader – one person leads the group in a snaking line around the space. Leader calls out the name of a new person to take over at the front of the line. Leading dancer introduces different ways of moving (music: Tarmac, Je Cherche)
- Warm up stretches – all main muscle groups (music: Marvin Gaye, I Heard it Through the Grapevine).
- Circles – dancers find as many circular moves as possible using different body parts and whole body moves (music: Buena Vista Social Club, Chan Chan).

Main section

- Create a motif using letters of name as a starting point (note, this is not drawing the name in the air – more using the shape or energy suggested by the letters). Find four short gestures and join them together to form a motif.
- Join with a partner and have a movement conversation using motifs:

  A moves, B watches
  B moves, A watches
  Repeat
  Both move together

Join with another pair. All perform individual motifs simultaneously then begin unison move (see Starting Points for Choreography for details)

Variation/development. Scatter and reform

(Music: Louis Crelier, Morna della Puglia, from *Azzurro* Soundtrack)

Final section

Dancers watch each other perform (half the group observes then change over). Short feedback discussion.

Cool-down – all over rub, calf stretches.

Breathe in and raise arms. Breathe out with a sigh. Repeat 3 times.

Starting Points for Choreography

The following ideas are useful starting points for creating motifs and movement phrases. By selecting and combining movement phrases they can be used as a one-off 'make a dance in a session' piece or, alternatively, developed into a performance piece. Many of these ideas can be adapted for seated participants.

Pass the move

This activity can be used as an ice-breaker or warm-up activity. It can also form a useful structure for making dances. The first person makes a short, simple movement that everyone copies. After a few repetitions the mover indicates that the leadership is passed to the person next to them. This person can choose to keep the move the same or change it. They can also just pass the leadership on to the next person if they wish.

Name game – pass the move

Each dancer says their name and accompanies it with a gesture. Everyone copies this a few times and then it is the turn of the next person.

This can be developed as a whole group without the names. Add music; develop in pairs or small groups by selecting three or four moves and joining them together. Practise the transition from one to another. When you can perform it in unison try it in canon. Finally perform it using a combination of unison and canon. This activity can be developed by trying it at different levels or different speeds. Basically, you use the movements from the group as a starting point for improvisation – give as much or as little structure as you think the group needs.

Shapes 1

Use photos, paintings or postcards to find a shape for a starting position. Work with a partner and learn each other's shape. Move from shape A to shape B and back to A. Lengthen the transition. Develop by varying speed, level, relationship (e.g. unison, canon, question and answer).

Shapes 2

Individual dancers move freely in the space until one dancer (A) stops and makes a shape. Other dancers notice and make the same shape. Some make their shape close to A; others notice and make the shape at some distance. When all are still A begins to move again. Try it with lively dynamic music, followed by unison move to a slower piece of music (see below).

Unison move

As an alternative to dancers learning a set piece to perform in unison, try working in groups of three or four with dancers forming a triangle or diamond shape. The person at the front begins to move slowly and the others follow. After a whilst the lead dancer turns to the right or left and, as the others follow, there will come a point where one of the other dancers can no longer see the leader so this person now leads the dance. This version of unison movement usually results in movement with a distinctive quality. The dancers focus intently on each other and seem to move as one body.

Props 1

Offer the group a selection of props – for example a hat, pebbles, driftwood, a fan, scarves, a large elastic band, and everyday objects such as a comb, pencil or tray. Encourage participants to keep using the prop as a stimulus for extending movement vocabulary. Dancers repeat the exercise without the prop. Each person has the chance to try several props.

Props 2

Use props as a starting point for devising a motif (e.g. hats, driftwood, stones, fabric). Dancers can either work individually or in small groups. If participants are uncomfortable without a structure you could give a score to accompany the props. The following scores for groups were developed during a training session at Powys Dance:

Plastic cup – roll cup/go to cup/go round cup/show off cup/balance it on someone else

Large scarf – Pass it/over it/under it/hold it away/hold it close/travel with it

Musical theatre

Use canes, hats and home-made 'tap shoes' to create movement phrases performed to songs from the musicals. For seated participants the tap shoes can be improvised using buttons sewn on to a wide strip of elastic with the ends fastened together with Velcro. The band can be slipped over shoes so the buttons form the taps.

Opening and closing dance – combining improvisation and set moves

Teach the group a short motif and intersperse it with sections of improvisation. This activity is a non-threatening way to support a group in discovering their own movement. It works well with a piece of music with a clear ABAB structure (for example, verse/chorus/verse/chorus). They have the security of set dance with a very short section where they devise their own movement.

Section A: Motif

Raise both arms together looking at hands (four counts)
Clench fists and pull down slowly to waist height (four counts)
Release tension, turn hands over and, with open palms facing the floor, make a large clockwise circular movement with the arms (four counts)
Repeat anticlockwise (four counts)

Section B: Improvisation

Encourage dancers to explore opening and closing movements with their hands. Develop this to involve movements with the arms, legs and whole body. After a period of experimenting, participants can choose to move just their hands or they can make bigger movements that travel.

Issues-based choreography

Start with a theme – for example, *Ageing* – and make a spider diagram of any connected thoughts. Collect words, phrases, photos, poems, pieces of clothing, newspaper articles, childhood memories or music. Explore these for movement potential and either improvise till you find a motif or select a piece from an existing dance. Develop this fragment in some of the ways outlined above. You may choose to accompany your movement with music, speech, projected still images or film.

Alternatively you might start with music and fit your choreography to it. Another variation on the theme of *Ageing* is to think of ways in which dancers can challenge stereotypes of ageing.

Poetry and Dance

I often work in collaboration with other artists – here are two poems that were produced during a project where Sylvia Christie, a writer and chronicler, observed some sessions with a seated dance group.

Mirroring

They danced so close –
Moving like one person.
In all her memories
She is one with him.
Now this stranger,
Like a mirror reflects
Her hands' soft motion.
She is complete
For this gentle moment.
Chiming together is never easy:
Anticipating –
Getting it right –
Brings her back to smiles.

String of pearls

In this gentle moment –
Glenn Miller is playing –
She strings memories together
And is complete again
Remembering how
They danced so close
Moving as one
His cheek warm
Against her hair
The tape has ended
But she still smiles
At a lingering sweetness.
Her hands recreate
Vanished rhythms,
Her feet recall old patterns
Intricate as lace

And all the time
Her dream partner
Is closer to her
Than her closed eyelids

Christie, S. (1993) *in Creative
Movement for Senior Adults*
(unpublished).

The following two poems were written by John Killick, using the words of people living with dementia. These poems were part of a collection that John and I used to create a performance at the UK Dementia Congress 2011.

On the Other Side

I'm just going round to see what's round the corner
I've lived here twenty-five weeks in the city.
Up and down the language, twice up and down...
I'd better just have another look...
I'll tell you if you can understand the language.
And I'm talking, talking all the time...
I'm just off to see if it's changed at all...
I didn't know if you would understand,
With you living on the other side...
I'll just see if it's all right over there...

Young girls wearing white on the other side
Of their dress getting married...
I'll just see if I can get far enough along...

The Key

Have you any openings?
Have you got a guide?
Could you come along
and turn a key in a lock for me?
You'll not find my room.
I've only got...nothing
This is my room? Not mine.

Not my room.
Not my clothes.
Not my bed.
I'm going home.

Killick, J. (1997) *You are Words: Dementia
Poems,* London: Hawker Publications.

Poetry as a score for devising movement

Using one or more of the above poems, work with a partner to explore
choreographic possibilities using the following exercise.

Exercise

- A reads the poem aloud whilst B moves
  B reads the poem aloud whilst A moves
  Repeat several times – each moving freely, creating fragments
  or impressions. Avoid miming a narrative story

- Make a sound recording of one of you reading the poems
  Play the recording whilst A moves and B observes
  Change over: B moves and A observes
  Both write or draw your responses
  Repeat several times

- If possible make a video recording of the session and discuss the effect of hearing
  the words and viewing the improvised movement.
- Select any movement material that you want to continue working on and repeat
  the exercises until you have a piece that you are both happy with.
- Share your work with another couple and continue to select and refine the
  material.

You may want to try this exercise using different poems. Remember these
suggestions are starting points; see where they take you. Don't aim for a
literal interpretation of every word – use the exercise to help you develop
new movement vocabulary and explore meaning. (See Chapter 16 for a
discussion on developing choreography that has meaning.)

When you have developed some interesting choreographic material, try
performing it to music, other sounds, a poem read aloud or a recording
of the poem over background music; introduce pauses, include movement
without poetry or poetry without movement.

Lucky Me

A dance performance and workshop package from Powys Dance, suitable for residential and day care settings for older people.

Stimulus/theme: 1950s fashion and domesticity

The dawn of the push-button age, with labour-saving devices such as washing machines, brought a welcome release from drudgery for many housewives...what could they possibly do with all this spare time in the domestic realm?

The Dance (10 minutes)

A humorous exploration for two or three dancers of:

1. Dancing with props: marigold gloves, yellow dusters and chairs.
2. Responding to fashion using tableaux from haute couture magazines and specially made costumes with hooped skirts (designed and made by Jill Rolfe) deliberately impractical for housework or dancing.
3. Breaking out of boredom and 'drudgery' through being 'silly' and playful.
4. Responding to a soundscape made up from 'Housewife's Choice', 'Listen with Mother' and 'Tico Tico'.
5. Social dance styles, for example rock and roll combined with a creative response to the stimuli.

Considerations

1. Very limited performance area
2. Carpeted floors
3. High temperature
4. Limited time or space for warming up
5. The need to use a portable sound system
6. Clear negotiation with setting managers and staff about appropriate timing, location, set up, space to change and staff support during the performance and workshops

How it was used

Lucky Me formed part of a community residency programme where Powys Dance was present in a particular geographic area for six weeks, working with a range of community groups. The performance was used as the second in a series of six participatory workshops in a residential or day care setting. *Lucky Me* also translated well into other settings, such as schools and day centres for adults with learning disabilities. The performance was often repeated twice.

It aimed to expand energy; provide fun; be visually appealing and colourful; stimulate reminiscence through the music and the costumes; provide an example of movement material or props that could be used in participatory workshops.

Sample workshop immediately following performance

There was very limited time following the performance, but it was important to use *Lucky Me* as an immediate stimulus for participants' own dance creation, particularly for those participants who found memory burdensome.

All activities take place sitting in a circle.

1. Gentle warm-up repeated from last week: check seated posture; curling and uncurling fingers and hands; gently reaching arms forwards one at a time; shrugging shoulders and circling backwards; extending one leg along the floor and replacing it (repeat to other side); rub hands together; gently circle hands over knees.
2. Yellow duster – improvisation. Pass one duster around the circle, so that everyone who wants to can explore some movement ideas from the performance, or of their own. Others can watch and enjoy. Use this time to talk about the performance and any thoughts or ideas it may have provoked in the group.
3. Group 'copycat' with dusters. Make sure everyone has a duster. Accept contributions and guide the whole group in an improvised unison duster dance.
4. Cool-down: link the circle by holding the dusters between each other. Gently sway.
5. Ending: discuss the development of the duster ideas for next week. What could we explore, add or develop?

Surprise and Delight

Chapter 16 referred to events and activities that surprise and delight. Here are some simple ideas that I have used occasionally to introduce an element of fun and unexpected pleasure.

- Lower the lights and use battery-operated tea lights for participants to hold during mirroring or solo improvisations.
- Make blossoming flowers by gathering up a chiffon scarf in each hand and slowly opening the hands, palm upwards. Make a 'bouquet' with several people's hands opening close together. Perfect surprise for someone's birthday.
- Bring in some unusual food to eat during the tea break – small pieces of fresh fruit on a kebab stick, or home-made buns with a poem or joke hidden on rice paper inside the bun case.
- Find an excuse to give prizes – for example, with a seated group you could have a warm-up activity where a scarf is tied to a large elastic circle. Elastic is passed through the fingers and the scarf moves around the circle. When the music stops, the person with the scarf gets a prize (a piece of fruit, a sweet or a flower).
- Bring dressing up clothes to the session, for example, a selection of hats. Play some music, let participants choose their hat and improvise with it. Alternatively, lay out a range of character clothing and encourage people to play around with movement ideas, changing their prop whenever they like.
- Change the lighting by drawing the curtains and introducing spotlights (a couple of reading lamps).
- If you are able to block out most of the light, participants can dance with LED sticks – in solo improvisations or connecting with other dancers.
- Similarly, encourage seated dancers to experiment with torches. In pairs, one person moves and the other follows the move with a torch – try it with very slow music and fast lively music.
- Introduce live music – a musician who can improvise to accompany dancers' movements or a trio to play popular music to suit the participants. (Sometimes I apply for a grant for live music; at other times I find musicians amongst the staff. One memorable musician was a therapy assistant who happened to mention that he played the violin.)
- Invite artists using other art forms such as poetry or visual arts. They might involve your participants or just make a creative record of what they see. Paintings, poems and other creations can be shared at celebration events.

Suggestions that require a little more preparation:

- Create a themed celebration by decorating the space and having special food and drink. For example a Spanish, Greek, Indian or African event – any of these offer scope for a delightful afternoon or evening.
- Tea dance – create your very own Palm Court, with afternoon tea, potted palms and dancing with spot prizes. Encourage participants to dress up in their best clothes. The palm effect can be achieved by sticking ferns into pots of sand; afternoon tea is tiny bite-sized sandwiches and miniature cakes. Spot prizes might be awarded during the dancing (stop the music and a blindfolded assistant follows instructions, 'forward five paces, turn to your left four paces' and so on until the winner is 'the person nearest your right hand'). Alternatively, have coloured spots on some of the chairs and announce the prizes partway through the event.
- Celebrate the end of a project by having a display of photographs, special food and invited guests. Show a DVD or PowerPoint presentation of edited highlights, and surprise participants by giving each one a personalised card with a photo of them dancing, or a poem created by your guest poet.

Most of these ideas cost very little; however, I often cost in a celebration event when I am submitting a funding application. This offers the flexibility to include live music, performance by other dancers, additional co-workers and outside caterers.

Props and Other Resources for Dance and Movement Work with Older People

Green Candle Dance Company

Activity box

A range of props to be used in movement sessions with older people – these include: a parachute, carnival sticks, a giant scrunchie, rubber balls, scarves, beach balls, balloons, percussion instruments and other items on request.

Falling About & Moving About DVD

A DVD resource for dancing with older people, showing Green Candle's most recent production *Falling About*, a light-hearted and informative performance that addresses the physical and emotional issues around falling. The DVD also includes two model workshops, one seated and one standing, providing both staff and participants with guidance on physical activities for those over 60. The resource also includes an information booklet giving background information and teaching guidance that can be used to support the DVD's content.

Jack Be Nimble Resource Pack and CD

The pack includes production notes from this show for older audiences, as well as original concepts from the show, soundtrack and lyrics, and practical information on exercise for older people.

Growing Bolder: a start up guide to creating dance with older people

By Sophie Hanson, Fergus Early & Sally Davies
The guide includes practical information on exercise for older people, including detailed exercises, ideas for classes, choreography and music, as well as case studies.

Prayers on the Wind DVD

A short (10 minute) documentary about a project in an older people's day centre. Beautifully filmed by Roswitha Chesher, the film includes interviews with participants.

Prices and further information from Green Candle Dance Company: Tel. +44 (0)20 7739 7722; Email: info@greencandle.com

JABADAO movement play specialists

The JABADAO online shop sells props to support dance and movement. The resources are designed to bring people together in active, sociable communication with one another, in groups or one to one.

Props available include: elastic rings from 2 metres to 10 metres in circumference – ranging from 'just elastic' to luxurious soft elastic with a stretchy, comforting Lycra velvet covering; giant (36-inch) balloons; long and short ribbon sticks; Lycra squares, circles and lengths in seven sizes and shapes and four bright colours; silky extra-light parachutes in three sizes; two kinds of scarf; boxes of feathers – white or assorted colours; CDs of music compiled by JABADAO; beanbags and Koosh balls.

Older people's kit

Contains a parachute, elastic, ribbon sticks, giant balloons, balloon pump, softy balls, feathers, beanbags, music CD, The Elderly Papers and a basket or kitbag to store them in.

Prices vary according to content (there is a budget kit available).

A Jig and a Caper CD

Six lively, longish tracks of jolly dance music played by the JABADAO band. Inspired by social dances that draw people together: polka, ragtime, farandole, circle dance and hornpipe.

FANDANGO

JABADAO's new online shop focusing on the oldest and frailest members of society. Gifts include: garlands and tiny bunting for walking frames; body-friendly shawls, rugs and blankets (with or without weighting for an added reassuring quality); things for grandchildren to make and give; a range of small, inexpensive gifts for when you 'pop round' and many more items.

Prices and further information about any of the above from JABADAO: Tel. +44 (0)113 236 3311; Email: info@jabadao.org

Liz Lerman dance exchange toolbox

A free, online resource with descriptions of warm-ups and activities to generate movement material. Detailed notes on a wide range of ideas.

http://danceexchange.org/toolbox/tool09b8.html?Line= 5 (accessed 21 August 2012)

Useful Contacts (UK)

As this is a rapidly developing area of work, there are many dance companies and organisations engaged in activities with older people. It is not possible to list all the agencies that are offering services and resources. Here is selection made in early 2012.

Foundation for Community Dance (FCD)

The professional organisation for anyone involved in creating opportunities for people to experience and participate in dance. The FCD website has information about events and training, member services, publications, professional development and current developments in community dance.

www.communitydance.org.uk

JABADAO

Works in partnership with the education, health, arts and social care sectors to change the way people work with the body and movement. Offers a range of resources and training courses.

www.jabadao.org

Kala Sangam

South Asian arts organisation creating and delivering creative and accessible activities: performances, classes, workshops and training.

www.kalasangam.org

Chaturangan

A company engaged in a diverse range of community projects and participatory educational work. Chaturangan brings together artists from different cultural backgrounds and organises national and international conferences.

www.chaturangan.co.uk

Carl Campbell Dance Company 7

A contemporary Caribbean dance company, which runs *Recycled Teenagers* – a programme for active older people.

www.ccdc7.co.uk

East London Dance

Provides a range of opportunities for older people to participate in dance. Includes Leap of Faith dance company.

www.eastlondondance.org

Green Candle Dance Company

Runs classes and performance opportunities for older people, as well as providing training and resources for working with older people.

www.greencandledance.com

Greenwich Dance

Runs a dance company for those aged over 60 years. *Dancing to the Music of Time* offers weekly classes in creative dance.

www.greenwichdance.org.uk

Lincolnshire Dance

The Freedom in Dance programme offers training and dance projects aimed at improving the provision of dance activities for the over 50s.

www.lincolnshiredance.com/freedom-in-dance

Sadlers Wells, London

Home of the Company of Elders, older people's dance company.

www.sadlerswells.com/page/education

Take Art, Somerset

Runs older people's projects within their participatory programme.

www.takeart.org/dance

Trinity Laban

Offers training courses in contemporary dance, professional development days for leading dance with older people and regular classes for over 60s. Has carried out research into the impact of dance on health and well-being amongst older people. The full literature review *Dancing towards Wellbeing in the Third Age* is available from their website:

www.trinitylaban.ac.uk/news-press/latest-news/dancing-towards-wellbeing-in-the-third-age.aspx

Yorkshire Dance

Offers creative dance classes for over 50s.

www.yorkshiredance.com

Generation Arts

In Scotland, Generation Arts, run by West Lothian Council in partnership with other organisations, offers a programme of creative activity for older people, and runs specialised training for carers and dance artists working with older people.

www.artfull.org.uk

NAPA

National Association for Providers of Activities for Older People is a charity that provides training events for staff leading activities in care settings. They have produced an *Exercise for Older People* training pack.

www.napa-activities.co.uk

Later Life Training

Provides specialist training for health and leisure professionals working with older people. Their website offers exercise booklets, which can be downloaded free of charge.

www.laterlifetraining.co.uk

Zumba fitness

Zumba Gold is a dance fitness programme aimed at active older participants. It is a modified version of the high energy 'fitness party', using Latin music such as salsa and meringue.

www.zumba.com

Age and Opportunity

Based in Ireland, Age and Opportunity is a national organisation promoting creativity and participation in the arts amongst older people. Part of their yearly programme is the Bealtaine Festival, which celebrates creativity in older age.

ageandopportunity.ie/bealtaine

Equal Arts

Works with professional artists to deliver arts and older people's projects in partnership with residential care homes, sheltered accommodation schemes, GPs and hospitals, arts and cultural venues and a range of community organisations.

www.equalarts.org.uk

First Taste

Small local charity delivering educational activities for frail older people in the Derbyshire Dales. Their activities include chair-based exercises for people living with dementia.

www.firsttastecharity.co.uk

Age UK

Charity formed by the merger of Age Concern and Help the Aged. It is the UK's largest charity for older people and offers a range of information about health and well-being.

www.ageuk.org

Beth Johnson Foundation

A national organisation that promotes positive ageing and hosts the International Consortium for Intergenerational Practice.

www.bjf.org.uk/
www.icip.info

Magic Me

A long-established provider of intergenerational arts projects. The website includes details of projects such as tea dances and cocktail parties in care homes. The bookshop resources include a practical handbook on setting up and running workshops linking young and older people.

www.magicme.co.uk

ARTZ is Artists for Alzheimer's (UK)

Links artists and cultural organisations to people living with dementia and their care partners.

www.artz-uk.org

Dementia positive

Website run by John Killick and Kate Allan. It includes useful information and downloadable handouts.

www.dementiapositive.co.uk

Arts Council England

www.artscouncil.org.uk

Arts Council of Northern Ireland

www.artscouncil-ni.org

Arts Council Ireland

www.artscouncil.ie

Arts Council of Wales

www.artswales.org.uk

Scottish Arts Council

http://www.creativescotland.com/

Useful Contacts (Outside the UK)

American Society on Aging

Publishes the journals *Aging Today* and *Generations.* The website contains articles on ageing and information about events such as conferences on ageing.

www.asaging.org

National Center for Creative Aging

Offers a range of information and activities including *Creativity Matters: Arts and Aging Toolkit*, which can be downloaded from their website:

http://www.creativeaging.org

Kairos Dance Theatre

An intergenerational dance company – home of *The Dancing Heart*, which is an evidence-based creative ageing programme.

www.kairosdance.org

Dance Exchange

Dance Exchange is an intergenerational company founded by Liz Lerman. Activities include concerts, interactive performances, community projects and professional training.

www.danceexchange.org

HelpAge International

Works in 60 countries across all continents to help older people lead dignified, secure, active and healthy lives.

www.helpage.org

Global Action on Aging

Reports on the needs and potential of older people within the global economy. The website includes current information from around the world.

www.globalaging.org/agingwatch/new/ngos.htm

Arts and Health Australia

A networking and advocacy organisation, which hosts conferences and training programmes. Their work includes a focus on creative ageing.
www.artsandhealth.org

ARTZ Artists for Alzheimer's (United States, Europe, Australia)

www.artistsforalzheimers.org

Index

Abraham, Ann, 13
acknowledgements, 144
age inclusive practice, xi, 73–88, 138,
    149
ageing
    global ageing, xvi, 30–3, 41, 240
    perceptions of, 13, 33, 76, 87
    positive ageing, 34–5, 40, 87, 94, 97,
        183, 238
    World Assemblies on Ageing, 31
ageism, 8, 14, 32, 71
Age UK, 3, 5, 32, 58
Agewell International, 33
Alzheimer's, 110, 238, 241
Annan, Kofi, xvii, 31, 41
arthritis, 100–1, 103, 189
arts and ageing, 18, 24, 27, 54, 179, 238,
    240
Arts Council England, 54, 58, 239
asthma, 105–6, 189

Baring Foundation, 11, 55, 58, 59, 63
Beazley, T., 125
Benini, M., 129
Body of Experience, 70–1
Bond, John, 17, 19
bones, 95, 100–2
Bonicca, J.J., 99
Borstel, J., 162
boundary management, 8, 151
brain, 96–7, 107–8, 110, 195–6
Brierley, M., 129
Brown, R., 19

Candoco, 72
cautions, precautions, 114–15, 134, 197
charter for the older dancer, 148, 154,
    183
choreography, 79, 84–6, 163–77, 222,
    224

Christie, S., 225, 226
circle dance, 138
circulation, 95, 104, 112, 193
City Arts, 54–5, 63
Coaten, R., 117
Coldicott, G., 128
Coleman, Elizabeth, xi, 55, 93, 100, 198
Colles, 102
Common Dance, 87, 165
communication, 11, 116
    non-verbal, 121–2, 189
community dance, xvii, 3, 6, 7, 21, 26,
    55, 56, 58, 75, 87, 117, 145, 146,
    154, 178, 183, 235
Company of Elders, 6, 49, 57, 58, 165,
    236
continuing professional development
    (CPD), 146–54
COPD, 194–5
Core Dance, 58
Corner, Lynne, 17, 19
Crichton, S., 117
Critical Response Process, 161, 162
cross-generational, 73–90, 219, 240
Crows Feet, 49, 50
Csikszentmihalyi, M., 121–2, 124
Cumbria Parkinson's Disease Dance
    Collective, 129
Cunningham, Merce, 67
Cushnie, D., 129

deep vein thrombosis (DVT), 106–7, 189
dementia, 46, 110, 116–24, 189, 199,
    226–7, 238, 239
    dementia care mapping, 122, 124
demographics, 13, 21, 31
    'demographic time bomb,' 39
depression, 98, 109, 113, 195
diabetes, 111
Dickie, Ann, 70

discrimination
   age discrimination, 14, 19, 32, 55
dowager's hump, 102
Dudley, Jane, 67, 70
Duff, J., 129
duty of care, 93, 132–45, 147, 178, 197, 200
Dyer, Richard, 14, 19

Early, Fergus, xi, 8, 64, 70
English National Ballet, 20, 52, 126, 205–6
Equality Act, 14, 17
evaluation, 57, 155–62
Everitt A., 18, 20
EXTEND, 147, 150, 154

falls, 110, 114, 144, 149
femur
   fractured neck of, 102, 103
Fogg, A., 44, 51, 127
Foundation for Community Dance, 145, 148, 150, 183, 235
Fourth Age, 4, 5
frail older people, 5, 96, 97, 98, 106, 111, 114, 238
Francis, Fi, 14, 15, 19
funding, 35, 54, 57, 59, 60, 153, 203–4

Gillespie, A., 129, 130, 131
global action on ageing, 32, 35, 41, 240
Global Alliance, 32
GODS (Growing Older Disgracefully), 47, 51, 52
Graham, Martha, 64, 66
Green Candle Dance Company, xi, 70, 71, 149, 232, 233, 236

Hall, Stuart, 14, 19
Hamilton, R., 18, 20
Hawker, M., 93, 99
Hazan, Haim, 16, 17, 19
health and safety quiz, 188, 189
heart, 95, 104, 105, 192–4
Hebdige, Dick, 15, 19, 88
HelpAge International, 32, 33, 34, 40, 41, 240
From Here to Maturity, 70, 71

higher education, 88, 150
Hill, H., 120, 124
hip replacement, 103, 138, 189

identities
   multiple identities, role identities, 8, 9
intergenerational, 37, 75, 76, 80, 136, 184, 238, 240
International Day of Older Persons, 37, 40
Ischaemia, 104, 192, 193

JABADAO, 46, 51, 124, 233, 235
Jackson, O.S., 99
Jackson, S., 204
Japan, 36–9, 71
joints, 95–6, 100–1, 109, 128

Kazuo Ohno, 71
Keirokai, 37–8
Kilián, Jiri, 69
Killick, J., 226–7
Kirkham, S., 165, 176
Kitwood, T, 115, 116, 123
Kunz, M., 99
Kyphosis, 102

labels, 5–6, 39, 82
Lansley, Jacky, 69, 70
Later Life Training, 150, 154, 237
Lautenbacher, S., 99
leadership, 137, 154, 179
Lee, Rosemary, 75, 84, 89, 165, 168
Lerman, L., 161, 162, 170–1, 176, 234, 240
Leventhal, D., 125
Life Circles, 58
limited lexicons, 7, 207
lincolnshire dance, 147, 149, 190, 210–11, 236
lungs, 95, 104, 105, 193–4

Macfarlane, Cecilia, 75, 80, 81, 145, 168
Magpie Dance, 72
Mark Morris Dance Company (MMDC), 125
Marple Movers, 44, 60, 63, 185, 220

Massine, Leonide, 65
McClean, G., 99
memory, 71, 96, 97, 109, 110, 120, 121, 164, 176
Murray, G., 164, 176
muscles, 95, 101, 111, 128, 134, 192–4
Musical Moving, 129, 130

Netherlands Dance Theatre, 69
NHS, 18, 55, 57, 58, 122

obesity, 111–13, 115
Older Americans Act, 36
older old, 4, 95
oldest old, 4, 31, 40, 97, 98
osteoarthritis, 100, 101, 103
osteoporosis, 100–2, 189

pain, 96–7, 99, 101, 102, 142, 192
Parkinson's Disease, 18, 20, 47, 52, 108–10, 125–31, 9, 205–6
participatory arts, 9, 11, 28, 54, 59, 85
partnership, 24–6, 53–63, 150, 154, 202, 204
PAT testing, 144
pensioners, 5, 6
performance, 48, 49, 70–1, 142–3, 163–4, 167, 169, 170–7, 228–9
Perrin, T., 118, 124
personhood, 116–17
playfulness, 117, 118, 120
population
    ageing population, xvi, 11, 13, 17, 18, 21–4, 30–2, 39, 74
Powys Dance, 59, 150, 203–5, 228–9
professional dancers, 8, 64–72, 183

Recycled Teenagers, 5, 49, 50, 52, 235
representations of older people, 13, 16, 18, 19
rheumatoid arthritis, 101, 189
risk assessment, 133, 139, 140, 143, 190
roles, 8–11, 65, 72, 140, 151–2, 167–8, 184

Rosetta Life, 45, 51, 117
Royce, A.P., 16, 17, 19

safeguarding vulnerable adults, 200
safe practice, 132–45
Sarker, B., 9, 159
senior citizens, 5, 22, 24, 35, 38, 53
senses, 96, 117
service provision, 4, 13, 57
Setterston R.A., 6, 11
short term, long term, movement memory, 124
sight, 97, 111
'silver tsunami', 39
skin, 96–7, 104, 137
Smith, Antony, 7–8, 11, 207–9
Spätbewegten, 49
stamina, 96, 101, 143, 173, 178
statistics, 4, 11, 18, 22, 158, 159
statutory provision, 4
stereotyping, 7, 14, 40, 168, 207
StopGAP, 72
Striking Attitudes, 50, 52
stroke, 107–8, 110, 112, 195–6
sustainability, 60–1

Take Art, 236
tendons, 96
Tepper, K., 6, 11
terminology, 3, 7, 8, 41, 75–6, 207
Third Age, 5, 236
    University of Third Age, 4, 11, 98
training, 59, 146–54, 201, 235, 236, 237, 240
Trauten M.E., 6, 11
Tyson Jones, R., 175

United States, 6, 21–9, 36, 39, 42

warm up, 134, 212, 215, 216, 217, 219, 234

young old, 4, 5, 30

Zumba, 46, 237